British Student Activism
in the Long Sixties

Routledge Studies in Modern British History

British Student Activism
in the Long Sixties

Caroline M. Hoefferle

Routledge
Taylor & Francis Group
NEW YORK   LONDON

First published 2013
by Routledge
711 Third Avenue, New York, NY 10017

Simultaneously published in the UK
by Routledge
2 Park Square, Milton Park, Abingdon, Oxon OX14 4RN

Routledge is an imprint of the Taylor & Francis Group,
an informa business

Library of Congress Cataloging-in-Publication Data
Hoefferle, Caroline.
    British student activism in the long sixties / By Caroline M. Hoefferle.
        pages cm. — (Routledge studies in modern British history ; 9)
    Includes bibliographical references and index.
    1.   Student movements—Great Britain—History—20th century.
    2.   College students—Political activity—Great Britain—History—20th
century.   I. Title.
    LA631.82.H64 2012
    378.1'98109410904—dc23
    2012006426

ISBN: 978-0-415-89381-7 (hbk)
ISBN: 978-0-203-10275-6 (ebk)

Typeset in Sabon
by IBT Global.

Printed and bound in the United States of America on sustainably sourced
paper by IBT Global.

Contents

Acknowledgments

I wish to give a big thank you to Professor Hamish Fraser, my mentor who read through this entire manuscript and provided me with guidance and perspective. I also want to thank my dissertation supervisor and mentor Professor Mitch Hall for all his long hours of working with my dissertation manuscript and guiding me through the process of writing up many drafts of this research. Thank you Annette Davis and the faculty in the Central Michigan University and Strathclyde University history departments for all of their support and help while I was there as a graduate student in the 1990s. I would also like to thank Willie Thompson and Sheila Rowbotham for graciously sharing their memories and thoughts with me. Thanks to Wendy Gordon, Neil Rafeek, and my other graduate student colleagues at CMU and Strathclyde, who through our long conversations and travel to various archives and conferences, helped me to develop my ideas and analysis more clearly. I extend my gratitude to the staff at the archives at Essex, Glasgow, and Hull Universities, the Warwick Modern Records Centre, the London School of Economics and Political Science, the British Library, the National Library of Scotland, and the Bodleian Library of Oxford University. I am also grateful to Central Michigan University and Wingate University for the financial support they provided for this research. Lastly, and most importantly, I want to thank my husband Mike for his support and encouragement in finishing this project.

Introduction

We were taking on the world, the political power structure, and we sensed that rebellion from below could change it. We were all agreed on that: students could start to change the world.

—John Rose, student at LSE in 1967[1]

... it is clear that out of the ideological wreckage of social-democracy and Stalinism, a new student revolutionary perspective is emerging – international, extra-parliamentary and returning militant politics to the street. These students have seen through the fancy dress of modern capitalism and found the irrational violence and the hopelessness which is its core. They have seen their community of interest with the working class – a community which should concern us as much as it should frighten those who rule us. There is a spectre haunting Europe and its banners read, in Berlin and Warsaw and Paris and London: 'Today the Students, Tomorrow the Workers!'

—David Widgery, student at the Royal Free Hospital Medical School in London, 1970[2]

They are out to destroy and disrupt. I hope that no one in this House or outside it will underestimate the long-term effect of this kind of activity ... They are wreckers who, whatever they may say, are concerned only to disrupt society. Their weapons are lies, misrepresentation, defamation, character assassination, intimidation and, more recently, physical violence. The activities of this tiny cell of people could do untold long-term harm in this country. In the short term, they are doing untold harm to the educational chances of the vast majority of students who are just as idealistic and just as bright and decent as ever they were.

—Edward Short, Secretary of Education, 1969[3]

For many of us who were born after the 1960s, these quotes may be puzzling. Were British student activists that much of a threat to the power structure? Were they really on the cusp of a revolution? Were they "wreckers of society"? What did they want? If they actually were a threat and a vanguard of revolution, what happened to them? Quite obviously, student protesters failed to achieve a revolution in Britain, so why should we even care?

Like much of what happened in the 1960s, the meaning of student activism in this era remains highly controversial and contested territory in the memory of the nation, as well as amongst historians and other scholars. Some former activists and leftists still defend the ideals of the era and point to its positive contributions in making British society more democratic and tolerant. Others, on the other hand, are embarrassed by the entire topic and look back upon the protests as the folly of their youth. Conservatives like to blame the whole era for the moral and economic decline of the nation, while even leading Labourites like Tony Blair have criticized the era for its excesses. Similar to many other conservative politicians, Margaret Thatcher blamed the "permissive" sixties for the social problems of the 1980s, including rising crime and divorce rates, and declining Christian values.[4] Indeed, scholars Christopher Connery and Hortense J. Spillers argue that the global Right has never stopped its struggle to defeat the energies and ideas of the sixties. They assert, "we remain in a postsixties era: many of the forces that arose to combat the sixties remain in power. These forces understood the challenge of the sixties. We should too."[5] As with all memories, however, remembrances of the sixties are intimately shaped by what has happened since then and by current events and needs. Because memories of the era are so clouded by all that has happened since that era, including the decline of the far Left, the rise of the new Right, and the massive student protests of 2010–11, it is essential that scholars thoroughly research all of the evidence and make sense of the history of student protest in a rational and objective way. Shedding new light on the issues of the era may allow us to better engage with these same issues as they continue to shape our world today; understanding the dynamics and impact of student activism in the Long Sixties may help us to better comprehend the larger meaning of student protests today and in the future. Considering the continued relevance of student protests and the contested meaning of the sixties, it is surprising that no scholarly work thoroughly studies the British student movement from the 1950s through the 1970s.

This volume attempts to fill this void in the scholarship. By compiling evidence from students and other eyewitnesses from universities across Britain, it traces the rise of the British student movement in the late 1950s, its escalation to its peak in the period between 1968 and 1974, and its gradual decline afterwards. By exploring the student movement throughout the entire era of the "Long Sixties," this study uncovers how the issues, ideas, and tactics of the movement evolved over time as different generations of students responded to changing international, national, and local conditions. Situating the British student movement within the context of individual university conditions, national cultural trends and political debates, and the global movements of the sixties, it reveals that the British student movement both responded and contributed to the changing British system of higher education, debates over British politics and culture, and international dissent movements in the era of the Long Sixties.

Popular memory of the student protests of the sixties continues to be based primarily upon narratives constructed by contemporary national media accounts. Television and newspaper journalists interviewed hundreds of activists and eyewitnesses, especially during the height of media interest in student protest when students across the nation and world rose in massive protests in 1968 and 1969. Journalists, however, were guided by their desire to cover sensational material and chose to quote the most extreme views of the protesters and to portray them in the most shocking manner. Contemporary journalist accounts of student activism consequently portrayed protesters as foreigners (mainly Americans) and criminal hooligans bent on revolution and destruction. The most heavily-covered protests by far were those at the London School of Economics and Political Science (LSE) from 1966 through 1969, and the massive 1968 demonstrations of the Vietnam Solidarity Campaign, in which students seemingly played a dominant role. Coverage of these events reveals a divided response from the public. Some supported the student demonstrations, especially on the issues of nuclear disarmament and the Vietnam War, while others saw students as a privileged elite, wasting tax-payers' money on irrelevant demonstrations which blocked traffic and annoyed the public. Overall, contemporary news media accounts reveal a contradictory narrative of the student protests: that they were violently revolutionary and dangerous, and when they failed to be violent or cause a revolution, that they were weak and insignificant compared to those in France and the United States. [6]

Although contemporary newspaper accounts demonstrate widespread concern for the domestic student protest movement in the late 1960s and some indicated a fear of student violence or revolution, they also expressed a contradictory belief that British student protests paled in comparison to the much more violent and powerful student movements in West Germany, France, and the United States. This latter belief was largely supported by contemporary scholarly analysis and most accounts written in the decades which followed. For example, in 1969 the Department Head of Social and Administrative Studies at Oxford University A.H. Halsey published several scholarly works analyzing British student politics in this period, trying to explain why British students were not as radical as students elsewhere. He argued that the structure of the university system, with its small class sizes and brief three-year programs and the existence of an organized political Left to direct student activism toward off-campus activism were primarily responsible for the low level of student protest in Britain. [7] In 1970, Vice Chancellor of Essex University Albert Sloman argued that British universities were still the envy of the world because of their relative lack of protest and disruption. [8] He claimed that this was due to the progressive nature of British universities, and their extensive efforts to respond to student demands and make substantial reforms accordingly. This narrative, viewing the British student movement as insignificant compared to student protests elsewhere, became dominant in the late 1970s and it remains unchallenged by most scholars today.

The best-known historian to build upon this thesis is Arthur Marwick. A history professor at Edinburgh and the Open Universities in the 1960s, Marwick began writing commentaries and histories of the decade in the 1970s. He consistently argued that Britain witnessed a cultural revolution in the sixties, which included a new distinct youth culture, unprecedented international cultural exchange, and a new permissive attitude toward behavior and personal freedom, expressed in liberal legislation on censor-ship, racism, divorce, abortion, and sexuality. He asserted that the cultural revolution and student protests were largely a result of structural changes in British society and culture following the Second World War, including the baby-boom, economic prosperity which gave young people security and the money to become more independent from their parents, educational reforms which allowed more of the working class to attend university, tech-nological advances in travel and communications which drew more people into an international economy and culture, and a thaw in the Cold War which allowed more people freedom of political expression.[9] As part of the new youth culture, university students were in the vanguard of cultural change, but Marwick argued that they had virtually no impact on politics or society in general, and their protests were much smaller and calmer than in the rest of Europe and the United States because British universities were more student-friendly to begin with, and the police and those in authority responded with more understanding and tolerance.[10]

A number of more recent histories of sixties Britain have challenged many of Marwick's conclusions, but have supported his argument on the insignificance of the British student movement. A number of these assert the importance of the rise of the New Right alongside that of the New Left in the decade. In a 1999 essay, Richard Cockett argued that the popular memory of the sixties, that of "revolting students, permissiveness, and per-sonal freedom" is not the historical reality. He asserted that high politics completely ignored cultural changes at the time and that the real impor-tance of the decade lay in the emergence of the widespread belief among both the Left and the Right in "meritocracy," or that individuals should be rewarded according to merit and that they had the right to keep the money they earned. They also agreed that "the individual was responsible to make their own choices about the lifestyles that they wanted to lead and when obstructed in this by the state, the personal, for the first time became the political."[11] Both the New Left and New Right appealed to this liberation ideology and modernism, but in the end, the New Right, which dominated the policies of Margaret Thatcher, was more successful because it was more in touch with the economic aspirations of the British majority.[12] The true picture of the sixties is, thus, portrayed as far more complex than previ-ously believed.

In *White Heat: A History of Britain in the Swinging Sixties* (2006), Dominic Sandbrook agrees with the political complexity of the decade, but includes a section specifically on the British student movement. Reflecting the contemporary narrative, he argues that it was much smaller and more conservative than elsewhere in the world because students had nothing to complain about:

> . . . British students really were 'better treated than anywhere else in the world'. Tuition was free and almost all living costs were covered by

the state grant. Teacher-student ratios were extremely low. . . . . What was more, during the late sixties most universities responded to student pressure by mildly relaxing their rules and admitting student representatives to university committees. . . . what really stands out about the events of 1968 is the contrast between the parochial, small-scale events in Britain and the genuine upheaval and bloodshed in, say, France and the United States.[13]

Sandbrook concludes that students made little impact on British history because they were only a tiny fraction of the population, making up only ten per cent of young people of university age. Most were politically apathetic or conservative, and the tiny minority that led protests had little sympathy from the wider public.[14]

While both Marwick's and Sandbrook's arguments on the student movement reveal important dimensions of the sixties, they are greatly skewed by their lack of archival evidence on the student movement and the narrowness of the time period they discuss. They rest their claims about the British movement primarily on contemporary newspaper accounts from the late sixties, ignoring student activism in late fifties, early sixties, and early seventies. Historian Nick Thomas, however, offers an important partial corrective to their flawed assessments. He is one of the only historians to have used archival sources in an in-depth exploration of the British student movement. His doctoral thesis was especially useful in bringing together information from a wide range of student and popular newspapers to create an overview of the student protests in the late 1960s.[15] More recently, he has used some of this research to challenge some dominant myths about the student movement. Thomas argues that the beliefs that student protests were caused by permissive parenting, the influx of anti-authoritarian working-class students, and the influence of an extremist revolutionary minority of students from Britain, the Continent, and especially the United States were myths created in the 1960s by a contemporary press and university authorities who felt confused and threatened by the protests.[16] He asserts that these myths were useful for ignoring the issues at the heart of the protests and undermining their validity, but they have contributed to an inaccurate understanding of student activism and the sixties as a whole.

Thomas uses contemporary surveys of students at various universities in the late 1960s to argue that most students were politically apathetic and did not regularly take part in protests. A small minority of British-born student activists, however, did gain the support of the majority of students by provoking the authorities to over-react, leading the majority of students to join protests against these undemocratic and unjust actions, and to demand increased participation in university decision-making. He argues that most students wanted a say in reforming their government and university rather than a revolution to overthrow that government. He explains that the increase in student activism took place in the sixties because of larger political, social, and economic changes. He includes most of Marwick's list of structural changes, but adds that the Cold War emphasis on freedom and democracy led young people to expect that "democratic institutions live up to their democratic rhetoric."[17] The student protests in Britain were similar to those in other countries not because they imitated others or were led by foreigners, but because they "were part of wider social and political changes taking place throughout the post-war period in numerous Western countries."[18] He concludes that student protests helped to create "a social revolution of sorts" in the 1960s by challenging accepted norms of behavior and social and cultural deference.[19] Thomas's research offers an important corrective to the dominant narrative of student protest in the sixties, but it is weakened by its focus on the late sixties. Although he partially addresses this problem in a recent essay which finds considerable similarities between the 1950s and 1960s, even he has not yet fully connected the student activism of the 1950s through to the 1970s.[20] Without this wider historical lens, Thomas's work and all the other existing accounts of the British student movement are necessarily limited in their ability to truly comprehend its origins, evolution, relationship to local, regional, national, and international factors, or overall significance in British history.

This wider periodization, however, has been used by scholars of the global sixties for a number of decades. American political theorist Fredric Jameson published a ground-breaking analysis of the ideology of the global sixties in 1984, which first explicitly framed them as "the Long Sixties," beginning in the late 1950s and ending in 1974.[21] He argued that the ideas and the "politicocultural model" of the "first world" sixties originated in the decolonization movements in British and French Africa in the 1950s. These movements gave the marginalized peoples in the first world (including students, racial minorities, women, and homosexuals) a model or process for recognizing their own subjection and fighting for their own human rights with a collective voice.[22] Jameson concluded that the Long Sixties ended with the withdrawal of American forces from Vietnam after 1973 and the worldwide economic crisis of 1974. This periodization has shaped most subsequent histories of the global student movements of the sixties.

Although a number of important histories of the global sixties have focused specifically on 1968 as a high point of the era, most of these now place that year within the larger "Long Sixties" framework.[23] For example, scholars Martin A. Klimke and Joachim Scharloth argue that "1968" was a "magical year" because it was

> the climax of various developments that had been set in motion by the immense speed of the social and economic transformations after the Second World War: demographic changes and dramatic increase in university enrolment, a globalization of communication channels, an unprecedented economic prosperity that brought the arrival of consumer society, and a generational gap expressed in differing expectations

and hopes for the future. . . . "1968" thus stands as a metaphor used to capture the broad history of European protest and activism.[24]

The year 1968 was important in the history of the global student movements, but primarily as a symbol for trends extending far beyond that calendar year.[25]

The existing scholarship on the British student movement also leaves us with many unanswered questions about the British student movement. Were British students relatively radical, apathetic or conservative? Was the British student movement in the sixties unique in any way? How, why, and when did it begin and end, and did it have any effect upon the government, wider British society, or the world? This volume systematically answers these questions by studying the history of student activism from its first phase in the late fifties and early sixties, through its distinct phases in the mid-sixties, 1968, 1969–70, and 1971–74. Organized chronologically in chapters around these phases, it plumbs archives from across the nation to trace the extensive activism which surrounded specific student protests and the ideologies which informed them, placing them within the wider political, social, and cultural history of the nation and the world in the Long Sixties. Each chapter begins with a significant protest that introduces wider trends within the student movement as a whole during that particular phase. Each of these protests was important in their own way, but they are not necessarily the most important protests of the era and none is exactly typical of protest elsewhere in the nation. As will become apparent throughout the chapters, each student protest was the product of a unique combination of student personalities, local university leaders and structures, and specific national and global issues. As such, the protests varied widely across the nation and across the era. Altogether, however, all of this student activism formed an amorphous, expanding and contracting, rising and falling social movement using collective action to shape the world.[26]

This research indicates that the British student movement of the sixties, far from being an imitative and insignificant element of the global student movement, was a vibrant, globally-conscious movement with its own unique blend of issues, strategies, and theories. It was an important part of the global dissent movements against the Cold War, human rights injustices, and the problems of modern capitalism. Mass communication technologies, such as nightly news reports on the television, aided in the spread of a transnational New Left ideology and helped British students to see themselves as part of a wider youth movement transforming the world. International student organizations, student and faculty exchanges, and student travel connected British students in more direct ways with student movements in other countries, especially West Germany, France and the United States, further facilitating the spread of protest rhetoric and strategies. In many ways, therefore, the British student movement was indeed intimately connected to the global student movement of the sixties.

As with most transnational phenomenon, however, global ideas were reshaped within local and national contexts, and were thus translated and applied in unique and diverse ways by British students. In part, the British student movement was a continuation of a long British tradition of similar types of student dissent reaching back centuries to the beginning of the university system.[27] What distinguished the British student movement of the Long Sixties from that of earlier eras, however, was its higher level of consistent activism and consequent increased public visibility, its political and ideological orientation, and its contribution to the wider social, economic, and political discourse of the nation in this era. The unique national inspirations for the British student movement of the Long Sixties were the modernization of the British system of higher education, the Campaign for Nuclear Disarmament, and the British New Left. The latter two movements connected students in the Long Sixties to ideas and traditions drawn from Britain's long history of leftist and pacifist dissent. Contrary to the student-centered New Left in Germany and the United States, Britain's New Left had no powerful central organization for students and little organizational presence in the universities. Despite this weakness, however, the student movement clearly reflected New left ideology until the late sixties, when Britain's revitalized traditional Left gradually shifted the ideology and identity of the student movement towards the working class. This latter development set the British student movement apart from previous generations of British students and from its counterparts elsewhere in the world.

The combination of global and national influences on the British student movement was clearly reflected in its protest issues. While the American New Left focused much of its energies on protesting the Vietnam War in the late sixties, British students interpreted the issue within a uniquely British context. Because of their nation's more extensive history of imperialism and decolonization, British students viewed Vietnam primarily as a colonial issue and expressed their opposition to American involvement as a third party passing judgment on the issue. Vietnam protests in Britain were consequently less passionate and involved fewer students than in the United States. While the post-war baby boom and Cold War ideologies led most Western European countries and the United States to expand their systems of higher education, Britain's commitment to increasing enrolment in higher education as a means to train more white-collar workers to regain the nation's dominance in the global economy uniquely shaped the British student movement. Beginning in the early 1960s, the British government committed the nation to providing free higher education to those who qualified and greatly expanded the numbers of students enrolled in higher education institutions. Students were convinced by mainstream political rhetoric that their time at university was crucial to the nation and that as intellectual workers their grants were their pay for this important national work. Whenever student grants came under attack, students used this rhetoric as a weapon to defend their rights to full grants. Primarily because of this issue, the British student movement escalated in the 1970s while student movements elsewhere declined.

Britain's unique national context also resulted in distinctive outcomes for its student movement. Through the effective deployment of rhetoric and strategies drawn from British traditions and discourse, student activists gained support from students, staff, and workers for their successful struggle for student's rights to tax-payer supported grants, autonomous student unions, free assembly and speech, and participation in university decision-making. These student rights protests ultimately contributed to the democratization of most British universities and indeed the entire system of higher education. Their campaigns against nuclear weapons, the Vietnam War, racism, and sexism, while smaller than student rights protests in terms of numbers of participants, effectively raised public awareness of these issues, and were a significant factor in national decisions on each of these issues. Specifically, the student movement contributed to debates over Britain's foreign policies, to the national debate over permissiveness and the limits of democracy, to the fight against racism and apartheid, to the rise of feminism and gay liberation movements, to the fall of the Wilson and Heath governments in the late 1960s and early 1970s, and to the rise of working-class protests in the early 1970s. Indeed, as this volume shall reveal, the British student movement was an integral part of post-war national political, economic, social, and cultural history, and as such, deserves a history of its own.

1 Beginnings

Student Activism in the
Fifties and Early Sixties

It was Sunday, the 4th of November 1956, and for the first time since the General Strike of 1926, Britain was witnessing a massive protest in Trafalgar Square, in the heart of London. Under overcast skies, white banners flew everywhere with big black letters spelling out "Law not War!" Thirty-thousand clean-shaven young men (and very few women), most of whom were dressed in conservative drab overcoats and neckties, completely filled the famous square at the center of the nation's capital city. They listened intently to a succession of speakers denounce the British and French invasion of the Suez Canal in Egypt, cheering and occasionally chanting, "Eden must go!" The star speaker was Labour's left-wing foreign affairs spokesman Aneurin Bevan. With his shock of white hair, this charismatic senior statesman made an impassioned speech, scattering a host of pigeons into flight and rousing the crowd to great cheers. He railed against the Conservative government of Anthony Eden: "They have besmirched the name of Britain. They have made us ashamed of the things of which formerly we were proud. They have offended against every principle of decency and there is only way in which they can even begin to restore their tarnished reputation and that is to get out! Get out! Get out!"[1] The speech made a lasting impression on those in the crowd and was reported widely in the national newspapers the next day. But the real importance of the day lay not in the speeches or even the chants and banners. The real importance of this particular rally in Trafalgar square was the fact that in the midst of supposed political apathy and consensus, 30,000 young Britons had turned out to register their dissent, and by doing so, began the reinvigoration of the nation's political Left and the era of the Long Sixties.

The protest had been brewing ever since Egyptian President Nasser had nationalized the Suez Canal in July of 1956 and the Conservative British government led by Prime Minister Eden had threatened retaliation. When the leader of the Labour Party Hugh Gaitskell initially supported Eden taking "precautionary steps," two small leftist organizations called Victory for Socialism and the Movement for Colonial Freedom formed the Suez Emergency Committee to mobilize public opinion against armed intervention by British forces. In the first week of September, the Trades

Union Congress passed a resolution opposing any use of force in the Suez without the backing of the United Nations. On 29 October, however, the British and the French secretly encouraged Israel to invade Egypt, and then sent in troops to occupy the area on the pretext of keeping the peace between Israel and Egypt. This spurred the Suez Emergency Committee to book Trafalgar Square for the November demonstration to use public pressure to stop the invasion before it began. At this point, the Labour Party threw its weight behind the protest, calling the Suez invasion a breach of international law and using its influence to ensure a large turn-out for the demonstration.[2]

The high turnout of students at the protest especially surprised everyone, including the participants, organizers, police, and government. One young socialist organizer Stan Newens, who would eventually become a Labour MP, later recalled:

At the height of the proceedings, a great chant went up in the north-western corner of the square as a massive column of student demonstrators began to come in and went on endlessly. "One, two, three, four! We won't fight in Eden's war", they chanted. The whole square and its environs were engulfed in a vast array of protesters who were jammed in tight. The sense of mass solidarity in a just cause held us spellbound and instilled in us all a common will to carry our protest forward. At the end of the protest speeches, part of the crowd made for Whitehall, perhaps hoping to besiege Downing Street, and bitter clashes with the police followed in which 27 people were arrested. It was clear that the rally had awakened many thousands from their apathy . . .[3]

Partly because of this large outpouring of dissent, Newens and many others on the British Left saw this rally as "a seminal event in British Labour history" and a turning point in the post-war era.

Stuart Hall was another young protester at the Trafalgar Square rally, but he was there for very different reasons. A postgraduate student at Oxford University, Hall and his left-wing friends, Alan Hall, Raphael Samuel, Peter Sedgwick, and Raymond Williams, had been discussing imperialism, racism, capitalism, and the possibilities of a new form of socialism for years. Inspired by their radical professor G. D. H. Cole, they had revived the Socialist Club at Oxford and were busily gathering together other like-minded students to plot out a new way forward for socialism. Born in Jamaica in 1932 to successful middle-class parents of mixed racial heritage, Hall was especially conscious of the evils of imperialism and racism. With a Rhodes scholarship to help him, Hall had arrived at Merton College in 1951. When the British invaded the Suez, he and his friends saw it as a reassertion of imperialism and they vowed to fight this action any way they could. The Trafalgar protest seemed to be the most important way of demonstrating their opposition to imperialism, and so they too found themselves in the crowd of thousands there in the center of London on that gloomy Sunday afternoon.[4]

The anger and excitement felt by Smith and Hall was echoed in the faces and attitudes of thousands of others there that day. For many, it was their first political demonstration and it was inspiring. Workers and students together were challenging the authorities for the first time that any of them could remember. Participation in the protest gave the protesters hope in other ways. When thousands surged towards Whitehall and Downing Street, anything seemed possible. United together, the masses of people might be able to exert real political power. Similar to countless activists in countries around the world in the twentieth century, this generation awakened to the realization of the power of demonstrations as a "visible fraternity," a "gathering of bodies into a single moving material form . . . intended to say 'we' are here and 'they' (the powerful, the others, those who do not enter into the composition of the 'we') should be afraid and take our existence into consideration."[5]

In 1956 their protest appeared to succeed. By the time the slow-moving Anglo-French invasion force arrived in the Suez, the fighting there had already stopped, and the British and French were forced to agree to a cease-fire without fully occupying the Suez. The United States, which was eager to gain the support of the Middle East in its Cold War, was quick to condemn its allies in this case and threatened the collapse of the pound if Britain did not pull out. Over the next few months, United Nations peace-keeping forces replaced French and British forces to the embarrassment of the two governments.[6] Although this withdrawal was due to international opposition much more so than to the Trafalgar protest, the demonstration had united the Left in a renewed political initiative and introduced students and young people as a major mobilizing force for the first time since the Second World War. The year 1956 would be a turning point in the history of British Left, and the beginning of a new student movement centered on upholding the high ideals of fair play and democracy espoused in British discourse for generations.

STUDENT "APATHY" IN THE POST-WAR PERIOD

The entrance of a large contingent of university students in the Trafalgar square demonstration of 1956 was a surprise because many social commentators in the fifties were convinced that most students were apolitical. Despite the long history of student activism and protest in British history, and a number of important national and international crises and transformations in the late 1940s and early 1950s, these years were relatively quiet years for the nation's universities. Students seemed to be most concerned with working hard at their studies and starting their professional careers. The leading student organizations, including the National Union of Students, National Association of Labour Student Organizations, and the Federation of Conservative Students, had no mass following among students and engaged in no significant direct actions in the early fifties. Local student clubs and student unions were preoccupied with social events and fund-raising, with little interest in issues outside of the universities. Indeed, students such as David Goldberg from Glasgow University complained of student inaction and apathy as late as 1955, calling them a "Generation Gone Wrong."[7] All seemed quiet on the university front in the forties and fifties, but a number of important changes in British society, politics, and the economy were taking place which would pave the way for the beginning of the student movement in 1956.

Popular memory recalls the post-war forties and fifties as docile years of consensus and conservatism in contrast to the years of social upheaval and liberalism in the sixties. In recent years, however, historians have uncovered considerable evidence demonstrating that many of the rapid changes associated with the sixties actually began as early as the forties.[8] One of the most important changes that would affect all generations since the forties was the creation of a modern social welfare state. The Labour government of Clement Attlee oversaw the passage of the National Insurance, National Health Service, and National Assistance Acts, the nationalization of the Bank of England, the railways, coal, and steel, and the implementation of the 1944 Education Act, hoping that these policies would eradicate long-term economic inequalities.

The 1944 Education Act, which was proposed by Conservative Minister of Education R. A. Butler, was especially important in shaping the experience and expectations of post-war students. Designed to guarantee equal access to a state-funded education for all children through the age of fifteen, its creators hoped that it might allow more working-class children to enter higher education by basing educational advance on merit and achievement, and thus help to eliminate the class inequalities which plagued the nation. At the age of eleven, children would take a Common Entrance Examination determining the type of secondary school the pupil would attend. Those scoring in the upper 25th percentile could choose to attend a grammar school, which would prepare them to go on to university. Those in the lower 75th percentile would attend a secondary modern school, which emphasized "practical" courses for children who would end their education at fifteen and enter the labor market. After age fifteen, pupils could study for entrance examinations for universities, attend further education courses, or end their formal schooling. With several years of study in two or three subject fields, grammar school children could take Advanced Level Examinations which would be used to determine their eligibility for entrance into universities. Although the Labour government began implementing this act in the 1940s, successive Conservative governments extended educational benefits even further in the 1950s in their efforts to modernize the economy. In 1953, for example, Local Education Authorities were required to provide student grants for higher education, the amount of which depended upon their parents' expected contribution. To ensure that the universities could accommodate all qualified students, Conservatives upgraded a number of colleges to university status and planned seven new universities in 1958. At least in theory, therefore, both Conservatives and Labour leaders agreed on access to higher education as a right for all qualified British children.[9]

As a result of these educational reforms, the number of students attending universities nearly doubled between 1946 and 1962, increasing from 69,000 to 119,000.[10] Overall funding of the universities and education in general also increased dramatically in the post-war period, rising from 6.8 per cent of public expenditure in 1951 to 12.5 per cent in 1975, as the nation increasingly perceived higher education as the key to solving Britain's social problems and to helping the nation to compete in the global economy.[11] Despite this emphasis on modernization and reform, Britain's higher education system was slow to change in many ways. Housing, facilities, and staffing often failed to keep pace with the expanding student population, and a myriad of university regulations limited student freedoms and reinforced traditional power hierarchies between staff and students. The reality of university life fell far short of the high expectations raised by the rhetoric of modernization and reform of the period.

The high cost of social welfare programs and recovery from the damages of the Second World War also contributed to a flagging national economy throughout the late forties and shaped national politics in the fifties. The stagnant economy, together with continued rationing, led to the loss of electoral support for Labour and the victory of Winston Churchill's Conservative Party in the 1951 general election. Because of the narrowness of this victory, the successive Conservative governments of the fifties made only minor and gradual adjustments to Labour's domestic economic policies.[12] As the nation recovered from its economic difficulties, the Conservative party became increasingly popular among voters and dominated politics throughout the fifties and early sixties. Despite occasional fluctuations, by 1957 the nation had entered into a period of affluence which would last until the late sixties. In a speech that year, Prime Minister Harold Macmillan famously declared, "Let's be frank about it; most of our people have never had it so good. Go around the country . . . and you will see a state of prosperity such as we have never had in my lifetime— nor indeed ever in the history of this country. What is beginning to worry some of us is, 'is it too good to be true?'"[13] This dual perspective on the period, delight in affluence but anxiety about the future, would shape British culture throughout the sixties.

Uncertainty over the economy and new consumerism was paralleled by anxiety about the social changes which accompanied this transformation. Historian Arthur Marwick convincingly shows that this economic growth and consumerism transformed the societies and cultures of all of

Europe and North America in the late fifties and the sixties, contributing to a revolution in consumer spending, leisure, popular culture, and standards of living.[14] The fastest growing group of consumers in the fifties were the baby-boomers. Like many other countries in Europe and North America, Britain had experienced a "baby boom" in the late forties which resulted in the number of young people under age twenty growing from three million in 1951 to over four million in 1966.[15] This population bubble attracted considerable attention from the media and from corporations seeking to target this new generation of consumers. Marwick and many other social commentators then and now believe that this generation was raised in affluence with new "permissive" child-care techniques, giving children more personal freedom than previous authoritarian generations.[16] This generational thesis, which was first outlined by social commentators in the late fifties and early sixties, perceived a resulting generation gap between baby-boomers, who were raised to view all people as equals, and their parents, who were raised to respect their elders and social hierarchy. The baby-boom generation, which came of age in the sixties, has thus been associated with permissiveness and youth rebellion.

More recently, however, historians of the post-war period have found that so-called permissive trends and worries about youth rebellion date back to the 1940s, a generation before the baby-boomers. Historian Nick Thomas points to a number of studies which have demonstrated the existence of rising rates of juvenile delinquency in the 1940s, and a rising tide of public hysteria in reaction to it dating to the 1950s. Social commentators and the news media in the fifties worried about youth rebellion and blamed the lax discipline associated with the banning of flogging and birching in 1948.[17] Thomas has also shown that a number of other social changes, such as the decline in church attendance and class deference, which have been blamed on the sixties, actually began in the forties. The sixties and the baby-boomers, therefore, are best seen as part of a continuum of long-term changes taking place within British society.[18]

More important for the creation of a student movement was the social construction of youth as a new social group. As youth emerged as a discrete social group with their own needs and money to spend, new commercial markets expanded dramatically to satisfy their needs and desires. Sales of rock 'n' roll singles especially benefitted from the emerging youth market in the 1950s. Although many early rock artists, such as Bill Haley and Elvis Presley, came from America, by the mid-sixties, British rockers, such as the Beatles and the Rolling Stones, overtook them on the national and global youth music scene. Young people loved this new music, but older generations and the government routinely condemned it as vulgar and paternalistically refused to allow it to be played on the BBC. Although pirate radio stations emerged in the early sixties to satisfy young Britons' demand for rock 'n' roll radio, in the fifties, most young people had to borrow friends' records or go to the cinema to discover new music. Historian Peter

Hennessy argues that one of the most important turning points of the fifties came with the introduction of rock 'n' roll music in 1956, specifically with the 1956 film *Rock around the Clock*.[19] Young people mobbed the cinemas to watch the film, singing and dancing in the aisles, and generally drawing attention to their special love for the music of the film. Indeed student newspapers were filled with advertisements for rock and roll films, as well as folk and jazz concerts. The famous historian Eric Hobsbawm told Hennessy in 2002 that "For the first time you could feel things changing. Suez and the coming of rock-and-roll divide twentieth-century British history."[20] Rock, folk, and jazz appealed directly to young people and gave them an increased sense of being part of a new global youth generation, distinct from their elders and authorities.

While the media "often presented youth culture in glowing terms, as an energetic and uplifting force, displacing the dead hand of tradition," especially in reference to youth music and clothing fashions, some social commentators displayed considerable anxiety over the impact of Americanization, affluence, and "permissiveness" on the youth of the fifties and sixties.[21] Most of this concern centered upon working-class youth subcultures, such as the Teddy Boys, the Rockers, and the Mods, which were defined primarily by their clothing styles. Teddy Boys were the dominant symbol of youth rebellion in the mid-fifties. They were first noticed in the working-class neighborhoods of south London in 1954 primarily by the way they dressed— a variation of the American zoot suit, with long, draped jackets.[22] It was their flick-knives and brawling, however, which attracted condemnation by social commentators. By the end of the decade, the Mods and Rockers had taken over the mantel of youth rebellion. The Mods were more upwardly mobile and influenced by continental "modernist" fashions including expensive suits with short jackets and tapered trousers, whereas the Rockers emulated American rebels with their motorbikes, leather jackets, jeans and boots.[23] These two groups also attracted negative media attention when they began brawling with each other in the early sixties. All of these groups were criticized for their foreign influence. Indeed, sociologist Bill Osgerby argues that young people intentionally embraced American and European styles as a symbol of their "rejection of the drab conventions of 1950s Britain" and "fundamental disrespect for the old class modes and manners."[24] These youth subcultures reveal how young Britons interpreted an emerging global youth culture within their own national context.

The working class youth cultures of this era, however, had little influence over the predominantly middle-class student culture in the universities. Because most working-class teenagers left school at sixteen and entry-level jobs for them were plentiful and well-paying throughout the fifties and sixties, their incomes increased more rapidly than the population overall.[25] Without families of their own, they were free to spend their money on consumer items, especially clothing and music. Middle-class teenagers, on the other hand, tended to stay in school longer to sit for university exams and go on to universities, thus delaying full employment and the independent spending power it would entail. As a result, middle-class students had little time or money for the activities of the youth cultures of the period. Peter Lewis, who was a teenager in the fifties, confirms that "Boys like me tried to dress (tweed jackets, grey flannel trousers) and talk like men . . . There was no space in between being a boy and becoming a man for any distinctive style or assertion of identity."[26]

Some middle-class youth, however, rebelled against the consumerism, conservatism, and classism of post-war British culture in other ways. They first found a voice in Beat writers from America and the group of British writers called the "Angry Young Men." First derived from the play *Look Back in Anger* (1956), "Angry Young Men" referred to writers who were influenced by the American Beat movement and French existentialism, and like them attacked class hierarchy and "the Establishment" or those in authority.[27] They inspired Britain's middle-class "bohemian" culture in the fifties and early sixties.

Sheila Rowbotham was one middle-class bohemian who has written extensively about her life as a teenager in the fifties, a university student in the early sixties, and a social movement activist in the late sixties and seventies. Like most middle-class teenagers, Rowbotham had little interest in or knowledge of elections or political parties at that time. The Suez crisis merely confirmed her belief that imperialism was long outdated. She did, however, grow up firmly convinced that racism and class inequality were ridiculous— beliefs that were reflected in most polls of middle-class teenagers in the Long Sixties.[28] These attitudes separated her sharply from her father, who had been a civil official supporting the British Raj. From an early age, she felt a distinct generational gap between her father's generation and her own. Rowbotham was among those middle-class rebels who identified with *Look Back in Anger*. She felt it portrayed people as they really were and exposed the hypocrisy of the way most people abandoned their ideals and squandered their meaningless lives in pursuit of material comforts. She had read all the existentialists by the time she was seventeen and considered herself a beatnik by the time she arrived at Oxford University in 1961. [29]

Like many middle-class youth of the fifties and sixties, Rowbotham was heavily influenced by French and American cultures. Part of this influence was gained by travelling abroad for student exchanges and family holidays, as many of the middle-class increasingly did in this era.[30] Rowbotham spent a term in France, absorbing the exciting bohemian culture there in the late fifties. She also absorbed beatnik culture through the arts journals, jazz music, and coffee houses flooding into Britain from the US in the fifties. The *Evergreen Review*, an arts journal from New York, was Rowbotham's "beat etiquette manual." From it, she absorbed the writings of Jack Kerouac and Allen Ginsberg and the clothing fashions which beatniks adopted.[31] Indeed the widespread accessibility of publications from

the United States and English translations from the continent greatly facili-
tated the internationalization of global youth cultures. As a result of the
emerging discourse of distinct youth cultures and the increased exposure
of Britain's youth to international ideas and cultures, the student generation
of the Long Sixties would see themselves as a distinctive generation, having
more in common with youth in other nations than with older generations
of their own nation.

Another important historical development of enormous importance to
the emerging student movement of the late 1950s and early 1960s was the
global political context of the era created by the Second World War and
the Cold War. Indeed, Prime Minister Harold Macmillan once said that
the Cold War "really dominates everything."[32] The Cold War obviously
shaped the foreign policies of all countries involved, but each country was
uniquely situated within the larger web of this complex war of ideologies.
Britain's position was distinctively influenced by the legacies of the Second
World War, its imperial past, and its special relationship with the United
States. These legacies not only influenced decision-making at the highest
levels, but they informed the perspectives of the British media and public.
The emergence of the British student movement, therefore, must be situated
within these wider contexts.

The Second World War was enormously important in shaping Britons'
perspectives of themselves throughout the Cold War era. Popular memory of
the war held it as Britain's shining moment, as a time when its people united
in a common victorious effort to overcome the forces of evil. In the post-
war period, national pride in this "people's war" replaced a former identification with imperial might and shaped the nation's domestic and foreign
policy discussions. Although the Second World War resulted in military
victory, it also eventually led to a decline in the nation's overall standing in
global politics. The war directly undermined British imperialism and hastened decolonization. The decline of its empire, together with its domestic
economic troubles, led the nation to seek further assistance from the United
States. Britain's economic dependence on the US strengthened their special
relationship in the post-war period, but also made Britain third in world
power behind the United States and the Soviet Union. Although Britons
still took pride in their heroic performance in the war and saw themselves
as a moral force, a growing sense of national decline increasingly took hold
of the nation's consciousness as the Cold War wore on.[33]

During the Second World War, the nation had conceded to a Charter
of Human Rights, which supported the right of all nations to free and
independent governments. In the years following the war, many of Britain's colonies demanded this right and rose up in revolution when Britain
hesitated to grant full independence. Mohandas Gandhi's Indian independence movement using nonviolent civil disobedience especially inspired
other colonial revolutions. The impressive demonstration marches, massive sit-downs on the railroads, and slogans of freedom and human rights

resonated throughout the world. One by one, Britain willingly and unwillingly negotiated independence for its colonies so that by the end of the sixties much of its empire was gone. The British commitment to human rights and decolonization, however, was contested throughout much of the fifties and early sixties. While most on the Left supported and applauded this retreat from imperialism, viewing it as one more step towards the economic equality and justice embodied in their socialist ideals, many Conservatives firmly believed in the value of Britain's empire and fought to maintain British bases of influence throughout the world. The Suez invasion was only one such attempt to maintain this international power.

To prove its claims to moral superiority despite its imperial past, Britain also opened its doors to the citizens of its former colonies. By the late fifties, immigrants from former colonies numbered over half a million. The nation, however, remained divided on the issue of immigration throughout the Long Sixties. Many white Britons feared an erosion of British culture and society with the influx of thousands of non-white immigrants with very different national traditions. Many working-class whites feared that this wave of immigration meant increased job and housing competition and a consequent lowering of their living standards. Much of these fears rested upon a persistent racism noticed by many social commentators at the time. To many middle-class young people, however, racism seemed to be not only irrational and unjust, but contrary to the democratic, liberal, and tolerant heritage of the nation. Professor of British history Wendy Webster explains that this national identity was shaped by a long history of self-representations which emphasized "the kindliness and friendliness of its people. . . . their attachment to democracy, and their qualities of decency, reasonableness and common sense. The idea of racial tolerance had particular resonance for a country . . . which portrayed imperialism as a benevolent paternalistic project, concerned with the welfare of the colonized, and invoked a tradition of asylum for refugees."[34] This contradictory legacy of imperialism and tolerant ideals would play an important role in the emerging student movement.

The Second World War also saw the rejuvenation of the "special relationship" between Britain and the United States. The war forced the British into a closer alliance with the US, but post-war economic troubles forced the British to continue to rely heavily on American aid to rebuild their bombed-out country. This economic dependency put considerable pressure on the British government to support American foreign policy through the 1950s, but the two nations also had similar foreign policy goals, especially in that both wanted to create a liberal-democratic world order to counteract the perceived totalitarian tendencies of the Soviet Union. Britain consequently joined the US in creating the United Nations, the World Bank, International Economic Fund, and the North Atlantic Treaty Organization.[35] With these and other actions, Britain clearly sided with the US against the Soviet Union in the Cold War. This alliance would continue throughout the Cold War and benefit both nations in a number of important ways, but as the Cold War wore on, increasing numbers of Britons came to resent American influence and see the "special relationship" more as a liability than a benefit.

These foreign policy initiatives were an important part of the common vision of Labour and Conservative leaders never to allow Britain to let its guard down as it had in the 1930s and to retain its place as a world power. Similar to other countries, part of this effort to maintain a strong global military presence was the building of a nuclear weapons program. In this endeavor, the British government needed to at first rely upon the direct aid of the US, which was the only nation to have nuclear weapons in the first years after the war. Over the course of the late forties and the fifties, the British government began building and testing its own nuclear weapons. The government justified its decision to spend enormous amounts of money on its nuclear weapons program by claiming that "only an independent British deterrent would give the government any ability to influence Cold War diplomacy" and despite the enormous cost of the nuclear program, it was still much less expensive than maintaining large numbers of military bases. [36] Throughout the Cold War, every British government would continue to support this general foreign policy agenda.

Many Britons, however, wanted the world to be rid of nuclear weapons and demanded a more independent British foreign policy. Polls in the mid-fifties showed that although most Britons supported their nation's manufacture of nuclear weapons, most also favored an international agreement abolishing nuclear tests and weapons.[37] Some were more vocal and active in their opposition to nuclear weapons, fearful that they and the "special relationship" would involve the nation in a disastrous third world war. Pacifist groups, such as the Peace Pledge Union, Direct Action Committee, and War Resisters' International, were among the first to oppose the manufacture of nuclear weapons in Britain. The Peace Pledge Union (PPU) first stated its opposition to nuclear weapons in 1951 when it proposed "Operation Gandhi" to adopt Gandhian nonviolent civil disobedience to pressure American forces to withdraw from Britain, stop the manufacture of atomic weapons in Britain, force Britain to withdraw from NATO, and disband the British Armed Forces.[38] Over the next few years, it sponsored a number of small-scale sit-downs, pickets, and vigils outside British military installations and changed its name to the Non-violent Resistance Group.

Britain's position within the Cold War also inspired considerable discussion amongst university students in the mid-fifties. According to Stuart Hall, even Oxford University had a small group of rebels interested in challenging the existing system.[39] These outsiders, like Hall, joined the Communist and Socialist clubs, endlessly debating how to apply Marxist theories to contemporary society. Although Hall appreciated Marxism, he strongly criticized Stalinism as brutal, authoritarian, and undemocratic. He was also critical of Marx's ignorance of the Third World issues of race and ethnicity, which were so important to Hall.[40] Many students were antagonistic towards both the

USSR and the US, viewing them as equally extremist and dangerous. Peter Sedgwick, then a Communist Club student at Oxford University, wrote in 1954 that the world was menaced by the hydrogen bomb and its escalation of the stakes of the Cold War. He felt that the US treated Britain as "the pawn to Washington's king" and a "shock absorber" in the Cold War. He accused the US of political bullying and cultural imperialism, claiming "Britain the colonizer has herself become a colony."[41] Many others on the Right and Left echoed this sense of decline in the fifties and sixties. Its economic decline in the 1940s, its loss of colonies, and its playing second-fiddle to the US all seemed to point to Britain's deterioration.[42] Sedgwick argued that the only solution to this state of affairs was for Britain to completely reject imperialism and form an alliance with colonial independence movements. Britain was no longer a political or economic leader, but it could still be a leader of a third ideological force in the Cold War.

Other students across the political spectrum were increasingly aware of international political issues in the fifties. This is partially due to the extensive media coverage of these issues in this period. Politicians and mainstream news media discussed international events such as the colonial independence movements, the civil rights movement in the United States, and the hydrogen bomb, but they contradicted this information with rhetoric portraying the US and Britain as the defenders of freedom, human rights, and peace throughout the world. The contrast between Cold War rhetoric and the actions of the governments involved increasingly disillusioned many people on both sides of the Cold War and fostered a growing global culture of dissent in the fifties. Frustratingly for most students, however, much of this discussion of international affairs was moot because few of them could vote. Since the age of majority was twenty-one until 1969, they would have to wait until they graduated from college to fully participate in the political system.

1956 AS A TURNING POINT

Prior to 1956, therefore, the preconditions for a new student movement were already in place: the new expectation that all worthy students had a right to a state-funded higher education and the resulting over-crowding of universities, a new discourse about a special post-war youth culture as progressive and problematic, and anxiety about the nation's overall decline in international standing all laid the foundations for the student movement of the Long Sixties. All that was needed was a spark, a shock to the system to jolt students and the nation to mobilize a protest movement. The Suez crisis of 1956 provided that shock and in this way can be seen as a turning point in post-war British history and the history of the student movement.

In the aftermath of Suez, Prime Minister Anthony Eden resigned because of ill health and was replaced by Harold Macmillan. Macmillan believed that the Suez crisis proved that the Conservative Party must reform itself and become a leader in modernizing the nation if it was to survive. As a result, Macmillan launched a series of reforms, which would contribute to the expansion of the university system, liberalize morality-based laws, and transform the nation's military. At the heart of Macmillan's military reform was the reduction of the size of the armed services and the strengthening of Britain's nuclear deterrence program.[43] The detonation of the H-bomb later that year seemed to put an exclamation point on this new policy. The threat of military conflict in the Suez and Macmillan's new defense policy sparked a dramatic escalation in the nuclear disarmament movement which would become the focal point of the emerging student movement.

Although the Suez crisis and the reforms of the Conservative government were an important starting point for the student movement, it took a different sort of shock to socialism to open up a space for a new form of socialism to guide the new student movement. That second shock of 1956 was the Soviet Union's invasion of Hungary. While Stan Newens and most others turned out at the Trafalgar square demonstration to protest the Suez invasion, he and the Socialist Review Group produced and distributed 6,000 double-sided leaflets which not only called for industrial action to stop the British attack on Suez, but also for a protest against the Russian army's invasion of Hungary.[44] Although the latter elicited less student protest than the Suez crisis, it critically wounded the credibility of Britain's stalwart of the Old Left, the Communist Party of Great Britain (CPGB), and thus opened the door for a third path on the Left between Soviet Communism and Social Democracy.

The CPGB had been the largest organization on the Left outside of the Labour Party for decades. Despite rising anti-communism and heavy surveillance by MI5 in the early years of the Cold War, it had a membership of over 40,000 in the early 1950s, 200,000 "fellow travelers," and about 3,500 in the Young Communist League.[45] Hierarchical and disciplined, it flourished within the British Left. It had a thriving newspaper, *The Daily Worker,* which was mostly funded by Moscow and translated Soviet communism within a British context. In its 1951 publication, *The British Road to Socialism,* the CPGB had laid out its plan to take over the leadership of the labor unions and unify the Left to defeat the Conservatives in Parliament. By MI5 estimates, it had largely succeeded in the former of these goals by 1955, with more than one in eight top union officials being party members.[46] The CPBG indeed dominated the Far Left through the early fifties.

The CPGB's influence on the British Left, however, was seriously damaged in 1956. The year began with Soviet Premier Nikita Khrushchev's "Secret Speech," which exposed and denounced Stalin's excesses. This sent a shockwave through communist parties around the world. The CPGB, rather than publicizing the speech and strongly condemning Stalinism, was divided on how to deal with the new information. Communist groups around the world began to break away from a unitary party line and discuss alternative models of communism. Then Hungarian students led a massive uprising against their pro-Soviet government, calling for widespread reforms and democracy.

Soviet troops invaded and crushed the rebellion in November, destroying large areas of Budapest and killing 2,500 Hungarians. Thousands of British students joined exiled Hungarians, Czechs, and Poles in a 12 November protest march through London to the Communist Party headquarters, calling upon the British government to defend the Hungarians and British students to volunteer to fight in Hungary.[47] Although few students actually followed through, British communists were deeply disturbed by these events and looked to the CPGB to take some leadership in denouncing the heavy-handedness of the Soviet Union. The CPGB tried to "twist the Russian invasion into some triumph of socialist internationalism," but it failed miserably, alienating many of its own members in the process.[48] Because of this, thousands left the Communist Party that year and the British Left was fractured into dozens of tiny Marxist sects, competing for membership and struggling to create a new vision of socialism.

While the Labour Party criticized both the Suez and Hungarian invasions, it too disappointed the Left by moving towards the political center that year. Its new orientation was outlined in Tony Crosland's *The Future of Socialism* (1956), which argued that "post-war capitalism had solved the problem of production and that the mixed economy could ensure material well-being for all."[49] The Labour Party would thereafter abandon its commitment to nationalization, deemphasize class conflict, support capitalism, and focus more attention on "welfare, personal freedom, culture, and leisure."[50] Access to education was an important part of this recipe for progress. Through increased access to education at all levels, incomes would rise and many social problems would disappear. Crosland's more moderate platform for the Labour Party was part of a larger battle taking place within the Labour Party in the fifties between those who supported the radical reforms of the Labour government of the late forties and those such as Crosland and the new Labour Party leader Hugh Gaitskell, who advocated a more conservative stand on domestic and labour policies in order to attract more voters and win back leadership of the government from the Conservative Party. Although many moderate and right-wing Labourites supported Crosland's ideas, many on the Left who still agreed with Marx's critique of capitalism and supported a working-class revolution were disillusioned. For them, the Suez invasion demonstrated the continued threat of imperialism; the Hungarian invasion proved the dangers of Soviet communism; and Labour's version of social democracy would not end imperialism or the inequality fostered by modern capitalism. The events of 1956, as a result, opened the doors of dissent, forcing many students on the Left to look towards a New Left for leadership and inspiration.

THE FORMATION OF A NEW LEFT

Socialist Societies, which would lead the student movement later in the sixties, were especially affected by the rise of a New Left in the late fifties.

This New Left provided students with a distinctive ideology and outlook that would become one of the hallmarks of the student movement of the Long Sixties. As such, the history of the New Left warrants some in-depth discussion here.

The British New Left emerged out of twin shocks of the Suez crisis and Hungarian Revolution. Stuart Hall, who was a founding father of the New Left, later recalled that these events "unmasked the underlying violence and aggression latent in the two systems which dominated political life at that time—Western imperialism and Stalinism—and sent a shock wave through the political world. . . . They symbolized the break-up of the political Ice Age."[51] The next year, Hall and his friends who had recently graduated from Oxford created the *Universities and Left Review* (*ULR*). They hoped to use their publication to include a wider audience in their discussions and to contribute to the debates over the future of socialism emerging throughout the nation and the world that year. In their first issue, they explained that:

> Those who feel that the values of a capitalist society are bankrupt, that the social inequalities upon which the system battens are an affront to the potentialities of the individual, have before them a problem, more intricate and more difficult than any which has previously has been posed. That is the problem of how to change contemporary society so as to make it more democratic and more egalitarian, and yet how to prevent it degenerating into totalitarianism.[52]

Hall and his friends proposed to begin this process by using their magazine as a forum for socialist ideas and inviting their readers and supporters to join them in their Left Review Club in London to work towards this goal.

The authors and editors of the *ULR* were most interested in revising Marxism to apply it to the conditions of contemporary British capitalism. Drawing from the work of Richard Hoggart and Raymond Williams, they debated how consumerism and television had reshaped capitalism and changed working class mass culture. Hall argued that because of their new role as consumers, much of the British working class had lost its class identity and developed a false sense of classlessness. This explained their current conservatism. In order to help the working class to re-identify with working class politics and develop their full revolutionary potential, he asserted that modern socialism must address working class culture and provide a more authentic cultural politics.[53] Hall's new cultural emphasis within the *ULR* was a clear challenge to the economist doctrines of the Communist Party which had dominated British Marxism for decades. In this sense, these theories were "neo-Marxist," and represented the beginnings of a New Left.

At the same time Hall was creating the *ULR*, older leftists in the north of England were creating the *New Reasoner*. The editors of this magazine, Edward and Dorothy Thompson and John Saville, were former members of the British Communist Party who left it in 1956 after Khrushchev's secret speech and the Soviet counter-revolution in Hungary. They reflected the interests of older intellectuals in the northern labour movement in creating a new form of socialism as an alternative to the Communist Party. Like the students who had formed the *ULR*, however, the editors of the *New Reasoner* also hoped to influence the Labour Party and help it to win the general election of 1959. When the Conservatives won the election once again, the *ULR* and *New Reasoner* editors agreed to join forces, creating the *New Left Review* in 1960, hoping that a united New Left front might be more effective.[54]

The *New Left Review* became the central publication of the British New Left and a major influence on the global student Left throughout the Long Sixties. It drew from a wide variety of emerging leftist perspectives from Britain and abroad. It appealed to its readers to "build socialism from below": in small groups, people could take action and make a difference, moving their lives and the entire country closer to real democratic and egalitarian socialism.[55] The New Left agenda centered on participatory democracy, in which every person directly participated in the decisions which affected their lives.[56] They also argued against the Old Left's strict focus on class struggle, asserting that changes in the economy, such as new forms of corporate organization and the spread of consumerism, required new theories and analysis.[57] Drawing on the theories of C. Wright Mills and Raymond Williams, the New Left broadened its definition of politics to include cultural issues, such as alienation, apathy, and the breakdown of community.[58] It thus encouraged activists to understand their own lives and experiences within a wider cultural system of exploitation and oppression.

The New Left, however, was never politically or culturally monolithic. It had no central organization outside of the *New Left Review* or individual leaders or spokesmen. It was more of a diverse socialist discussion group to encourage people to actively participate in politics and organize themselves to transform the world around them. It spawned dozens of clubs across the country, many of which were student clubs. Some clubs were closely linked with local workers' groups, while others helped to organize activism around the most important issues of the day, including nuclear disarmament and racism. The *ULR* Club, for example, held weekly meetings in London, attracting up to four hundred participants from the broad Left. They invited famous speakers from the Left to their debates, including Labour leaders Hugh Gaitskell, Anthony Crosland, and Richard Crossman. They discussed racism, imperialism, education, literature, film, and jazz. They applied Marxist theory to their lives and contemporary British society, connecting the political and the personal.[59]

Although many focused on forging a new domestic politics, many New Leftists were also explicitly internationalist in outlook. Their leftist opposition to capitalism and imperialism led them to condemn Britain's alliance with the US and NATO. Many eventually came to advocate a foreign policy of "positive neutralism," hoping that by unilaterally renouncing nuclear weapons and breaking its ties with the US and NATO, Britain could ally with newly liberated Third World countries and be the leader of a third force in global politics.[60] Some New Leftists advocated working toward these goals within the Labour Party, while others argued that more revolutionary extra-parliamentary tactics were needed. Indeed, the pages of the early *New Left Review* are filled with heated arguments and debates over strategy and the meaning of socialism.

While many people played important roles in the New Left's publications and ideological formation, E. P. Thompson more than any other was the voice of the early New Left. He was the leading figure behind the publication of *Out of Apathy* in 1960, the first book produced by the New Left. This collection of essays emphasized the creative potential of individuals, asserting that "humanist socialism must seek to liberate men and women as creative, moral beings; that socialism should above all increase our capacity, individually and collectively, to shape our lives according to fundamental human values and ideas."[61] He rejected the bureaucratic socialism of the Communist parties of Eastern Europe and called for a more libertarian form of socialism.[62] Thompson's humanist socialism originated in the work that he had done with Christopher Hill, Eric Hobsbawm, and John Saville in the Historians' Group of the CPGB in the 1930s, as part of their larger project "to recover and reinterpret the indigenous British radical heritage in order to reactivate popular radicalism and ally it with the Communist cause."[63] As such, this humanist socialism which would become a central organizing principle of the New Left originated in a uniquely British context.

Thompson and other New Leftists drew upon a deep British Marxist tradition, but increasingly engaged with ideas from the United States and Europe through the late fifties. One of the most important intellectuals of this global New Left in the early sixties was C. Wright Mills, a sociology professor from the United States. Deeply critical of the United States and the Soviet Union already, the events of 1956 also spurred Mills to forge a new way forward toward humanistic socialism. At that time, he was in Europe on a Fulbright fellowship and was deeply affected by the New Left he witnessed emerging in Britain. He toured Eastern Europe with Ralph Miliband, another early member of the British New Left in 1957. He was so impressed with Thompson, Mills tried to get him a job in Castro's Cuba.[64] After visiting and lecturing at the LSE, he wrote to its director: " . . . from what I have seen, I cannot believe that there is in [the world] any intellectual center more stimulating than the London School of Economics."[65] Mills returned to Britain and Europe many times over the next few years, meeting with many of the British New Left and sharing his own ideas in publications and lectures across the region.

Since Mills is viewed by many historians as a seminal influence in the global New Left and student movements, it is worth exploring some of his ideas as they relate to the British New Left and student movement. Probably the most important piece of evidence in this regard is Mills' "Letter to the New Left," which was published in the *New Left Review* in 1960. In it he agreed with Thompson's *Out of Apathy* and went on to argue his own points about what the global New Left should be and who the primary agent of radical change might be. He briefly stated that instead of the morally bankrupt Communist Left, the New Left should be "guided morally by the humanist and secular ideals of Western civilization—above all, reason and freedom and justice" and should connect the cultural and the political. [66] He then posited that while the working class was too conservative to lead a socialist revolution, young intellectuals might be "a possible, immediate, radical agency of change."[67] He supported this last point by referencing the powerful and successful radical student movements that had emerged in the spring and summer of 1960 in Turkey, South Korea, Cuba, Taiwan, Japan, Poland, Hungary, and the US South. This argument would help a generation of British students to identify themselves as part of a global student movement with the potential power to lead a revolution.

Inspired by Mills and other leading intellectuals, students in West Germany and the US formed powerful New Left organizations: the West German Socialist Student League (SDS) and the American Students for a Democratic Society (SDS). Both had origins in national social democratic organizations, but had become disillusioned with their parent organizations' unwillingness to challenge nuclear politics or the military draft, which they considered to be the worst aspects of the Cold War status quo. Both split from their parent organizations in 1960 and began to build student movements which would stress participatory democracy and social humanist values. Each movement, however, was distinct in that they chose to focus on issues of special concern within their respective national contexts. For example, the American SDS was mostly involved with the African American civil rights movement and racial justice, whereas the German SDS was more concerned about opposing West German rearmament and renouncing its Nazi past.[68] Despite their unique national contexts, both groups learned from each other as well as from the British and French New Left, and in turn transmitted their own ideas and strategies back to the British student movement in the mid-sixties.

The American SDS's famous *Port Huron Statement*, which was widely read by student activists in Britain and elsewhere, articulated some of the values of this emerging global student movement in 1962. Drawing from their experience within the civil rights movement, their reading of Mills, Herbert Marcuse, and Albert Camus, and the dissenting tradition at the University of Michigan where most of its leaders lived, American SDS leaders critiqued the Cold War ideology of anti-communism and the build-up of a deadly nuclear arsenal, and expressed discomfort and disillusionment with the inequality, political apathy, and stifled atmosphere on campuses and in society. They suggested that participatory democracy was the key to reforming the system in order to prevent a nuclear holocaust and allow all "men" to fulfill their capacities for reason, freedom, and love.[69] This New Left rejected "traditional" socialism's emphasis on redistributing wealth, declaring that they did not want more wealth. They wanted something qualitatively different; they wanted to *be* more.[70]

Expressing themselves as members of a distinctive generation, SDSers also helped to create an image of the global New Left as a product of the baby-boom generation. The British New Left, of course, began earlier than the American New Left and its members predated the baby-boom. The British New Left was also different from that of the American and West German New Lefts in that it had no central activist organization to mobilize students and would remain far more attached to the socialist goal of wealth redistribution. It did, however, engage with the discourse of the global New Left, translating it within the British context and spreading it to its readership.

The British and international New Lefts would have a tremendous influence on the student movement of the Long Sixties. The *New Left Review* became an influential forum for activists throughout the era, spreading the hodgepodge of New Left ideologies and discourse to student audiences. New Leftist professors, like Thompson and Hall, encouraged students to question the system, try to reform it, publish their ideas, and rise up in protest as a last resort. A great example of how New Left professors could inspire and politicize their students is the case of Sheila Rowbotham. She remembers that she was rather apolitical when she first arrived at Oxford University and thus not really interested in any of the male-dominated political clubs on campus. She first became interested in New Left politics, however, through her professors. Her medieval history tutor was Trevor Aston, editor of the radical social history journal *Past and Present*. Aston encouraged her to read Marxist historian Eric Hobsbawm, and together Aston and Hobsbawm awakened her interest in learning more about Marxism. Two socialist dons at her college encouraged this interest and directed her to study with European social historian Richard Cobb. Cobb in turn introduced her to "history from below" and to Dorothy and Edward Thompson, whom she visited during the summer. They became her very good friends and important influences on her life. Soon after that, she met another key New Left activist, Bob Rowthorn, who was then twenty-three and had become a committed socialist through the left-wing friends he had met while studying in Berkeley, California. Rowthorn then introduced her to a new generation of the New Left, which included Robin Blackburn and Gareth Stedman-Jones. These personal contacts with New Leftists played a major role in Rowbotham's decision to become a political activist and remain politically active for the rest of her life.[71]

Although there was no central activist organization to coordinate a New Left student movement in Britain, many students formed independent New Left clubs and many existing student Labour and Socialist Societies reflected New Left rhetoric and perspectives. Indeed, members of New Left clubs at universities were usually also members of Socialist and Labour Societies, effectively blending the groups. For example, while he was a student at Aberdeen University in the late fifties and early sixties, Willie Thompson was a member of both the New Left Club and the Socialist Society, which was still affiliated with the Labour Party. These two clubs invited speakers, such as Stuart Hall, who helped to spread New Left ideas. Thompson was concerned about apartheid in South Africa, decolonization, the Cuban revolution, and nuclear war, and the New Left club helped him to explore these issues further. Both clubs met infrequently and organized no direct actions, but were instrumental in shaping students' views, convincing many of them, like Thompson, to become activists later in the sixties.[72]

Many other students applied the New Left's rhetoric of human liberation, humanist socialism, and participatory democracy to their age-old struggle to increase student personal freedoms and student participation in university decision making.[73] In 1959, for example, Oxford's Labour club began what would become a long-term movement to demand university reforms to make their institution more democratic and just. Voicing their demands in the student newspaper in 1961, they especially wanted more student participation in decision-making when it came to student discipline and called for a central students' union, which most other universities already had.[74] The university administration responded by allowing students the right to form a Student Representative Council. Each of Oxford's colleges would elect a student representative to the Council, which represented student interests in general when called upon by the administration. This was enough to appease the students at that time, but the demand for a student union and further reforms would remain central to the Oxford student movement throughout the Long Sixties and eventually lead to its largest protests in 1973–74.

New Left ideas entered into student discussions at many other universities across the nation in the late fifties and early sixties. The New Left group at Hull University dominated the Socialist Society and published its own magazine, *Partisan,* discussing national and university issues from a New Left perspective. In describing Hull's student political groups, the student newspaper *Torchlight* claimed that students in the Socialist Society had a close relationship with staff who provided intellectual stimulation and leadership.[75] Its Socialist Society was active in supporting a Hull dock workers' strike in the late fifties as well as participating in its Student Union Council. As a result, Hull's Student Union began agitating for increased student representation on university committees in November of 1959 and continued to press for this demand over the next several years.[76]

Similar to other universities, Hull students expressed most of their dissent through their student newspaper. In January of 1963, when it published articles calling the food in the refectory "dung" and the editor satirized University authorities, a staff and administrator Disciplinary Committee banned the *Torchlight* for one year and reprimanded the editor. This enraged more students who pressed even harder for student representation. At last the Vice Chancellor approved the creation of a student-staff Liaison Committee to make recommendations to the Vice Chancellor on the advisability of increasing student participation in university decision-making. He additionally allowed students to print an abbreviated newspaper, *Hull*, during the year that *Torchlight* was banned.[77] At the end of the semester, the Liaison Committee was made permanent to deal with disciplinary matters and students were allowed minority representation on one further committee, the Grounds and Gardens committee. The Student Union leadership, however, was "bitterly disappointed" with the result and the next year, the president of the student union Clive Pratley, a 34-year-old ex-regular army officer, resigned his presidency when the Vice Chancellor failed to treat him as a serious negotiator.[78] Despite these set-backs, Hull university students would continue to work towards making their university a participatory democracy throughout the Long Sixties, resulting in spectacular sit-ins in 1968 and the early seventies.

The National Union of Students (NUS) was a national organization of student union representatives from universities and colleges across the nation. Although it was much more conservative than the student Socialist Societies, it continued its long-term effort to increase personal freedoms and university representation for students at all universities in the early sixties. One important impetus for a renewed campaign towards this end was the government's decision to use the NUS as the representative for the nation's students for the first time in 1960. Perhaps coming as a result of Macmillan's wish to modernize the university system as well as the new tendency to view youth as a unique group in society with their own needs, the University Grants Committee on University Expansion officially asked the NUS to make recommendations on basic educational development.[79] The NUS Executive Council felt that this was an important responsibility and devoted considerable time and resources toward presenting a complete report to the University Grants Committee. Partly because of this initiative, the NUS also began to view university students as a distinct social group, uniquely qualified to weigh-in on how the university system should be modernized. The NUS and other student groups, while voicing perspectives similar to the New Left, rarely took direct action on the issue of student rights before the mid-1960s. Operating through traditional channels, they politely petitioned, negotiated, and published their requests. It would take a more powerful social movement to mobilize students in sustained protest and forge a student movement.

THE CAMPAIGN FOR NUCLEAR DISARMAMENT

While the Suez crisis disillusioned students, educational reforms heightened student expectations, and the New Left provided students with a discourse of dissent, the nuclear disarmament movement got them out of their lecture halls and onto the streets in sustained activism. This movement was the dominant extra-parliamentary social movement of the late fifties and early sixties. It not only involved students in its national actions, it inspired them to use direct action and civil disobedience in their own independent protests. As such, it introduced students to the excitement of being part of a larger protest movement and inspired future generations of students to create similar protest communities and cultures throughout the Long Sixties.

Similar to the New Left, Britain's nuclear disarmament movement was rejuvenated by the dual crises of 1956. Some like Martin Smith joined in the "Ban the Bomb" movement as part of his rejection of established politics, while others became much more afraid of nuclear escalation once Britain and the Soviet Union had committed their militaries to Suez and Hungary.[80] The nuclear disarmament movement absorbed many members of the New Left, who worked actively within the disarmament movement to direct it towards other New Left goals as well. Unlike the New Left, however, the nuclear disarmament movement focused on extra-parliamentary activism and had strong national organizations, giving it a stronger presence within the mainstream news media, national politics, and the student movement. Although the two movements maintained distinct identities, they joined together in their efforts to break the political stalemate of the Cold War.

As public fears of a nuclear holocaust escalated and both the Conservative and Labour parties continued to support the policy of nuclear deterrence, novelist J. B. Priestley published an article in a November 1957 issue of the *New Statesman* in which he called upon Britons to mount a moral crusade against their politicians' acceptance of nuclear deterrence. Drawing on Britain's popular memory of the Second World War, he wrote: "Alone, we defied Hitler; and alone we can defy this nuclear madness into which the spirit of Hitler seems to have passed, to poison the world."[81] The overwhelmingly positive response from the public inspired the editor of the *New Statesman,* Kingsley Martin, to invite prominent supporters of nuclear disarmament, including elderly philosopher Bertrand Russell and canon of St. Paul's Cathedral John Collins, to a meeting to discuss how to implement Priestley's suggestions. They decided to form a new single-issue campaign to "Ban the Bomb" in early 1958.

Called the Campaign for Nuclear Disarmament (CND), it adopted a cooperative attitude towards other activist groups, but it made it clear that it would be a separate organization to focus on the single issue of unilateral nuclear disarmament in Britain. CND leaders believed that British unilateralism would restore Britain's moral leadership in the world. Student organizer of the Oxford CND Nigel Young explained that this idealistic moral national vision was especially appealing to the young, the apolitical middle class, and "the older politically alienated and disenchanted."[82] He believed that this movement not only responded to escalations in nuclear weapons technology and the Cold War, but also "arose as a direct response to the change of Britain's world status revealed by Suez" and reflected many Britons' worries about their loss of empire.[83] At the first public CND rally, nearly 5,000 people crammed into Central Hall in Westminster to hear speakers such as renowned historian A.J.P. Taylor and author Alex Comfort. Comfort especially stressed the morality of their cause, explicitly comparing nuclear war to the Jewish holocaust of the Second World War. Drawing on the legacy of the "people's war," Comfort exhorted: "We can make Britain offer the world something which is virtually forgotten—moral leadership. Let us make this country stand on the side of human decency and human sanity—alone if necessary. It has done so before. If it does so again I do not think we need fear the consequences."[84] This blend of moral and national idealism was especially intoxicating to many young people who had missed out on the war, but still looked for national moral leadership.

The CND's moral witness in the defense of all human life attracted Christians, pacifists, and humanists, while its emphasis on individual action and challenging state authority appealed to anarchists, and its challenge to the Cold War status quo attracted New Leftists and socialists. Many in the New Left, including Stuart Hall and E.P. Thompson, were especially excited about this new dynamic force for change. In the spring of 1958, Thompson wrote: "At last it is beginning to move. The frozen formations of the Cold War era are beginning to break up. . . . the rapidly gathering success of the Campaign for Nuclear Disarmament: these are signals of a new temper among the people."[85] CND's famous fifty-mile Easter marches from the weapons research center at Aldermaston to London were especially successful in engaging young people in an exciting adventure away from home, and in helping activists of all ages to feel part of an international community of dissent. For New Leftists in particular, the Aldermaston marches manifested a new creative form of democracy, where the common activist rose up to directly confront the "tyranny of destruction."[86]

By the end of 1958 the CND was enormously successful. Over 200 groups had affiliated with the CND, and the CND and other peace groups were organizing hundreds of pickets, vigils, lobbying campaigns, and marches across the country. The confidence of the CND reached an all-time high in 1960 with its incredible turn-out of 100,000 participants at its Easter Aldermaston March.[87] By 1961, the CND had over 800 local groups. According to Canon Collins, the CND symbol, which was a circle encompassing the symbols for "N" and "D", or a broken cross, "became as well-known as the Union Jack . . . and to thousands the world over it became a sign of sanity and hope."[88] Polls in the early sixties showed overwhelming public support for halting nuclear testing and securing nuclear disarmament treaties. Although the Macmillan government repeatedly refused to meet with CND representatives, a March 1958 memorandum from his undersecretary of state warned that the movement could damage his policies and required immediate attention. As a result, Macmillan approved measures to undermine the CND through the use of propaganda and press contacts to ignore CND news.[89]

Despite the apparent success of the movement, the CND began to change directions and fracture in 1960. When Cold War tensions remained high in 1959 and 1960 and the Labour Party lost the general election, many within CND believed that they needed to go in new directions. A small group within CND, led by Bertrand Russell, felt that CND marches would never convince a majority of either party to renounce nuclear weapons. Influenced by Gandhi, the British Direct Action Committee, and the American civil rights movement, they wanted to use nonviolent civil disobedience in an effort to gain more public support for their cause. Russell argued that since all the major organs of publicity were against them, they should use civil disobedience purely as a practical method of propaganda.[90]

One of Russell's closest advisors at this time and a powerful force within the CND was Ralph Schoenman, an American postgraduate student studying at the LSE. His argument for civil disobedience was very different. Influenced by the American New Left, including Herbert Marcuse and C. Wright Mills, he viewed nuclear weapons as one symptom of the larger problem of modern technological society, and how it had repressed and alienated humanity.[91] By using civil disobedience, activists could reassert humanistic, moral values and be an example of how people can make their society more humane. If the government reacted brutally to suppress them, the CND could use this to expose the violent corruption of the entire system and gain more public sympathy for broad radical change. The frustration with the lack of change within political parties and global New Left ideas about participatory democracy and direct action thus encouraged thousands of CND activists to advocate civil disobedience after 1960.

The majority of CND leaders, however, rejected civil disobedience for a number of reasons. Many felt that it was too radical, "would alienate the labour movement, and confirm the already current notion that the movement was extreme, 'cranky', and not a serious political phenomenon."[92] This opposition to civil disobedience reflected the dominant political culture in mid-century Britain which emphasized parliamentary democracy and rational debate.[93] In polite British society, marches and rallies were acceptable means of voicing opinions, as long as they obeyed the law. No matter how activists justified civil disobedience, the press, public, and government would view it as breaking the law and frame it as criminal behavior. This tactical change would therefore change the nature of the entire movement.

Angry with this reaction, Russell and his supporters broke with the CND and formed a separate organization devoted to using civil disobedience to achieve nuclear disarmament. Called the Committee of 100 (C100), this new organization worked alongside the CND and eventually absorbed the Direct Action Committee into its ranks. From late 1960 until 1962, C100 was very successful in generating publicity for its actions and in attracting more young people to its ranks. A number of celebrities such as John Osborne, Vanessa Redgrave, and John Braine joined and enhanced the popularity of the group. The C100's first formal demonstration was a four-hour sit-down outside the Ministry of Defense in Whitehall in February 1961 to protest the arrival in Scotland of the first nuclear submarine from America. An estimated 2,000 activists sat down and at least another 3,000 supported them. They marched in silence and were quiet and disciplined throughout the demonstration, with the police and press remarking on the good behavior of the protesters.[94] Another 10,000 marched in Glasgow in one of the largest nuclear disarmament protests ever held in that city.[95] The C100 leaders were satisfied by the actions overall, but some, including Schoenman, were frustrated by official tolerance of the protests and the lack of confrontation because they believed that only confrontation would force the government and press to react to their protests. At the next Aldermaston March, which involved 150,000 participants, Schoenman led about 500 protesters off to the US and Soviet embassies in an unplanned and unsanctioned sit-down protest. This was much more confrontational than anything before, with protesters charging the police cordons and the police arresting twenty-five of them. The media focused on this small sensational aspect of the four-day long protest to the fury of the CND and delight of Schoenman.

As the C100 became more confrontational and successful, the government and police became less tolerant and the media more critical. In April 1961, 2,500 sat down outside of Whitehall, but this time 826 were arrested and fined one pound each. Their most successful and publicized action was a protest later that year. Just prior to the event, the authorities tried to prevent the demonstrations by forbidding the use of Trafalgar Square and arresting thirty-seven members of the Committee for inciting a breach of the peace under the Justices of the Peace Act of 1361.[96] Russell, who was then eighty-nine, and several of the other leaders were sentenced to two months in prison. Russell used the trial to voice his eloquent plea to the British people:

> You, your families, your friends and your countries are to be exterminated by the common decision of a few brutal but powerful men. . . . Our ruined, lifeless planet will continue for countless ages to circle aimlessly around the sun, unredeemed by the joys and loves, the occasional wisdom and the power to create beauty which have given value to human life. It is for seeking to prevent this that we are in prison.[97]

Although his sentence was reduced to seven days due to health concerns, the media and the public viewed his imprisonment as a travesty of justice and Russell became a worldwide hero to peace activists.

As a consequence, the C100 protest that September was wildly successful. In Scotland, only 500 demonstrators turned up in the heavy rain, but over 12,000 sat down in Trafalgar Square and were joined by many thousands more. The crowd jeered the police and tried to break through their cordon, and the police treated them roughly, arresting over 1,000.[98] A National Council for Civil Liberties report contained thirty-one allegations of police violence during the protest and the media generally sided with the protesters. Although the magistrates treated the protesters leniently, many activists were outraged when the police blatantly lied in giving their evidence.[99] This experience radicalized the protesters even further.

Despite these victories, the government's strategy of using the legal system and media to undermine the movement was working. As C100 members began to organize demonstrations against US bases in late 1961, the authorities arrested six Committee members under the Official Secrets Act and sent in thousands of police and soldiers to protect the bases. The judge refused to let the Committee members state their beliefs or otherwise use the trial to help their movement, and sentenced them to twelve-to-eighteen months prison. This demoralized the movement and contributed to an overall sense of decline among its leadership. The sentences, however, did generate considerable anger and publicity, which contributed to another turnout of 150,000 for the 1962 Aldermaston March.[100]

By that time, however, the Labour Party, trade unions, and media had turned against the C100. Reflecting the widespread belief that Britain was a respectable, tolerant nation, the *Times* argued that breaking trivial laws was inappropriate in a democratic society, where the protesters had a wide range of civil and political freedoms to express their views legally.[101] Others, steeped in the British tradition of rational debate, accused the C100 of hooliganism and getting carried away with an emotional mob mentality. Indeed, while the C100 stressed nonviolent civil disobedience, most activists had no training in the difficult tactic of Gandhian nonviolence and consequently were unprepared to respond non-violently to police violence. This led a small number of protesters to react angrily when pushed by police, resulting in skirmishes and arrests. These small incidents were then publicized by the press and used to reframe direct actionas violent and criminal, and thus unacceptable even when used for a moral cause. As a result of the non-traditional tactics of the C100, legal actions against the protesters, and the consequent reframing of the movement, the public identity of the nuclear disarmament movement changed from rational and respectable to irrational and criminal. As the image of the Aldermaston march shifted from "a pilgrimage of dedication" to a "national threat" in the eyes of the media, public support for and participation in the movement declined rapidly.[102] By the time Bertrand Russell resigned from the C100 in late 1962, it had begun to decline and the CND soon followed suit.

Regardless of its divisions and eventual decline, the nuclear disarmament movement was an especially important origin of the student movement of the Long Sixties. The inspirational rhetoric of the CND was very attractive to an idealistic younger generation, eager to do something to affect world politics. Student activist David Widgery said of CND:

> Once a year the march passed through the streets with great clamour and glamour. People with battered top hats playing the cornet out of tune and girl art students with coloured stockings—the whole parade of infamy came through the town. It was terribly enticing . . . They were passionate, evangelical, calling upon you to do things now, to sit down, to stand up and be counted.[103]

The nuclear disarmament movement thus introduced a whole generation of young people to the joys, tactics, and challenges of direct action. It was so successful in appealing to young people that joining CND became "the thing to do" amongst teenagers and an important part of the emerging middle class youth culture. A Youth CND branch secretary recalled that, "We got a lot of young people who joined us because this was the thing to do among teenagers. They came on Aldermaston or wore the CND badge because they thought this would annoy the grown-ups."[104] The movement's anti-adult, anti-authoritarian character especially appealed to young people who saw the Bomb "as a symbol of the older generation's moral and political bankruptcy."[105] By 1962, up to 90 per cent of CND participants in the Aldermaston march were young people.[106] This youth participation in the CND would have an enormous impact on the participants, radicalizing and politicizing them, and preparing them to continue their protests as students in universities.

CND actions not only gave participants a strong sense of community, of "us" versus "them," but it was also a way to get involved in politics without having to join the bureaucratic and boring youth organizations of established political parties. Sociologist Frank Parkin wrote in 1968:

> The excitement of a four-day march, with its attendant personal sacrifices and discomforts suffered for the sake of a cause, the fellowship and conviviality, and the creation of *Gemainschaft* relationships, combined to create an appeal which could not be matched by the daily round of routinized politics . . . Protest against the Bomb was, for many, their first major political experience, and one which thrust them dramatically into the midst of the ideas and personnel of the radical left.[107]

Teenager David Triesman, who would become a leader of the Essex student movement in the late sixties and eventually a leading member of the Labour Party, was "turned onto politics by Youth CND." He remembers: "taking part in one of the Committee's mass sit-downs in Trafalgar Square. It was a very festive event. People were having a good time because they felt positively involved and emotionally engaged. The enjoyment had as much impact on your politics as the physical events that were taking place around you."[108] The CND thus provided an introduction to radical cultures and an exciting alternative to parliamentary politics, which was irresistible to many teenagers.

As a result, large numbers of university students joined in CND marches and in 1960 formed their own affiliate of CND: Colleges and Universities Campaign for Nuclear Disarmament. A CND survey of 2,919 students from eight British universities that year revealed that 37 per cent had attended nuclear disarmament activities.[109] There were 150 CND-affiliated chapters at universities and colleges by 1962.[110] Although each club functioned independently of the larger organization, each served to transmit the rhetoric and strategies of the wider movement to each local context, serving as a focal point for most peace-related activism in the student movement through the early sixties.

Individual student CND groups reveal important clues not only about the nature of the emerging student movement, but also of how nuclear disarmament groups varied according to local circumstances. Among the first wave of CND societies formed in universities in 1958, Hull University's CND group became the most active organization on that university's Left through the early sixties. They organized protests of 100 to 300 students (approximately 10 per cent of the student population) against the French A-bomb, the Russian explosion of the 7-megaton bomb, and the Cuban missile crisis. After the Cuban missile crisis, Hull CND exhorted other students to join them, saying "Self-interest alone should be sufficient motive for you to realize that the way in which the world is being run is wrong and criminal. Join us in attempting to find a path to world sanity and peace."[111] Reflecting the strategy of the wider nuclear disarmament movement at this time, Hull students framed their movement as rational and respectable, and the nuclear policies of governments as irrational and criminal. Using the student newspaper and pamphlets, these students effectively portrayed the issue as a crisis in governmental authority and drew upon a British national identity of rationality and respectability to gain support for direct actions against nuclear weapons.

While Hull CND's framing of the movement as respectable and rational kept them out of trouble with university authorities, Oxford's chapter of the CND, which formed in 1959, immediately ran afoul of university administrators. Although this group too framed their protest as respectful and law-abiding, Oxford's Proctors worried about the university's non-partisan reputation and fined CND students for carrying an Oxford University banner at a CND march, stating that they had not gotten approval to do this beforehand. When students attempted to organize their own march from the military base at Brize Norton to Oxford in November 1959, the Proctors refused to allow them to organize the march under the name of a university organization. The students then got the town CND group to officially sponsor the demonstration.[112] The protest was a great success, attracting over 700 participants, most of whom were students. They marched in organized lines to a jazz band and banners reading "US Friendship, not US Bombs." [113] Fifty protesters stayed behind at the gates of the base for an all-night vigil. Despite harassment from university authorities, Oxford's CND continued to sponsor local protests and send busloads of students to national protests throughout the early 1960s.

Explaining her own motivation for this activism, Oxford student Catherine Fiske wrote in the student newspaper *The Cherwell* that "the Campaign offers the only positive step towards world peace that we have today. It opposes the general apathy which allows war to happen." She went on to quote C. Wright Mills' *The Causes of World War Three* in discussing the danger of this apathy and its cure in activism. She told her fellow students, "The need to awaken people to a critical and appraising attitude towards government policy is still absolutely essential. The Campaign is still working against the great mass of apathy and disinterest seen at all levels of society in this country."[114] Echoing New Left rhetoric, Fiske and many other student activists in the early sixties saw apathy as the primary problem confronting their society, and used the nuclear disarmament issue as a way to change society at a deeper level.

Scottish students were just as active on the nuclear disarmament issue as their southern counterparts. Glasgow University students formed a Nuclear Disarmament Club in 1960 to protest nuclear testing and manufacturing in Britain.[115] In February 1961, this group participated in the CND march of 10,000 to protest the decision to build a new American Polaris submarine base at Holy Loch.[116] The Glasgow Nuclear Disarmament Club, however, stressed more nationalist reasons for their protests. They objected specifically to Britain's powerlessness to control nuclear weapons in the Cold War conflict between the United States and the USSR. In a 1961 statement, they asserted:

> At a time when Polaris is so close as to serve as a continual reminder that our strategy is now wholly integrated with the US, that our function is now to provide bases for bombers, missiles and submarines over which we have no control. . . . We adhere to the almost forgotten doctrine that control of Britain's policy and safety should be kept in Britain's hand. . . . The US may engage in a war with Russia because of a dispute in which we have no interest, or in which we may think the Americans to be wrong, yet despite this the first Russian blows would be struck at the US bases in our country and around our shores.[117]

As this excerpt reveals, these CND students rejected Britain's subservience to the United States in the Cold War. They distrusted American control over the fate of their country and lives, and demanded that their own government stand up to the super-powers in defense of morality and disarmament. This type of argument would appeal to even conservative students' sense of patriotism and contribute to CND's success at Glasgow University throughout the sixties.

ANTI-RACISM CAMPAIGNS

In addition to the New Left and the CND, a third strand of social dissent that emerged in the late fifties and became a vital part of the early student movement was the struggle against racial injustice at home and abroad. Similar to the nuclear disarmament movement and the New Left, this crusade was greatly influenced by and connected to international developments, in this case especially by the American civil rights movement, decolonization, and the South African anti-apartheid campaign. The American civil rights movement, itself inspired by the post-war discourse of human rights and the Gandhian struggle against imperialism and racism, burst into the British newspapers in the mid-fifties with photos of white police brutality against peaceful civil rights marchers and reports of widespread racial segregation and hatred. These made white Americans seem racist, violent, and hypocritical, while the heroic actions of the marchers were an inspiration to all those seeking to use mass direct action to change the world. The African-American sit-in movement, which began in 1960 and was led by college students, was especially inspirational to young activists in Britain, showing them that young people like them could make a difference through collective action.

Young South Africans who challenged apartheid in the fifties and sixties similarly gained the sympathy and respect of many in Britain. The African National Congress and other civil rights groups used massive protests and nonviolent civil disobedience to fight the creation of the apartheid system in the fifties, but their government violently suppressed and imprisoned them. They turned to international allies to pressure the South African government through diplomatic measures and economic sanctions. The 1960 Sharpeville Massacre, in which South African police killed sixty-seven African demonstrators, especially outraged human rights activists around the world. These civil rights movements not only embarrassed two of Britain's closest allies and former colonies, but they also framed racism as a global problem linked to imperialism, making many Britons feel a moral responsibility to do something about it. The British student movement consequently added the fight against racism to their list of protest issues in the late fifties, and this issue would remain a central focus of the student movement throughout the Long Sixties.

The National Union of Students took the lead in voicing its support for civil rights campaigns in the late fifties and early sixties. Although its constitution forbade it from taking political stands, even against nuclear weapons, NUS leaders defined racism as a moral issue and thus opened the door to include it as part of its wider agenda. The NUS was very interested in what its American counterpart, the US National Student Association, was doing to help the civil rights movement, and repeatedly expressed its solidarity with and support of American student civil rights initiatives.[118] Since the civil rights movement seemed to be achieving its goals on its own in

America, British students did little more than express solidarity in writing and took no direct action on the matter.

The case of South Africa, however, was different. The South African government seemed determined to preserve apartheid and violently repress all dissent against it. As a consequence, the South African situation seemed more appalling to Britons. A 1959 Gallup poll revealed that 80 per cent of British citizens strongly opposed apartheid.[119] Many felt that as a former colony, member of the Commonwealth, and one of Britain's largest trading partners, South Africa would respond to strong pressure from the British government. When British diplomats protested against its violent racial repression, however, the South African government merely left the Commonwealth and continued to enforce apartheid. In 1959, African Chief Albert Luthuli raised the stakes by appealing to the international community for an economic, cultural, and sports boycott of South Africa to pressure the South African government to end apartheid.[120] English activists responded by forming the Anti-Apartheid Movement (AAM) in 1960 to use education and direct action campaigns, as well as continue the boycott, to fight apartheid. In response to the Sharpeville Massacre, it joined with trade unions to organize a March 1960 rally of 14,000 in Trafalgar Square.[121] Drawn by its moral rhetoric as well as its tactics, many students and members of the CND and the New Left joined AAM campaigns for the next two decades.

The NUS gave considerable publicity and financial aid to the AAM, encouraging its member chapters to discuss the issue of racism at home and abroad. For example, in 1959 when South Africa passed a bill creating racially segregated universities for its students and the South African Student Union called upon other nations to boycott South African goods, the NUS demonstrated its opposition to apartheid and a sense of global student solidarity by asking British students to participate in the boycott. It urged its members not to participate in sporting events with segregated South African teams and it sponsored several national demonstrations. These actions were very well attended, with up to 10,000 students participating and expressing their moral opposition to racism to the world. [122]

Independent groups against apartheid and racism also formed at many universities across the nation, joining CND groups in the emerging student movement. By 1964, there were twenty-two student societies affiliated with the AAM and 53 per cent of AAM's total membership consisted of students.[123] LSE students were among the first to hold demonstrations at their university against South African apartheid and racial segregation in 1957.[124] Because of its large proportion of overseas students, the LSE's Student Union felt compelled to take a firm stand against racism. It supported many anti-apartheid actions and took up collections to aid black South African students in fighting their government's attempt to restrict them to segregated colleges. Over a thousand LSE students participated in a 1959 national protest march against apartheid in South

African universities, and many joined the 1960 AAM demonstration of 12,000 in London.[125]

Oxford students mobilized against racism in 1959 with the formation of a Joint Action Committee Against Racial Intolerance (JACARI). Their first action was to adopt a resolution to join the international campaign against apartheid by participating in the boycott against South African goods.[126] JACARI went on to sponsor silent vigils in memory of the Sharpeville massacre, organize protests against visiting South African teams, and send Oxford students to national anti-apartheid protests in London. The Oxford Labour club additionally supported the fight against apartheid by demonstrating against the all-white South African cricket team which played Oxford in May of 1960. The Proctors forbade the club from this demonstration beforehand, but fifty-six dons voiced their support for the protest. In the end, fourteen Labour club students, led by club secretary Robin Blackburn, picketed the game.[127]

Luthuli's call for international support in the fight against apartheid also resonated with Glaswegian students. In October 1962, University of Glasgow students elected Luthuli as their rector. The rector was a symbolic representative of the student body who was typically some popular figure elected by students each year. Student activists had hoped to publicize their support for Luthuli's cause with his election. A riot during the rectorial elections, however, stole much of the media attention from this statement of solidarity with African freedom fighters. Carrying on a long tradition of student election mayhem, some students threw flour and other foods at supporters of other candidates. Unlike earlier elections, however, the police arrived to break up the crowds and randomly arrest students. Thousands of students then turned against the police, pelting them with bags of flour. The riot police eventually dispersed the crowd and charged thirty two students with breach of peace and obstruction. The significance of the Luthuli election, however, was not lost. When the South African government refused to allow Luthuli to attend his installation as rector in Glasgow, students protested by wearing black armbands and holding a teach-in in South Africa. For Glasgow University's students, Luthuli remained a powerful symbol of the South African civil rights movement for the remainder of the decade.[128]

The South African and American civil rights movements not only gave British students a chance to express their moral outrage against racism abroad, but also raised their awareness of racism at home. Until 1958, most British students assumed that their national tradition of fairness and tolerance would eliminate any chance of racial violence in Britain. This self-image, however, was shattered in the summer of 1958, when race riots erupted in the disadvantaged Notting Hill area of London. Racial tensions there and elsewhere in the country had been building throughout the fifties as immigrants from the Caribbean settled there and competed with poor whites for housing and jobs. Expressing working-class anger, gangs of Teddy Boys openly harassed blacks and smashed Caribbean cafes that summer. Finally, at the end of August, the black community fought back and Notting Hill erupted into full-scale rioting. Mobs of hundreds of whites and blacks roamed through the streets attacking each other. By the time the fighting finally stopped after 5 September, 108 people had been arrested for rioting and possessing offensive weapons, and many others were seriously injured.[129]

The riots shocked the nation. Peter Hennessy remarks that "The comfortable shared notion within a nation which prided itself on its tolerance and civility that race riots were a blemish on other societies such as South Africa or the southern USA was gone for ever."[130] Although many in the New Left blamed white racism for the riots, many conservative whites blamed immigrants for the problem and demanded new restrictions on immigration. The Macmillan government responded to this anti-immigrant feeling with the Commonwealth Immigration Act of 1962, the first law restricting migration from the Commonwealth to only those who held work permits upon entry and their dependents. For many young people, however, the Notting Hill race riots and the Immigration Act demonstrated that Britain had its own problems with racism.

With their awareness of racism raised by apartheid, the American civil rights movement, and the Notting Hill riots, British students across the nation mobilized to protest racial discrimination in their own cities.[131] The NUS began discussing Britain's "colour bar" in 1960 in conjunction with its continuing discussion of racism abroad. Its Vacation Work department had seen "a large measure of racial discrimination" as it encountered many employers who "operated a colour bar."[132] The Union was also "disturbed by recent instances of overseas students being refused lodgings in University towns . . . with the agreement and connivance of the University Authorities."[133] Later that year, the NUS again discussed these issues, and although all agreed that they should take some action against racial discrimination, they disagreed on strategy and in the end, did nothing.

It was up to local student groups to begin implementing direct action techniques, borrowed from overseas civil rights movements and the CND, in the fight against racism in Britain. The London School of Economics took an early lead in this effort. In June 1960, an LSE student newspaper investigation revealed that a popular student bar in Soho refused to admit black students. The manager confirmed this, explaining that if he allowed "coloured" people they would fight with white students. The newspaper editor Don Esslemont wrote "British students are deeply committed in the struggle against apartheid in Africa. We must be equally firm about apartheid in London."[134] LSE students formed a Society Against Racial Discrimination to fight racism at the bar by boycotting and picketing it.[135] At the request of an LSE delegate, the NUS passed a motion that condemned the "colour bar" and called on all students to boycott the club.[136] As a result, the club eventually agreed to admit students regardless of race.

Similar protests against racism occurred at other universities. For example, students at Glasgow University began a campaign against the House of Fraser retail chain in 1961. Minority students in Glasgow, including Asians, Indians, and Africans, had long faced discrimination in private accommodations. The problem, however, only became an issue for the student government when several of these students, working with the student council employment bureau, were immediately rejected when they applied for employment at clothing stores owned by the House of Fraser.[137] The House of Fraser denied accusations of discrimination, but many students remained unconvinced. After some small demonstrations and pickets, the student council asked the owner of the clothing stores to resign from the Glasgow Students Charities Appeal and the student council employment bureau refused to send students to work at the House of Fraser stores.[138] Reflecting on the issue two months later, student Hugh Macpherson explained:

> One of our most cherished beliefs is that we are above any of the racial troubles that afflict various parts of the world, and our own ideas of superiority were rudely shattered with the outbreak of the Notting Hill riots. Still, at least in this town we clung to the idea that, being, of all the cities in the land, the most friendly, it did not apply to us. It is most unfortunately true that this belief is not founded on fact. . . . The hard fact of the matter is that the vast majority of the landladies on the official university list will not have dark coloured people in their houses as boarders. . . . In this, and the other evidence of a creeping colour consciousness we are not only being immoral but are also showing a complete lack of appreciation of the true political suicide of this policy.[139]

He added that since Africa and India were becoming politically powerful regions, Britons needed to gain their respect by treating future leaders fairly and showing them the best of British behavior. Once again, while the fight against racism had strong international origins, British students translated the issue within the context of Britain's vanishing empire and a desire for Britain to regain international prestige through moral leadership.

While incidents like these may seem insignificant in hind-sight, they were in fact signs of an emerging student movement in Britain and the world and, as such, reveal some important dimensions of the history of Britain and the global history of student movements in the Long Sixties. The origins of the global student movements of the Long Sixties lay in long-term postwar developments, but the turning point and spark for the British student movement was the Suez crisis of 1956. Dissent from the bipolar divisions of the Cold War had been growing prior to that fateful year, but the Suez and Hungarian invasions shook the global Left and awakened them to the necessity of forging a New Left between Soviet communism and social democracy. The most important forces of dissent to emerge in the years that followed 1956 were the New Left, the Campaign for Nuclear Disarmament, and the civil rights movements in South Africa and the United States. These groups had a tremendous influence on the student generations of the Long Sixties, introducing them to new perspectives on politics and strategies for challenging injustice and immorality, and inspiring them to begin their own student activist movements. As a consequence, the British student movement that emerged in the late fifties focused on many of the same issues as these groups: humanist socialism, including human rights and participatory democracy, and nuclear disarmament.

The emerging British student movement also resulted from a conjuncture of other historically specific factors, including the rise of global youth and dissent cultures and the "modernization" of the British educational system. Similar to other nations in the late fifties and early sixties, a youth culture, or at least an awareness of youth as a special social group, emerged in the post-war years. This youth culture led many young Britons to identify with youth in other countries, especially the United States. As products of this youth culture, students perceived themselves as the harbingers of modernity, with a special mission in life. Movements that expressed this idealistic desire to improve the world, such as the New Left, nuclear disarmament movement, and civil rights movements, would therefore be especially appealing to students of this generation. Actions taken by the British government in the forties and fifties also contributed to British students' hopes and expectations of a new future for their nation and themselves. The creation of the social welfare state in the years after the Second World War raised their expectations that social inequalities would eventually disappear, while educational reforms led many young Britons to assume that they would have equal opportunity within a reformed higher education system. The state did fund higher education for more students in this era, but not enough to keep pace with the greater numbers of qualified students applying for university admission. Once in the universities, students quickly realized that the university system had remained steeped in tradition and hierarchy. The youth culture and educational reforms thus raised student expectations and set the stage for the beginnings of student dissent in the late fifties.

The most important inspiration for the student movement in the late fifties, however, was the Campaign for Nuclear Disarmament. This movement gave young people experience in dissent and direct action, raised key issues such as the importance of challenging evil through moral leadership, and showed students the difference that activism could make in the lives of the activists and in the course of national events. Its extra-parliamentary organizational style and rhetoric framed international politics as a crisis point, in effect feeding upon and raising public fears of nuclear war and Britain's lost political prestige in the Cold War. It also provided students with methods, rhetoric, and solutions to face this crisis.

The movement's strategy of mass direct action, however, rested on the belief that Britain's government was essentially democratic and would indeed bow to massive demonstrations of opinion. But even hundreds of thousands of people in the streets were not the majority of Britain's population, and throughout the era, election results continued to support politicians who did not follow a policy of nuclear disarmament. As a consequence, the British government could and did ignore the nuclear disarmament movement. Yet this lesson was lost on thousands of students who believed that the movement was achieving its goals of creating a new culture and society through direct action, and pressuring governments to cool off the Cold War through nuclear test bans and other conciliatory efforts made in the early 1960s. For them the lesson of the nuclear disarmament movement was that one should stand up for one's ideals and take action in the name of morality, even if it meant breaking the law.

External social movements, including the New Left, CND, and AAM inspired students to form their own related activist groups at universities across the nation. These new student organizations, together with the Socialist Societies, became the foundations for the student movement of the Long Sixties. Inspired by other movements' use of mass direct action, the new student movement planned and organized events including demonstration marches and pickets. Using direct action, however, raised the stakes of involvement. It made activists' names known to university administrators and the wider public, and thus risked punishment for breaking rules or laws. This meant that only small numbers of the most dedicated students would directly participate in activism. Although the student movement in this early period involved small numbers of students and had no national organization to unite their political activism, they were unified in a similar commitment to direct action and moral causes. While the National Union of Students could not lead them in explicitly political actions, it did organize student activism around moral issues and foster a sense of student solidarity not only among British students, but also with students in other countries. This unique combination of moralistic idealism, New Left rhetoric, and widespread use of protest techniques such as the demonstration rally, picket, and boycott, were what defined the student movement of the Long Sixties as distinct from student activism before and afterwards.

The British student movement originated in both British and global forces. It was inspired not only by the ideology, rhetoric, and tactics of the British New Left and CND, but also by the Indian independence movement, American civil rights movement, and anti-apartheid activists in South Africa. The British student movement was a manifestation of a global culture of dissent emerging in the late 1950s, yet its perspective remained uniquely British. The nation's long history of imperialism and liberalism had created a national identity based upon the belief that their government led the world in tolerance, moral responsibility, and concern for the welfare of the colonized. Although the nation recognized its third place behind the United States and Soviet Union following the Second World War, the discourse of moral leadership pervaded the British student movement, uniquely shaping its perspective on nuclear disarmament and racism. From the beginning, therefore, Britain's student movement framed its protests as rational and moral responses to irrational and immoral events, and applied international strategies and rhetoric in ways uniquely situated to Britain's political culture and international standing. As such, the British student movement helps to reveal the extent and limits of transnational connections within global student movements.

When compared with student movements emerging in other countries around the world, British students shared much in common with their foreign counterparts, but also some distinctive features. While national left-wing student organizations formed in West Germany and the United States in the early 1960s, neither organization sponsored national protest demonstrations in this period. British students, however, led the world in protesting against nuclear weapons and apartheid. Unlike West German and American students, British students were much more free to take political action and form political groups at their universities. Under anti-communist pressure in the 1950s and early 1960s, West German and American students faced enormous pressure to support their respective governments in the Cold War and extreme repression of left-wing political perspectives. In that context, their activism against nuclear weapons remained tiny compared to that of British students. While American and South African students took the lead in fighting racism in their own countries, British students took the lead in supporting these battles against racism from abroad and in fighting racism in Britain, even though Britain had a tiny population of racial minorities and its racial troubles paled in comparison to those in other countries. The British student movement, therefore, was at least as significant as student movements elsewhere in the world in this period.

British students participated in student activism at or above the level of their counterparts in many other countries in the world in this period, but like them, student activists were only a small percentage of the student population. As such, it has been easy for many contemporaries and historians to overlook their significance. The student movement may not have ended racism or the nuclear arms race, but it did help to raise public awareness of these issues and contribute important moral and financial support to organizations working towards the same ends. Perhaps more importantly, student protests allowed participants to feel as though they were a part of a much larger community of dissenters, part of a significant new force emerging in the world. This feeling would inspire longer, more powerful protests later in the era of the Long Sixties.

2 "The Troubles" of Universities in the Mid-sixties

Sir Sydney Caine, the clean-shaven, graying, soon-to-be-retired Director of the London School of Economics and Political Science (LSE), stared at the crumpled body of the old porter, Edward Poole. That cold night in January of 1967, Caine had come to the Old Theatre to explain to the students why he had banned their meeting, had all of the light fuses removed, and posted an army of porters around the theatre to keep students out. He knew the students were upset about his replacement as Director of the School, Walter Adams, principal of a university in the hated racist regime of Rhodesia, but the students had no right to slander the man or to use university facilities for their campaign to prevent him from taking up his post next year. Things had just gotten out of hand and the foreign-born student ring-leaders had to be stopped. He had spoken to one of these leaders, David Adelstein, a South African born student and president of the LSE Student Union, and Adelstein had just agreed to move the students out of the theatre and down to the student bar, when another group of students began to scuffle with the porters in an attempt to enter the Theatre and Poole had fallen to the ground.[1]

Colin Crouch was a second-year LSE student attending the meeting that night. He described what happened next:

> The scene inside the darkened theatre was extraordinary. Some students had lit candles, and small points of light illuminated agitated and gesticulating human forms as the theatre gradually filled. Several students were on the stage ready to start the scheduled meeting. Caine ascended the platform to announce that the porter had been hurt and to say that if the students would now leave the theatre there would be no victimization. The theatre continued to fill, and was very noisy. Caine returned and made a vain attempt to still the noise. "The man has now died," he said, "Does that satisfy you?" There were enraged screams of "No!" from all sides of the theatre. Then the mood changed dramatically. It fell quiet, and students began slowly to leave.[2]

The Director closed the School for the rest of the evening and went to the students' bar to comfort weeping students. Crouch appreciated his support and felt sick with guilt at the mob mentality of the students that night. This was a turning point for him. He had fully supported direct action and mass participation up until that point, indeed, he had even helped to organize the meeting, but this night changed his mind on all that. For the rest of his days at the LSE, Crouch would be the voice of moderation within the Student Union.[3]

In the days that followed the Old Theatre incident, the newspapers had a field day with the story, deeply embarrassing Caine and many other administrators and staff who had been so proud of their university. The porter's death was tragic, but he was a frail man, with a weak heart, and he was not even on duty that night. Although no one had attacked him and he could have had the heart attack at any moment, many people felt that the students' irresponsible actions were to blame. School Secretary Harry Kidd, was outraged with the entire thing and wanted to take action against the student radicals who had caused it. He begged the Director to bring them all up on disciplinary charges and show them their proper place in the university. Eventually, Caine gave in and allowed Kidd to bring disciplinary charges against Marshall Bloom, an American graduate student who had helped to organize the Theatre meeting, Adelstein, and four others.[4]

Some LSE students also blamed the organizers for the events of that tragic night. They attempted to remove Adelstein and Bloom from their offices and gave evidence against them. Other students felt badly about the events that night and as a result simply gave up protesting about Adams. The announcement of the proceedings against the student leaders, however, reignited student anger against School authorities. Over 500 students had been present at the Theatre and Adelstein had actually been trying to get them to leave the premises. There was no evidence that Bloom or Adelstein had published any of the leaflets which libeled Adams and encouraged students to attend the meeting despite the ban. The Board of Discipline took several weeks to announce its decision. During that time, the annual Student Union elections were held and chairman of the Conservative Society, Peter Watherston, was elected president of the Union. He and the sitting Union Council organized a meeting to coincide with the announcement of the Board of Discipline's decision on 13 March. Approximately 800 students attended the meeting and heard the decision that Adelstein and Bloom would be suspended until the end of summer term in July. Watherston proposed that the Union should organize a boycott of all lectures and classes and a sit-in at the main entrance to the School demanding their reinstatement. This was overwhelmingly approved and the seven-day boycott and sit-in began immediately.[5]

Colin Crouch was busily involved in the sit-in and later wrote about the experience in several different publications, attempting to help his readers to gain a sense of the exciting atmosphere of the sit-in, as well as the feeling of community it generated. As he described it:

Meetings would go on long into the night in the Old Theatre, usually presided over by Richard Kuper, a brilliant orator, who would sit on the platform cross-legged, smoking a pipe . . . the sense of intensity was greatly increased by the surprising prominence accorded to us by the Press, television and radio. If the comment was often hostile and distorted, this only led to a feeling of solidarity. . . . A shop steward who brought a resolution of support from his branch late one night was received ecstatically. Sometimes the meetings would take on the characteristics of an early revivalist meeting, as individuals would tell us how they had come to experience a new view of life in the course of the sit-in. . . . Emotional tension was of course high. We had embarked on a novel, potentially dangerous course of action; we were tired; we were aware of the almost unanimous hostility of the outside world. . . . This experience, on an incredibly small and acknowledgedly unrealistic scale, was what the revolutionaries had spoken of when they dreamed of a new kind of politics, a new freedom from the constraints of mundane authority, a new immediacy of personal relations, a breaking down of the requirements of the roles we were forced to occupy in everyday life.[6]

This sense of revolutionary excitement and community was reflected in the reminiscences of many LSE students who participated in the sit-in that March. John Rose recalled, "when we decided to occupy, it was like the revolution had started! I was just a typical student, like most of those sitting in. But we discovered what is meant by collective strength, we felt our power."[7] The sit-in was thus an empowering experience, giving students a new sense of solidarity and community; of the power of collective action to not only effect change, but to change the lives of the participants.

On the second night of the occupation, a small number of students decided to add two more innovative protest tactics to increase the pressure on authorities to give into their demands. A group of thirteen started a hunger strike the next day and reported it to the *Times*, who noted in its headline that "girls" were among the volunteers. They quoted sociology student Elliott Isenberg saying that he had already gone on a five-day hunger strike against the Vietnam War, and that he wanted to use the hunger strike now "to dramatize to the public that we have a commitment."[8] Another group of eighty students, led by the Socialist Society, snuck into the main administrative building, Connaught House, early on Wednesday morning to confront administrators more directly with their protest. Harry Kidd warned them to leave the building immediately, and when they refused, told them they were suspended and brought in the police to carry them out one by one.[9] This was the only time the administration brought in the police, and even though it resulted in no arrests or even suspensions, it increased students' sense of solidarity in persecution.

This feeling of solidarity was only confirmed and heightened by messages of solidarity pouring in from students all over the country, the National Union of Students, and the newly formed Radical Student Alliance (RSA), as well as from the students at Berkeley University and prominent adults such as Bertrand Russell and New Leftist Ralph Miliband. The NUS and RSA helped to coordinate a demonstration march on Friday, 17 March, in which over two thousand students from all over Britain marched down Fleet Street in the center of London in support of the sit-in. Called the "Daffodil March" (presumably because many of the marchers carried daffodils), it looked like another CND march, with students dressed in respectable suits, ties, and dresses, playing music, and flying banners, peacefully winding through the streets of London. This time, however, students marched for themselves, for their own rights as students. Viewing the suspension of Bloom and Adelstein as "victimization" of their student government leaders, they felt that they needed to demonstrate to show solidarity with these victims of injustice. Other students added that they were there to demand the right of students to participate in university decision-making and in protest of the "pedagogic gerontocracy" which ruled their universities with an iron fist. This march and the the LSE protests illustrate how the student movement was beginning to evolve from a small, decentralized movement primarily over external issues in the late fifties to become more wide-spread and include well-organized, large-scale protests over student rights.[10]

At the end of the Easter break, the administration agreed to suspend the penalty on Adelstein and Bloom "as an act of grace" and to allow the rest of the students to get on with their work.[11] When students returned after Easter break, the School returned to normal, but the issues of student representation remained on everyone's minds. Watherston wrote in the student newspaper that the university was continuing to delay implementing any real reforms, complaining that "amazing as it may seem the powers that be at LSE seem determined to carry on in the same unresponsive, paternalistic ways that led to the open conflict at the end of last term. . . ."[12] In response to these criticisms and pressure from staff, LSE administrators and staff created a Machinery of Government Committee, which included five student members, to study the cause of the protests and make suggestions for reforms. This committee, however, failed to resolve the issues. The Student Union, Socialist Society, and student newspaper continued to demand a complete restructuring of the university throughout the Long Sixties, but the authorities offered only minor reforms and token student representation in return.

The LSE protests of 1967 shocked the university authorities and the nation. School authorities did not know what to do with students who occupied the school and refused leave. The police had no precedent and no idea if students had the right to occupy their own university. The national news media had an incredible story unfolding literally at their doorsteps, but did not quite know what to make of it all. They read the banners and the leaflets students handed out, they interviewed School officials and students, but they struggled to understand what was really going on.

The occupation seemed so unusual and so out of place in a British institution, many authorities and journalists were quick to assume that foreigners must be leading it. Most of them were aware of the growing student protest movement in the United States at that time, but knew little of Britain's own student movement. The massive student sit-in at the University of California-Berkeley in 1964 was the most well-known and observers were quick to assume that British students were trying to imitate the Americans, since they had clearly adopted American protest songs and slogans in an October 1966 occupation. By the time of the March 1967 protest, therefore, the press and public assumed that this was an imitative action inspired by foreigners. It was only a small step for them to believe that foreigners also were leading the protests. The *Guardian* argued that LSE demonstrators "had the California pattern before them and assumed from the start that the affair had to run the same course." [13] The *Times* also concluded that a small minority of foreign students, who opposed all authority and all restrictions on their freedom, had fomented the discontent and led the unrest.[14] The media thus framed this protest in a way that would discredit the protesters, shifting public opinion away from the real problems of higher education and confirming conservative fears of foreign contagion of their society and culture. This media frame for the British student movement would prove extremely influential and long-lasting.

In addition to characterizing the LSE as a hot-bed of foreign-led radicalism, the media was generally critical of the entire premise of the protests. The *Daily Telegraph* called a November 1966 protest "an outrageous piece of impertinence." They argued that to demand "all the rights of a grown-up on trial before a court of law is no more defensible than it would be if demanded by a schoolboy about to be beaten." Although they agreed that some participation in university government was acceptable, they asserted that "It is not, however, for the young people themselves to lay down the conditions under which they should be taught and cared for at lavish public expense."[15] A journalist for the *Daily Express* complained that "the overwhelming majority of adults in this country . . . are sick and tired of coming home from a hard day's work and reading in the evening paper that, while they themselves were busy providing taxes to sustain the universities, a university mob was protesting against something which is not a matter for protest at all."[16] English lecturer Alan Shelston later recalled, "the Adams affair at LSE was the first of a series of incidents to make a dramatic impact through the mass media on the general public, and to reinforce a popular image of the student as an outspoken and often unkempt and anti-social element, suspect in matters of personal morality and social aspiration and certainly unreliable in his political allegiances."[17] This media stereotype, while confirming students' sense of persecution and solidarity in the short-term, created a narrative of student protest that would dominate all public discourse of the British student movement for the remainder of the Long Sixties.

Because this stereotype conflicted with the students' own perception of their protest and the views of some of the LSE's staff, a group of social administration and statistics professors on the LSE staff, including Tessa Blackstone, Kathleen Gales, Roger Hadley, and Wyn Lewis, were determined to clarify exactly what the student protesters did and why they did it. Towards this end, they sent out surveys to all LSE students seven weeks after the sit-in and published their findings based on over 2,000 responses in *Students in Conflict, LSE in 1967* (1970). They determined that the majority of student activists were born in Britain and that overseas participants rarely took on leadership roles. Only two out of eleven student government representatives who organized the protest came from overseas. Although some Americans were involved in the protests, the proportion of activists among American students was no greater than among British students. Contrary to the image created by administrators and the press, British students led and provided the bulk of support for the LSE protests. The majority of students (over sixty per cent) thought the sit-in and boycott were justified. Thirty-six per cent of students participated in the sit-in on at least one day, while forty-nine per cent missed at least some classes in support of the boycott. Only four per cent of LSE students identified themselves as Communists and only two per cent as Trotskyists, Marxists, or Anarchists. Clearly, the sit-in was not the result of a tiny minority of radical students. Most student activists participated primarily because of the unjust disciplinary actions, rather than a desire for student power or control. While the vast majority of LSE students wanted representation on matters directly concerning students, such as student discipline, only thirty-five per cent wanted representation on appointing the Director.[18] Obviously, the protests at LSE were quite a bit more complicated than first portrayed by the press.

Dubbed "the Troubles," these events were actually a culmination of long-term international, national, and local factors. The New Left and nuclear disarmament movement of the early sixties, growing awareness and moral revulsion of the racism in southern Africa, an increasing sense of solidarity with students in other nations, the example of student movements in America and France, growing disillusionment with a new Labour government and its changes to higher education, and questionable decisions made by LSE authorities all laid the foundations for this outburst of student protest. The "Troubles" also signaled a new wind blowing in the British student movement. Students, university administrators, the government, the media, and the public realized that large-scale student unrest *could* happen in Britain and from that point on, everyone was increasingly aware of the potential power of the British student movement.

THE TROUBLES AND THE SWINGING SIXTIES

The student movement had pre-dated the Troubles at the LSE, but by 1966 few seemed to remember the student activism of the late fifties and early sixties. That student generation had graduated and gone on with their lives, although many remained active in left-wing causes throughout the sixties. University students in the mid-sixties were born after the war, during the baby boom, and were a product of the post-war era even more so than their predecessors at the beginning of the Long Sixties. As a consequence, the raised expectations generated by the new welfare state, and especially its educational system, and the nation's admiration for modernization and all that was new had a stronger impact on students in the mid-sixties than it had even a few years earlier. This ethos of reform and progress was taken up by the new Labour government of Harold Wilson after 1964, giving many students hope that their nation would leave behind its old-fashioned traditions and move into a new age of freedom and prosperity for all. Indeed, those years between 1964 and 1968 were heady with the anticipation of change sweeping through the nation. Fueled by this national climate of high expectations, anxiety over social and economic change, and disappointment with the lack of radical transformation, the student movement grew stronger, more insistent, and more organized.

An important driver and reflection of Britain's infatuation with the modern and new was its youth culture. Although it emerged in the fifties, by the mid-sixties Britain's youth culture had come into its own and was exporting its own music and fashions to the rest of the world. In addition to the music of the Beatles, the Rolling Stones, and the Who, clothing designers helped to make London the center of global fashion in the mid-sixties. John Stephen and others in Carnaby Street sold clothing specifically designed to appeal to the Mods' desire to show off their good taste. Designers like Mary Quant deliberately defied the conventions of established fashion and appealed to the young middle-class "Chelsea Set" with her mixture of bohemian and modern fashions for women. By the mid-sixties, Quant's fashions, including the mini-skirt, had become the standard of the global sixties generation.[19]

London's reputation as the center of the fashion world peaked in 1966 with *Time* magazine's cover story officially dubbing London "The Swinging City." It exclaimed, "In a decade dominated by youth, London has burst into bloom. It swings; it is the scene. This spring, as never before in modern times, London is switched on. . . . In a once sedate world of faded splendor, everything new, uninhibited and kinky is blooming at the top of London life."[20] This article went on for several more pages, describing the London "scene" for all the world. More than any other single publication, the *Time* article drew the world's attention to London, beginning a flood of media attention for the city and its inhabitants. While much of "swinging London" was media hype, this image had an impact on the imaginations of Britons themselves. Social commentators began speaking of the "swinging sixties" and hordes of teenagers flocked to the city or otherwise adopted the image of "swinging London": young, sexy, optimistic, and most of all "modern."[21]

Although much of the youth culture of the Long Sixties originated with the working class and "swinging London" only represented a small elitist and apolitical number of fashionistas, middle class university students could not help but be influenced by the new fashions in music and clothing. Student newspapers advertised the latest mini-skirts and music albums or concerts of the day, and these fashions provided working and middle class youth with a basis for a common culture and identity. People commonly spoke of youth as a special social category now, and regardless of whether they actually were a classless group, many young people perceived themselves as part of a separate, special group, which had more in common with other people their age than with people from previous generations.

Even the new Labour government of Harold Wilson used the discourses of youth and modernization to promote its agendas. Wilson had become leader of the Labour Party in 1963 by appeasing nuclear disarmament activists, voicing opposition to apartheid in Africa, and promoting a platform of economic, technological, and cultural modernization. Many New Leftists, CND supporters, and student activists supported and even campaigned for Wilson in the election, believing that he was their best chance to enact the reforms they desired. After winning the General Election of October 1964, however, Wilson rejected unilateral disarmament, greatly disappointing many activists. Most of his supporters, though, accepted his reluctance to initiate sweeping reforms because of his slim margin of victory. When Labour achieved a larger majority in Parliament in 1966, many expected Wilson to carry out the Labour Party program of returning power to the working class, and fighting against imperialism and racism.

Labour leaders, however, had other plans. Wilson's Home Secretary Roy Jenkins had laid out a program of modernizing the nation's laws and society in a series of essays published in 1959. Instead of economic equality, these focused on eliminating capital punishment and loosening restrictions on personal freedoms, especially laws regulating sexual behavior and restricting abortion and divorce. He eloquently wrote:

> Let us be on the side of those who want people to be free to live their own lives, to make their own mistakes, and to decide in an adult way and provided they do not infringe the rights of others, the code by which they wish to live; and on the side too of experiment and brightness, of better buildings and better food, of better music (jazz as well as Bach) and better books, of fuller lives and greater freedom.[22]

When the Labour government gained its majority, Jenkins went forward with his so-called "permissive" agenda, effectively reforming the nation's laws on divorce, abortion, homosexuality, capital punishment, and censorship. These reforms and the debate surrounding them made students and the public much more conscious of personal freedoms as a part of Britain's move away from its "archaic" authoritarian past towards a new, modern, and progressive nation.

The Wilson government, like that of Macmillan, saw higher education as an important component of the nation's economic modernization program. Many political and industrial leaders had called for a new investment in higher education to create innovative technologies to make the country more competitive in the changing global economy and to produce the larger numbers of highly skilled and educated workers required by a modern economy. To study how the system of higher and further education could serve the needs of industry and the nation, the Macmillan government formed a committee under the Chairmanship of Lord Robbins in 1961. This committee consulted Vice Chancellors and education experts, as well as the National Union of Students, and issued its report in 1963. The *Robbins Report* asserted that it was the government's duty to ensure the continued economic success of the country by investing more money in the universities to supply the increased demand for educated workers. It recommended the creation of several new universities, upgrading many colleges to make them universities, and providing funds for adding facilities to existing universities to allow more students to enter higher education. It claimed that this move would not only satisfy the needs of industry and government, but democratize access to higher education, ensuring that it became a right for all British citizens rather than a privilege for only those who could afford it.[23]

Although the Conservative government committed the nation to this vast expansion of higher education, the Labour party agreed with the need to modernize the nation's economy and education system, and thus also supported these recommendations. At the same time the Robbins Committee was working on its report, the Labour party had appointed its own committee to forge a radical new approach to higher education. The Labour report, which was issued in the summer of 1963, argued that "There must be a rapid and continuing expansion of higher education, on a scale never before contemplated." Higher education should be "a right for all able young men and women, regardless of their families' class, income or position." It argued that improving the system of higher education was "a matter of national survival," asserting that "economic expansion is only possible if university and technological education expands rapidly and continuously to provide the necessary brainpower and skill."[24] As a result, Wilson made the reform of higher education the lynchpin of his modernization campaign platform. Both political parties thus framed higher education reform as the key to national progress, raised public awareness of the importance of higher education, and provided the nation with parliamentary solutions.

The *Robbins Report*, together with the baby boom, contributed to a dramatic increase in enrollments in higher education from 166,000 in 1960 to 486,000 in 1975. In fact, education historian Brian Simon asserts that the years 1963–1967 were "the period of the most tempestuous growth in higher education in the country's history." [25] Despite the rhetoric of democratization, however, this growth was not equally distributed among all social classes and genders. Between 1961 and 1977, the proportion of middle class youth attending college rose from 19.5 per cent to 26.6 per cent, but only rose from 3.2 per cent to 5 per cent for their working-class counterparts.[26] The number of female students increased from 68,000 in 1962 to 214,000 in 1980, but remained far below the number of male students, which reached 310,000 in 1980.[27] The winds of change were sweeping through the universities, but inequalities remained.

Although Parliament, the public, and students agreed on the need to democratize and modernize higher education, there was no consensus on how to do this. Some of the newly founded universities, such as Essex, Warwick, and Sussex, tried to create innovative programs and curricula, but older universities barely changed at all, and hierarchical power structures within the universities remained virtually unchanged everywhere. The *Robbins Report,* however, did encourage several prestigious universities to reform themselves to contribute more to the needs of modern industry and society, and raised student expectations that all universities would indeed reform to become more democratized and modern.

Indeed, it was one factor behind student discontent at the LSE. The *Robbins Report* caused Sydney Caine to begin the process of reforming the LSE. His Director's report for 1963/4 noted that "The most absorbing activity of the School during the last session has been the re-examination of its general position and prospects, consequent on the publication . . . of the *Robbins Report.*"[28] As a result, the LSE committed itself to increasing undergraduate numbers twenty per cent by 1967. Over the next two years, the total number of full-time students consequently increased from 2,450 to over 3,000 in 1967. Although staff-student ratios improved in these years, resources became scarce, facilities overcrowded, and student accommodations in short supply. In light of these new problems, the Director was forced to propose an overhaul of the entire structure of the university. In an August 1966 memorandum to staff and the Board of Governors, he recommended that a Committee be created to study the relations between the Court of Governors, academic committees, and the overall committee structure.[29]

That same year, however, Caine noticed a growing discontent amongst students.[30] Many students, whose expectations had been raised by the "swinging London" image and the discourse of modernizing higher education, were unhappy with the overcrowded conditions, the continued physical compartmentalization of the university, and what they perceived as the relative conservatism of the staff and student body. Like other universities within the London system, the School did not really have a campus, but rather consisted of six buildings grouped around Houghton Street.[31] A system of bridges connected all of the buildings, including Connaught House, which housed the administration, and St. Clements building, containing the Student Union offices. There was no real central meeting place at the School and most of its students commuted over a half-hour's journey to and from the university.[32]

Many students came to the LSE because of its long history of radicalism. The School was founded in 1895 as a place where non-traditional working and middle class students could be educated in courses such as sociology, economics, and political science, which could help them reform British society. Until the 1950s, it had attracted some of the best and most radical professors in the country and world. By the sixties, students admitted to the LSE were similar to other universities in terms of their class background, with approximately 75 per cent coming from middle-class families. They were unique, however, in that a much larger proportion of LSE students considered themselves Labour supporters and LSE students scored higher in their A-levels than their counterparts at other universities.[33] They were also more diverse than other student populations, with overseas students comprising approximately one-third of the School's full-time undergraduates. Thirty per cent of its foreign students came from the United States, while Asia, Europe, Canada, and Africa provided the bulk of other overseas students.[34] As a consequence, LSE's student population was among the brightest and most diverse in the nation, all of which enhanced its elite, cosmopolitan reputation.

David Fernbach, a sociology student from Bournemouth, had been politicized by CND in school and had come to the LSE specifically because of its progressive and radical reputation, and its location in the center of London. When he arrived there in October 1963, however, he was "profoundly depressed" with the drabness and career-orientation of his fellow students and the "uniformly reactionary" teachers.[35] Colin Crouch, arrived at the LSE in 1965 from the London suburb of Isleworth as a first-year sociology student. He agreed that the School exuded conservatism in the mid-sixties, but he argued that it derived primarily from the Government and Economics departments, and he felt that the student body was remarkably politically engaged.[36] This clash between the high expectations of the student body and the perceived conservatism of the School created a growing current of discontent which would eventually contribute to the high turnout for LSE's protests in 1967.

At the same time, the Wilson government was also unwittingly creating a climate of frustration and disillusionment amongst many of the nation's activists. Although the Wilson government did push through liberal legislation and make equal access to higher education a priority, it also supported nuclear weapons, industry's demands for cheap and plentiful labor, limits on immigration, trade with South Africa and Rhodesia, and American involvement in Vietnam. This disillusioned many activists, but especially those in the CND and the New Left. Many activists moved on to new projects, but the CND and the New Left declined dramatically.

Failing to convince the Labour Party to support unilateral nuclear disarmament, the CND fragmented and was eventually taken over by Communist Party activists. It continued to limp along throughout the decade, but lost its large following and dynamism. The New Left also fragmented in 1963. E.P. Thompson wrote dispiritedly that year: "I am not, I think, betraying a closely-guarded state secret when I say that the movement which once claimed to be 'The New Left' . . . has now, in this country, dispersed itself both organizationally and (to some extent) intellectually. We failed to implement our original purposes, or even to sustain what cultural apparatus we had."[37] Like the CND, the New Left faded into the background in the mid-sixties, but retained its influence over the ideology of the student movement.

This was in large part due to a second, younger generation of New Left intellectuals, including Perry Anderson, Tom Nairn, and Robin Blackburn, who took over the production of the *New Left Review* in 1962 and brought new theoretical perspectives to the New Left in the later sixties. Turning away from Thompson's and Williams's admiration for the English radical tradition, this second phase of the New Left was more inspired by continental Marxism, the theories of Marcuse, Sartre, Gramsci, Althusser, and Foucault, and the Cuban revolution. Although this new group was similar to Marcuse and Mills in arguing that the working class lacked revolutionary desire and in looking to other oppressed groups in society such as students and racial minorities to lead the way to revolution, the second phase of the New Left was more interested in structuralist theories about the sources of power and non-class forms of oppression and identity.[38] Leaders of the New Left remained in academia– sometimes even participating in student protests– and continued to infuse student Socialist and Labour clubs with the rhetoric of participatory democracy and the left-wing struggle against apathy, imperialism, and "the powers that be."

Even staunch student Labourites voiced dissent over the government's policies in the mid-sixties. As early as 1965, the National Association of Labour Student Organizations (NALSO) criticized Labour's immigration policies and stance toward Rhodesia and Vietnam. A NALSO secretary wrote that "from 1966 onwards students lost all faith in the Labour government as it became obvious that even with a secure parliamentary majority, the Labour government was not going to put through any fundamental changes."[39] Disillusioned with government resistance to change, students and others on the Left would increasingly utilize extra-parliamentary action to achieve their demands in the mid-sixties.

The LSE's Socialist Society mirrored these wider trends on the national Left. Similar to other universities in the mid-sixties, LSE students formed a Socialist Society (Soc-Soc) in October of 1965, which became the center of radicalism at the LSE throughout the remainder of the Long Sixties. Most of the students in the Soc-Soc were disillusioned with the Labour government and formed their group as a left-wing alternative to the Labour club, which was the largest club on campus at the time. In the first issue of its society publication, *Agitator,* the Soc-Soc proclaimed its dedication to the spread of socialism and overthrow of capitalism through direct action.[40] LSE's Soc-Soc published articles analyzing the New Left in Britain and the US, claiming that the British New Left had failed because it was tied to the Labour Party, while the American New Left had succeeded because it had adopted the civil rights movement as its model and participatory democracy as its ideology. Although Soc-Soc students frequently used New Left rhetoric, they distinguished themselves from the New Left, emphasizing what they considered their more revolutionary brand of socialism.[41] David Fernbach, who was a member of the LSE Soc-Soc throughout the "Troubles," explained that their revolutionary ideology came primarily from the group's leaders, most of whom were members of International Socialists (IS), a tiny revolutionary socialist group affiliated with the Trotskyist Fourth International.[42] The IS had been actively recruiting young people since its formation in 1962, attempting to foster an understanding of classical Marxism and support for workers' rights and socialist revolution. Although LSE's Soc-Soc attracted students from a wide range of leftist political beliefs, the IS dominated its leadership and publications throughout the Long Sixties.

THE GLOBAL DIMENSIONS OF THE TROUBLES OF THE MID-SIXTIES

LSE's Soc-Soc also reflected an important new trend emerging within the student movement in the mid-sixties: the strategy of using the university and student union to support larger campaigns against racism and imperialism. LSE's Soc-Soc specifically wanted to use its Student's Union to oppose "American aggression in Vietnam" and "white racialism" in Rhodesia. By 1966, it had succeeded in bringing out hundreds of LSE students in protests against racism in Rhodesia and Wilson's handling of the situation, and in getting the Student Union to affiliate with the British Council for Peace in Vietnam and the Campaign against Racial Discrimination.[43] At dozens of universities, other independent Socialist Societies would similarly pressure their student unions to support international and national political campaigns. This strategy would eventually bring student activists across the nation into direct conflict with university authorities and mark the mid-sixties as a distinct new phase of the student movement.

This interest in international issues was, of course, nothing new. Students had been keenly aware of and interested in international protest movements since at least the late fifties, but public awareness of student protests and political crises in other nations increased dramatically in the mid-sixties as advances in telecommunications helped the news media to gather more information about international events and bring these events into more Britons' homes. The widespread availability of television especially made international news more immediate in people's lives. Through the news media, students were drawn into a world of increasingly publicized dissent movements and deeply disturbing international events. Just as press coverage of nuclear disarmament and civil rights movements had helped to generate a sense of crisis over these issues and of individual responsibility to do something about them in the late fifties, press coverage of international developments, such as the racist governments in South Africa and Rhodesia, the escalating Vietnam War, and the student movements in the United States and France, motivated student activists in the mid-sixties.

While international events in the news made more students concerned about the world's problems, student movements elsewhere in the world gave Britons examples of how students could mobilize by the thousands to confront authorities. In 1963 and 1964, British newspapers were filled with news of the French student movement. The national student organization of France, the *Union Nationale des Etudiants de France*, led this wave of protests. They began with protests for Algerian liberation and against the military draft in 1960. The French government of Charles de Gaulle agreed to Algerian independence in 1962, but outlawed student demonstrations. Students continued to protest, however, and in 1963 demanded educational reforms as well. Thousands of students peacefully demonstrated at the Sorbonne, but police troops smashed the demonstration and arrested as many students as they could. Hundreds of thousands of students then went out on strike, but the government continued to attack them and ignore their demands. In a February 1964 demonstration, thousands of frustrated students fought with police and occupied the Sorbonne to protest police actions, but won no concessions.[44] Student newspapers across Britain admiringly reported these events, helping to reinforce the idea of students as a powerful global force of change.[45]

Although student movements existed all over the world in this period, the most internationally famous student protest of the era was undoubtedly the Free Speech Movement at the University of California at Berkeley. Students there had been fighting California's ban on political speakers and organizing on campuses since 1961. The speaker ban controversy escalated dramatically when civil rights activists attempted to build a student civil rights organization at Berkeley in the autumn of 1964. When university officials suspended eight students for their political organizing, they formed the Free Speech Movement. Thousands of students attended their spectacular protest demonstrations and sit-ins, demanding free speech on campus and student participation in university government. Students saw themselves as defending the liberal ideal of the university against the corruptive bureaucracy of the administration, drawing upon an idealistic vision of the university where students and faculty freely exchanged ideas in the pursuit of truth and knowledge. As the protests went on, and hundreds of students were arrested and expelled, Berkeley activists appealed to students around the world to support them in their fight to defend student rights.[46]

British students were very much aware of and sympathetic to events at Berkeley. In university after university, British students applied Berkeley students' arguments against bureaucracy and for student rights to their own universities. For example, in a 1965 editorial, an Essex University student wrote of the Berkeley movement:

> It is not hard to think of similar cases nearer home where a university's benefactors expect gratitude at the expense of freedom of speech and action. . . . This paper and, we hope, this University, condemns the blatantly undemocratic and illegal attempts now being made to stifle the basic freedoms, and ultimately, the individuality of the Berkeley students, and would like to identify itself with them in their struggle.[47]

The NUS and student unions across the nation consequently sent letters of support and solidarity to Berkeley students. The international impact of the Berkeley protest should not be underestimated. As Mark Edelman Boren argues in his recent history of global student resistance, "the Berkeley uprising made political protest exciting to a lot of previously uninvolved students; it identified the university as the site par excellence for fashionable dissent, and popularized student organizations as had no other incident in US history."[48] Although hundreds of other student protests were occurring across the United States and around the world in this period, Berkeley had become synonymous with student protest worldwide, making British student activists feel as though they were indeed a part of a global student movement.

After the Berkeley Free Speech Movement ended, British newspapers focused their attention on the American student movement against the Vietnam War which emerged in 1965. American involvement in Vietnam had been escalating since the fifties, but in March 1965 the US government committed ground troops to prop up the pro-American government in South Vietnam and began extensive bombing in the North. The American SDS had sponsored the first national student protest against the Vietnam War in April 1965, just as the US had begun its extensive bombing campaign of North Vietnam. The timing of this protest made it a tremendous success with a turnout of over 20,000 students.

American students also formed hundreds of independent local anti-war groups and protests. University of Michigan faculty and students organized the first nationally publicized "teach-in" as an educational protest against the war in Vietnam in May of 1965. This national teach-in included leading authorities on Southeast Asian affairs and carried detailed information to students across the country through a television broadcast. To counteract accusations that teach-ins were unpatriotic or radical, the planners of the teach-ins stressed the importance of free policy debate in a democracy.[49] Similar teach-ins then took place at over 100 universities across the country that year.[50] They were crucial in sparking more anti-war activity because they provided participants with information on the war in an exciting atmosphere, showed them inaccuracies in government and media reports, and emboldened them to criticize the government.[51]

As SDS and other American antiwar organizations escalated their protests afterwards, they increasingly reached out to student and peace groups outside the United States. For example, the National Coordinating Committee to End the War in Vietnam (the leading national anti-war group in the US in 1965) appealed to the CND and other peace organizations to support their International Days of Protest in October 1965.[52] SDS, which was a supporter of this action, wrote to student unions all over the world, including many universities in Britain, requesting support for a world strike over the war in Vietnam. The NUS and student governments responded with messages of solidarity with the SDS and moral resolutions against US involvement in Vietnam.[53] In these ways, dissent movements were increasingly perceived as transnational and all activists could feel empowered by the global dimensions of their movements.

From this perspective, LSE student protesters made references to the American student movement not because they were imitating them, but because they saw themselves as part of the same global student movement. This identification with a global movement would give LSE students more confidence in their own power to win battles with administrators and give their movement a stronger sense of importance and deeper meaning. In this context, messages of solidarity from other student movements were very important to LSE students as they reified this belief in their role as contributing to a powerful global student movement. The perception of acting within a transnational student movement thus strengthened the LSE student protest and the British student movement nation-wide.

VIETNAM

The transnational movement against US involvement in the Vietnam War was an important, but relatively small part of the British student movement in the mid-sixties. British students followed the American anti-war movement closely, expressed solidarity and support, and adopted some of its rhetoric and tactics, but Britain's imperial past and its different position in relationship to the war, being an ally of the US but not an active participant in the war, led British students to approach the issue in their own unique way.

One of the first student Vietnam groups formed at Oxford University in February 1965. A leading organizer of this group was Tariq Ali, an overseas student from Pakistan. Growing up in a former British colony, Ali was particularly sensitive to any issues linked to imperialism. Ali had viewed the Chinese communists as heroes for throwing off the yoke of imperialism and admired the leaders of colonial independence around the world.[54]

He too had been raised with western governments' post-war rhetoric of freedom and human rights, but was appalled by their hypocrisy in continuing to uphold imperialism. Ali had helped to create Oxford's Vietnam Committee in February 1965 because he "was totally obsessed with the war in Vietnam and felt very helpless that one could not do anything about it miles away from Asia . . ."[55] For Ali and many other young opponents of imperialism, the Vietnam War was a colonial independence movement and American intervention there appeared to be a hypocritical attempt to recolonize Vietnam.

Oxford's Vietnam Committee urged the British government, as a leader of the Geneva conference which had ended the war between the French and Vietnamese, to take the initiative in negotiating an American withdrawal from Vietnam.[56] To publicize this goal, it joined the Youth-CND, Committee of 100, and the Young Communist League in organizing the first national demonstration against the Vietnam War in February 1965 (two months before the American SDS demonstration). He and forty other Oxford students joined 800 demonstrators outside the US embassy in London for a four-hour protest against US aggression in North Vietnam.[57] Ali was one of fifteen people arrested at the demonstration, charged with "threatening behavior," but the charges against him were dismissed when no witnesses could be found to confirm the charges.[58] Indicative of growing police frustration with protests following the civil disobedience campaigns of the Committee of 100, police in the mid-sixties were increasingly eager to arrest any protesters who defied their authority. Vietnam War protesters, for their part, also were increasingly confrontational, provoking arrests so as to gain more media attention, just as Bertrand Russell had done with the Committee of 100.

Ali's well-publicized Vietnam activism brought him to the attention of two young Oxford fellows, David Caute and Steven Lukes, who asked him to help them to organize a "teach-in" on Vietnam at Oxford University. They had heard of the teach-in movement sweeping across the United States that year and thought it would be an engaging and educational event for Oxford as well. The powerful political connections of Oxford's professors and students quickly elevated the stature of the teach-in to international proportions. The BBC became involved, as did the Labour Foreign Secretary Michael Stewart and Henry Cabot Lodge from the US embassy in Saigon.[59] Several hundred students attended the seven and a half-hour teach-in in June of 1965, and a few heckled and laughed at Lodge when he attempted to defend US policy. Although Ali felt the anti-war argument had won, BBC coverage cut out the anti-war arguments in favor of the pro-American argument.[60] Encouraged by the success of the Oxford teach-in, America's CBS television company and the BBC sponsored a debate on Vietnam between Oxford and Harvard Universities in December of 1965 in which the Oxford debate team clearly won. Although the debate was not shown in Britain, it aired in the US. Ali, who had been on the Oxford team, received 500 letters from the US, supporting him and his stand against US involvement in Vietnam.[61] This positive response encouraged Ali even further and as a result, he continued to lead the British movement against the war after he left Oxford in 1966.

It is understandable why overseas students like Tariq Ali and those from America were so opposed to American intervention in Vietnam, but why did the issue resonate with British-born students who supported the Vietnam protests? For one, the British media carried news of the Vietnam War on a daily basis, and although much of this coverage was sympathetic to the United States, many of those already active in the nuclear disarmament movement were predisposed to doubt American intentions in Vietnam. Peace activists, therefore, immediately interpreted the bombing of North Vietnam and the commitment of US soldiers to Vietnam as a new threat to international peace and stability. Some feared that Britain might commit its own troops to Vietnam as it had in Korea, while others feared that this small conflict would eventually engulf the world in another global war. Anti-imperialists on the Left, of course, had additional cause to oppose US intervention in Vietnam as yet another incidence of capitalist-imperialist aggression. Britons thus opposed US involvement in the Vietnam War for a wide variety of legitimate reasons.

The leading national organization opposing the Vietnam War in 1965 and 1966 was the British Council for Peace in Vietnam (BCPV). Founded in May 1965 and led by Lord Brockway, the BCPV was supported by a wide variety of groups, including the CND, trade unions, and church groups.[62] It expressed moral opposition to the war, claiming that the war was "a crime against humanity which challenges the conscience of the world. Weapons of destruction are being used more barbarous, short of the bomb, than known in human record. The people of Britain and the peoples of the world, already awakening to awareness, must be stirred and mobilized into action."[63] Their goal was to pressure the British government to lead the way in enforcing the terms of the 1954 Geneva Agreements, which called for a withdrawal of forces and the creation of a united independent Vietnam. In 1966 the National Association of Labour Student Organizations, Young Liberals, and Young Communist League additionally created the Youth for Peace in Vietnam Campaign, which attempted to mobilize students and other young people.[64]

As a result of the efforts of these organizations, as well as independent Socialist Societies, many universities saw small-scale protests in the mid-sixties, indicating a wide range of reasons for protesting the war. Hull University students, for example, revealed two very different reasons for their anti-war protests. Sensitive to colonial struggles all over the world, the Hull Movement for Colonial Freedom held a demonstration march of about 100 students and trade union representatives through the town in March 1965 to protest what they saw as American imperialist aggression in South Vietnam.[65] The Hull Liberal Society, on the other hand, framed their protest on moral and humanistic grounds, claiming that they:

want to stop bloodshed, whoever it is caused by, and object to racial discrimination regardless of which race exercises it; and [they] do so from some idealistic belief that human life and dignity still mean something. . . . [their] objections to aggression in Vietnam are based on the pointlessness of escalating a war which cannot be won, in order to uphold a puppet democracy that much of the South Vietnamese population does not want.[66]

Indicating the ideological diversity of Vietnam War activists, Hull liberal students thus saw the Vietnam conflict more in terms of human dignity and democracy for all people, while others opposed it as an imperialist war.

Student anti-war protests elsewhere in the mid-sixties likewise revealed a diversity of strategies and perspectives. A large student anti-war demonstration took place in Manchester in December of 1965. Organized by the Manchester University Peace in Vietnam Committee, it attracted 200 student participants, but ended in clashes with police and eleven arrests.[67] The Manchester group remained active for the next several years; even sponsoring a sit-in in February 1967 in protest against research being done at the university which they felt would help aid the US in Vietnam.[68] Liverpool, Birmingham, London, and Leeds students all held smaller protest demonstrations against the war in 1965 and 1966.[69] Although relatively small-scale, these actions indicate how British students began to participate in the transnational Vietnam War movement on their own terms.

CAMPAIGNS AGAINST APARTHEID IN SOUTHERN AFRICA

While the Vietnam War attracted scattered protests in the mid-sixties, student activism against apartheid in South Africa and Rhodesia grew considerably in this period. Perhaps because these were former colonies in the British Empire and Britons felt a special responsibility for the fate of these countries, anti-apartheid activism was stronger in Britain than anywhere else outside of Africa. The release of a few prisoners following protests in London in November of 1964 convinced British activists that their protests could indeed help to end apartheid. This success and new events in Rhodesia contributed the growth and diversification of anti-racism protests within the student movement in this period.

The National Union of Students helped to mobilize much of this student support for the campaign against apartheid. One of their largest actions was in December 1964, when 7,000 students from eighty-one colleges and universities marched through London in solidarity with the National Union of South African students, which was fighting against segregation in higher education.[70] In March 1965 representatives from student unions throughout England laid seventy-two wreaths at the door of South Africa House in London to commemorate the Sharpeville massacre.[71] After this protest,

Gerry Stinson of LSE Students Against Racial Discrimination wrote in the LSE student newspaper: "The South African Press is very sensitive to demonstrations in London."[72] The truth of this statement is debatable, but it reveals many students' belief that their actions mattered to authorities in Britain and elsewhere. As future leaders of the nation, many British university students expected that their polite and sincere demonstrations of protest and concern would indeed influence national and international politics.

Anti-apartheid activism thrived at many universities across the country in the mid-sixties. Tariq Ali, for example, had originally gotten involved in Oxford's student movement through anti-apartheid activism. Although he had attended numerous protests in Pakistan against racism in the US and the Suez invasion, his first protest at Oxford was a picket against the South African ambassador who spoke on campus in 1964. He and five other students were "rusticated" (suspended and removed from campus) for two months for attacking the ambassador's car after the speech and "bringing the good name of the university into disrepute."[73] Under considerable pressure from parents and MPs, the Oxford administration enforced the rustication over the summer break and allowed them to resume their studies as normal the next term. This incident was mentioned in the national press because it occurred at the nation's premier institution, but anti-apartheid actions elsewhere were rarely mentioned in the national media, even though they were widespread since the late fifties.[74]

While the movement against apartheid in South Africa would continue to play a role in the student movement throughout the Long Sixties, the issue of apartheid in Rhodesia burst into the nation's headlines in 1965 and briefly redirected student protest against this new outrage. In 1962 the United Nations had called on Britain to end apartheid in its African colony in Southern Rhodesia and restore political freedom and equality to non-Europeans. The white minority in Rhodesia, however, resisted this attempt to take away their privileged position. In November 1965 the Rhodesian Front Government, an all-white group representing five per cent of the population, made a Unilateral Declaration of Independence from Britain. Although Labour Prime Minister Harold Wilson was a vocal opponent of apartheid, he only responded to this action with economic sanctions, disappointing many in Britain's anti-apartheid movement.[75] Some British nationalists wanted the government to send in troops to bring Rhodesia back under British control; others wanted government troops to banish the racist white government and institute free parliamentary elections to include the black majority. The large majority of students who opposed racism in principal also condemned apartheid in Rhodesia. Thus this issue became a natural focus of activism at many British universities in 1966 and 1967.

The National Union of Students took the lead in pressuring the government to take a stand against apartheid in Rhodesia. As early as 1961, it had passed a resolution to that effect and in 1966, it sent Geoff Martin, who became the NUS president the next year, to the University College of Rhodesia on a fact-finding mission. He reported that that the college was racially segregated and actively discriminating against its African students.[76] Following this report, the NUS put further pressure on the Wilson government to help African-Rhodesian students who had been expelled for their activism and to use its financial backing of University College as leverage to end segregation there. On the local level, students at Manchester, Liverpool, Leeds, Birmingham, Hull, Lancaster, and Leicester Universities all held their own peaceful protests, ranging from small-scale marches to teach-ins, to raise awareness of the immorality of the situation in Rhodesia and encourage political leaders to end segregation there.[77]

LSE students were especially interested in the Rhodesia issue. In October 1965, the LSE's Soc-Soc helped to organize a Rhodesia "teach-in" which attracted 500 students. They invited Sir Peter Runge, leader of a group of British industrialists who had recently visited Rhodesia, but he walked out without giving his speech because of student hecklers. Students acknowledged that the idea of a teach-in originated in the University of Michigan's Vietnam teach-in, explaining that it was "neither debate nor protest meeting, its aim is to cover a topic as fully as possible, using speakers from all points of view, and to subject the views expressed and statements made to rigorous criticism in the style of an academic seminar." [78] The Soc-Soc also participated in several Rhodesia protests that November, including a demonstration march of 300 LSE students on 12 November to Downing Street, LSE, Covent Garden and finally to Rhodesia House, where police violently charged the students, arresting eleven and dispersing the rest. The Student Union condemned the police violence, paid the fines of the arrested students, and sponsored another march of 500 students on 19 November.[79] These protests reveal why the appointment of the head of Rhodesia's University College as the new Director of the LSE was so appalling to LSE's students and how the Troubles of 1966–67 were actually a year in the making.

A RADICAL STUDENT ALLIANCE

Student frustration with their powerlessness to influence their government or university on the issues of apartheid and Vietnam, together with the example of powerful student movements abroad and New Left rhetoric encouraging participatory democracy, all contributed to the creation of a national student protest organization in Britain in the 1966–67 academic year. Student activists had been trying to get the NUS to take political stands since the late fifties, but moderates and conservatives continued to dominate its Executive. These students argued that as an organization representing students of all political beliefs, the NUS could not advocate specific political goals. They consistently upheld Clause 3 of their constitution, which limited the scope of NUS policy and discussion to "students as such." In the mid-sixties, however, student activists wanted the NUS to act more like a trade union and social movement in taking a stand against class inequality, racial discrimination, and other systemic social problems. New Left rhetoric about students being a special marginalized group in society additionally fostered students' belief in the importance of having a powerful organization to represent their own special interests. They argued that even the issues of student rights and university reform had become political issues following the higher education debate in the 1964 election. Indeed, the *Robbins Report* and the rhetoric of the election had encouraged students to see their role as students as crucial to the economic well-being of the nation, warranting a more powerful organization to represent their interests to the government.

The campaign to politicize and empower the NUS as the leader of student political activism was begun by students affiliated with the British Communist Party. In response to the overwhelming involvement of students in the CND and anti-apartheid movement, the CP saw university students as a possible new source of support and formed a National Student Committee in 1963 to coordinate activities among students.[80] Willie Thompson, who had joined the Communist Party in Glasgow in 1962, helped to explain the CP's interest in the student movement in a pamphlet in 1965. He argued that the CP's *British Road to Socialism* (1951) had called for the building of an alliance between the working class and the middle class in the fight for social progress. As open-minded future leaders of the middle class, students would be an important group with which to start. He encouraged the CP to offer political leadership to student activists by providing speakers for their student societies, leafleting their universities and protests, publishing articles in student newspapers, and making the CP newspaper, *Daily Worker*, available in all university libraries and common rooms. Lastly, he explained key areas where the CP could address the interests which most concerned students: grants, student representation in university decision-making, ending *in loco parentis*, union autonomy, international student solidarity, and apartheid and racialism.[81]

To accomplish these goals as well as to forge an alliance of the broad Left and politicize the NUS, the Communist Party decided to create a new student organization. CP student organizer Fergus Nicholson invited prominent student union leaders, including David Adelstein from the LSE, David Triesman from Essex, and Anna Ford from Manchester, to a meeting in Manchester in October 1966 to discuss this new organization. All of these leaders had attended NUS meetings in the mid-sixties and were frustrated with its refusal to take a more political stand on the Vietnam War and student rights.[82] As a result, they were sympathetic to the Communist Party's goal of politicizing the NUS. Although most of them were not affiliated with the CP, they were willing to work with it on this one common goal. Toward this end, they created the Radical Students Alliance (RSA).

Throughout 1966–67, this small cadre worked very hard to build up student support for the RSA. They wrote a manifesto of their ideas and goals, much of which reflected New Left discourse and greatly expanded the purpose of the organization. The RSA manifesto stressed the importance of equality and democracy in education and society. It asserted that students should have the right to complete control over their unions, effective participation in all decisions which affected them, democratic university governance, and free access to higher education. More importantly, the RSA recommended that students take collective action on general social concerns and express solidarity with student victims of oppression. Its goal was to create "a democratic and active student movement, based on strong local and area unions and organizations, autonomous and democratic."[83] The RSA, therefore, not only worked within the NUS to get Clause 3 repealed, but it also worked with individual student unions to encourage activism on the local level. As such, the RSA was Britain's first national student organization to explicitly advocate direct action as a tactic to democratize the system of higher education.

The RSA began as a small organization, but quickly grew in size and influence. Triesman recalled that the RSA's first meetings "were very, very badly attended. They were dour as hell, they were humourless, grim discussions, conducted along that lethal supposition that you had to be deadly serious because the revolution was bound to take place the following week."[84] By early 1967, Triesman, Adrian Perry, and David Widgery had concluded that they had to work jokes into their speeches, so that they could make the audience laugh and liven up the meetings. Eventually the RSA meetings attracted hundreds of students at different universities, making Triesman feel a little like a rock star. The experience was intoxicating and exhausting, but it also taught student leaders how to speak in front of large audiences and built up a close-knit network of activists at the heart of the student movement.[85]

Revealing the popularity of the idea of a radical student organization, the RSA's January 1967 conference attracted 400 students from 108 colleges. The delegates, however, disagreed over the structure of the RSA. Communist delegates developed a plan for a hierarchical bureaucratic structure, but the majority preferred a more democratic organization based upon local groups and mass participation, similar to the New Left and the CND. Although Communist delegates comprised the organizing force behind the RSA, they compromised on the structure and agreed to a grassroots, mass participation model. The RSA, however, was not nearly as representative of student opinion as it hoped to be. Many students at this time cared very little about the NUS, and many student activists preferred to take political stands through local organizations, seeing the NUS as a distant, bureaucratic organization for careerist students. The RSA attempted to overcome this obstacle by connecting student concerns over political issues to their situation as students, to prove that student organizations must take political stands because politics did indeed affect them personally.[86]

THE OVERSEAS STUDENT FEES CAMPAIGN

Just months after the creation of the RSA, the Labour government gave them the perfect issue to unite student issues with those of broader international and moral consequence. In December of 1966, the government announced that to offset the rising costs of higher education, it would dramatically increase overseas student fees. Vice Chancellors, staff, and students were united in their opposition to this increase. A number of prominent leaders in higher education published their criticism of this "monstrous and inhuman" decision to discriminate against students who often had little access to higher education in their home countries and who contributed much diversity to Britain's universities.[87] Many British students also felt that this move was racist because it discriminated against overseas students, many of whom came from developing countries and desperately needed the inexpensive quality education that British universities provided.[88] The RSA criticized the NUS executive for taking no action on this issue and organized its own rally of 3,000 students in London on 3 February 1967. The RSA next held a National Day of Action on the overseas fees issue on 22 February. An estimated 100,000 students participated in strikes, boycotts, marches, meetings, rallies, and petitions at universities across the country. This was to be the RSA's most successful protest.[89]

At the core of the overseas student fees campaign were the 400 students who had attended the original RSA meeting and returned to their universities to organize support for its goals. Some of the largest actions took place at Leeds, Birmingham, and Manchester Universities that February. Student participation in these marches ranged from 2,000 to 3,000, and over 90 per cent of students boycotted their lectures at Manchester in protest of the fees.[90] Hull University also joined in the overseas student fees campaign. Their Union president attended an RSA conference as an observer the first week of February, but he judged that "they were a group of extremists with whom we should have no dealings."[91] The National Day of Action sparked intense debate over whether the Hull Student Union should declare a strike and boycott lectures. Voters at a Union meeting instructed the student president to call a one-day strike, but the Union president refused because he feared violence. At that, Tom Fawthrop, a second-year sociology and politics student and member of the university Socialist Society and the Hull Student Council, led 300 in a spontaneous march through the city to protest the rise in overseas student fees and helped to form an RSA committee to organize future actions. David Triesman then came up from Essex to speak at the inaugural meeting of the Hull RSA.[92] Both Triesman and Fawthrop went on to become leaders of other protests at their respective universities and key activists in the student movement.

Despite this initial outpouring of support for the overseas fees campaign, the RSA proved unable to lead the student movement for long. Comparing itself to the American and German SDS, the RSA admitted that it had a long way to go to develop that sort of student movement. Fatally divided on tactics and its own future, the RSA was much weaker and smaller in terms of membership than the burgeoning student organizations in West Germany and the United States. Because of this and the strength of its conservative opponents, the RSA failed even to strike down Clause 3 at the 1967 NUS conference and failed to force the government to abandon the overseas student fees increase.

STUDENT RIGHTS CAMPAIGNS

Although the RSA failed on these fronts, student unions did indeed become politicized and make student rights a priority after 1967. Since the fifties, student CND and anti-apartheid activists faced university regulations limiting their ability to effectively protest and punishing them for their activism. Some university authorities may have sympathized with the issues, but they were determined to protect the image of the universities as objective and non-partisan. Although student activists already felt frustrated by limitations on their rights to protest, the Anti-Apartheid Movement's call for universities to boycott South African goods and all connections with South African corporations brought these limitations into sharp focus and pitted students against university administrators. Both groups opposed apartheid and racism, but administrators felt bound to protect the best financial interests of the university, which often meant investing in South African companies and other kinds of economic relationships with South Africa. This division would raise the question of student rights in university decision-making which became the key issue of the LSE Troubles.

The Anti-Apartheid Movement's boycott campaign pushed the issue of student decision-making to the forefront of the student movement in a number of important ways. The AAM encouraged students to attack their university's relationship with apartheid in their literature, framing the issue in terms of personal moral responsibility:

> Almost all colleges have direct or indirect links with apartheid and racism in Southern Africa which effectively associates you with, for example, enforced migrant labour, inferior education syllabi and health provisions for blacks; discriminatory colour bar in job opportunity and the 'legal' negation of basic human and civil rights. It takes a concerted effort to break these connections but if you believe in justice and ending the exploitation, racism and discrimination of thousands, then you have a responsibility to try.[93]

When student unions responded by voting to boycott all connections with South African corporations as the AAM suggested, they found that they had no power to enforce their boycott and no support from the administrators who did. Activist students then directed their attention to the university power structure that prevented them from using university resources in support of moral and political causes.

While the AAM caused conflict over university decision-making, the discourse of the global New Left and student movements gave them an ideology to explain this authoritarian system and a solution in participatory democracy. Disciplinary action against student activists added fuel to the fire, leading many students to see this as an unjust infringement upon their right to free speech, press, and assembly. These factors led students to turn their gaze to the problems of student rights and power inside the university. In one university after another, radical activist students joined forces with moderate and conservative students who had been petitioning and politely requesting minor reforms to allow students more control over their own personal lives and more power in university governance for a number of years. These polite requests generally met with equally polite or, from the students' point of view, slightly condescending and paternalistic responses by the authorities who only agreed to take student wishes under consideration. Often this consideration meant forming a committee to study reform and a long bureaucratic process that rarely resulted in real reform. Facing this resistance on the part of the authorities, students grew impatient and disillusioned with the lack of change.

The NUS led the national campaign for student rights throughout the Long Sixties. Although this issue had been a central reason for its formation earlier in the century, it escalated this campaign in the mid-sixties because the nation seemed ripe for higher education reform. In April 1965 the NUS created a Students' Charter which set standards for university conditions and contained recommendations on student representation, appropriate disciplinary action, and the right of students to form independent student unions.[94] The NUS also met with national staff and administrative associations to negotiate for increased student representation in university government. In 1966 the NUS executive met with the Association of University Teachers and the Committee of Vice Chancellors and Principals to discuss this issue. The Association of University Teachers supported student representation on some committees, but not on university Senates, while the Vice Chancellors agreed that students should have some access to Senate proceedings.[95] The NUS also submitted recommendations to the Latey Commission on the Age of Majority which was established in 1965 under the chairmanship of Justice Latey and published in 1967. The *Latey Report* quoted liberally from NUS proposals when it suggested that the national government lower the age of majority to 18 and that higher education end *in loco parentis* rules. Although its recommendations would not be implemented until 1969, this report gave student rights activists powerful ammunition in their negotiations with university authorities.[96]

Socialist Societies were another important group in the debate over student rights and instrumental in interpreting the student rights issue within a broader socialist and New Left framework. A Canadian-born student in Oxford University's Socialist group, Stan Gray linked New Left analysis to the *in loco parentis* issue in a 1966 essay. He began by pointing out the fundamental contradiction between society's changing beliefs about personal freedom and their university's archaic authoritarianism, especially its *in loco parentis* regulations.[97] Gray called for a radical reorganization of the university power structure and a redefining of the university's goals and philosophy of education toward a conception of education as a means through which students could take an active and creative part in a democratic learning community. Reflecting the British New Left's emphasis on the working class, Gray asserted that this change could not come about without changing wider society, and so he recommended that students ally with the working class to build "a new social order based upon genuine democracy, social justice and full equality. The fight for student democracy and a free university is an integral aspect of a more generalized fight for a socialist society."[98] In this way, the New Left's rhetoric of participatory democracy, individual creativity, and freedom informed discussions about student rights in this period, and gave them a stronger ideological framework.

Although small student rights protests occurred at Aberystwyth, Liverpool, and elsewhere in this period, an intriguing student rights case at Glasgow University brought the issue to national attention and framed the issue in terms of the wider debate over educational reform. In 1966, Glasgow University authorities suspended the student president for life and five others for one year for making obscene phone calls to the secretary of the Student Council. Students objected to this discipline because the accused did not hear the evidence against them, they had no opportunity to answer the accusations, and the principal had ruled without an adequate investigation or solid evidence.[99] Students were outraged by this betrayal of their democratic rights. The Glasgow Student Council, together with the Student Councils of other Scottish universities and a Member of Parliament, called upon university authorities to set up an independent inquiry into the affair and suggested that student representatives be allowed to participate in future cases of student discipline.[100] The suspensions were eventually lifted, but no revisions in disciplinary procedures followed. This incident, however, provoked a national discussion in Parliament and in the press over the archaic disciplinary systems in universities, making student rights a national concern in 1966.

THE LOCAL CONTEXT OF THE LSE'S TROUBLES

Within this broad national context, therefore, the Troubles at the LSE can be seen as just one large-scale manifestation of the student movement developing at universities across the nation in the mid-sixties. Reflecting the rhetoric and actions of the NUS, the RSA, and student unions across the country, the LSE Student's Union began expressing increased interest in university decision-making and student rights in 1965. Before then, Sydney Caine had always reported that the relations between the administration and the Students' Union had remained "cordial," but in 1965 he had begun to notice "wide differences in the approach to staff-student relationships" between himself and student representatives. He rightly perceived this as a part of widespread changes taking place amongst students across the nation.[101]

Although the LSE conflict was part of a larger student movement against apartheid and in support of student rights, its local context shaped the unique form it took in 1966–67. The LSE's Troubles specifically began in 1964, when its Student Union resolved to boycott South African goods on school premises, but found it had no power to enforce the boycott.[102] Only School administrators had that power and they declined to support it. Student activists realized then that they needed power in university decision-making to fully carry out their moral activism. As a result, the president of the Union asked the Director for representation on School committees which discussed matters of direct concern to students. Although the Director was sympathetic, he argued that staff members did not wish to allow students on committees that dealt with confidential matters. Two of the most powerful committees, the Academic Board and General Purposes Committee, however, did agree to send the Union president agendas on the condition that they be kept strictly confidential.[103] This step, however, did not result in the desired university boycott of South African goods or any real change in student participation in decision-making. As a result, LSE students grew increasingly frustrated with traditional channels of communication and reform, and looked for alternative means to achieve their goals of increasing student power in decision-making, so that they would be able to meaningfully contribute to the causes in which they believed.

Throughout the 1964–65 academic year, the LSE Student Union also pressured administrators to ameliorate the crowded conditions at the university, but to little effect. Their dissatisfaction with their conditions and the university's ignorance of their demands led to increased student support for a strike by the spring of 1965. A student editorial asserted that "their objectives are not simply to pointlessly defy authority for its own sake. They are not just practicing at politics. They are trying to convince the school that no student . . . is happy with the overcrowded conditions here. But the school have refused to take their case seriously."[104] Finally, in March 1965, the Student Union threatened to strike over demands for student government freedom to make loans to union societies, more wardrobe lockers, more public telephones, a new snack bar, and establishing a Staff/Student Reform Committee to discuss student representation. The Director averted the strike by agreeing to form a Staff/Student Committee to discuss the other issues.[105]

After a year with little progress in these discussions, LSE students were ready to carry through with their threat of a strike. In January of

1966, the Student Union elected David Adelstein, a South African born second-year leader of Students Against Racial Discrimination, to the Union presidency on a New Left platform of student power and mass participatory democracy.[106] Adelstein and the new Union Council immediately attempted to gain more power for the Staff/Student Committee and representation on other more important School committees. They subsequently submitted recommendations to the Director requesting copies of the agenda for meetings of the Academic Board and General Purposes Committee, and the right to attend and speak at these meetings when matters directly affecting students were being discussed. Reflecting the national discourse on the democratization of higher education, they explained their demand for representation: "Students, as a necessary and important sector of a university, have a right to be represented in the government of their university." They asserted that taking student views into account "is fundamental to ensuring the effectiveness of the teaching we receive," and emphasized that the lack of representation "leads to a deep frustration amongst students over the tenor of staff-student relationships, which in turn leads many students to become alienated from the School in general." [107] They specifically wanted a voice in matters such as student facilities, welfare and health, and teaching methods.

The Standing Committee of the Governors and the Academic Board rejected the Union's request because, as School Secretary Harry Kidd later claimed, "the presence of students, who would not be able to take part in discussion as equals, would hinder constructive debate, and there was no evidence of student discontent on any serious issue that would justify their admission."[108] Whether the issue of student representation was of primary concern to the bulk of students is in fact debatable. Judging from Union comments about the lack of student participation and attendance at meetings, it is doubtful that most students cared about this issue to the extent that the leaders of the Union did. After all, as representatives of the students, Union leaders would be the most likely students to gain admission to these meetings. Because of the lack of interest among most students, the Union leaders made a campaign for greater student involvement in politics one of their primary goals for 1966–67.

This goal paralleled that of the Socialist Society. Although the LSE Soc-Soc was more interested in external politics, some saw student representation in university government as a way to involve more students in protests, which might radicalize them. In the March 1966 edition of *Agitator*, they discussed the upcoming appointment of a new Director for LSE as an opportunity to do just that. In 1964, the Director had announced that he would retire in 1967 and students were aware that the Court of Governors would be selecting the new Director in the coming months. *Agitator* announced that it would hold its own student election for the Director. It argued that the process of filling the post without consulting students or rank-and-file staff was undemocratic, asserting that "it must, and it can only be through students' participation and control over deci-sion-making that a university worthy of the name can be established."[109] Their mock election proceeded during the summer, but attracted little attention from students or university authorities.

Then the Court of Governors selected Walter Adams, Principal of Uni-versity College Rhodesia, as the new Director in June 1966. This action merged the issue of Rhodesia with that of student rights with explosive results. In October, the Soc-Soc published a pamphlet, *LSE's New Direc-tor: A Report on Walter Adams*, which was strongly critical of Adams and his appointment as Director. It alleged that Adams was unwilling to take a stand on the issue of academic freedom, avoided making important deci-sions, was isolated from staff and students, and was inefficient in his duties in Rhodesia.[110] Most importantly, it argued that he had not resisted the Rhodesian government's racist policies. Over 1,000 copies of this pamphlet were sold in the next month, stirring the waters of discontent.

Influenced by the Soc-Soc, the Student Union passed a motion "seriously questioning" Adams' appointment. It sent a telegram and mailed a copy of the pamphlet to Adams, requesting that he respond to the allegations within eighteen days. School Secretary Harry Kidd, however, sent Adams a telegram on behalf of the governors and Director, advising him to not reply to the Student Union. Some students wanted to protest the appointment and the authority's unwillingness to discuss the issue with a boycott of lectures. Colin Crouch and Richard Kuper, a member of the IS and graduate student leader of the Soc-Soc, brought a motion to this effect before the union, but it failed due to the lack of interest among the majority of students at that time. Although Crouch was in favor of taking action, he felt that the Socialist Society was really out of touch with the majority of students. He claimed it was trying to lead the student movement at the LSE, prodding and goading the Union into taking a more radical stance on the issues, but "their language was strange and unfamiliar to the bulk of students . . ."[111] If the authorities had done nothing more, perhaps there would have been no Troubles at the LSE after all.

Similar to the case of Berkeley and many other universities in the sixties, however, LSE's authorities felt that they had to retaliate against what they saw as impertinence from the students. Feeling embarrassed by the pam-phlet and the actions of the Student Union, the Court of Governors Chair-man, Lord Bridges, published a letter in the *Times*, deploring the attacks on Adams and defending his selection as Director. When David Adelstein, at the direction of the Student Union, replied to Lord Bridges in the *Times*, Secretary Kidd began disciplinary proceedings against him because of a regulation that students could not publish statements in the name of a uni-versity organization without the express permission of the Director.

The disciplinary proceedings against Adelstein then raised a storm of student protest. The Disciplinary Board had only met once since 1945 and was considered by many to be an archaic relic of the past. The Student

Union was shocked that their president had been reprimanded for an action taken on its behalf. It had been advised by two members of staff that Adelstein's letter was perfectly legal and well within his rights. Students also believed that they had a civic right to freedom of expression and opinion. The disciplinary action, therefore, seemed not only out-dated, but also unjust. The Board of Discipline itself seemed undemocratic, with no student representatives and no provision for Adelstein's defense. Student leaders, therefore, objected to the Court's actions, asserting that the disciplinary procedure itself was unjust and that the Court had infringed on the Union's independence and students' freedom of speech. Encouraging students to attend a meeting to discuss these issues, Colin Crouch wrote in the student newspaper:

> We are not schoolchildren, nor are we privates in the Prussian Army; we are consumers of an educational service and we have a right to say whether it is good or not. . . . The School [authorities] have broken the rules of gentleman's agreements. . . . When you find that constitutional procedures themselves are in dispute and you are not allowed to use them any more, you must look for other courses of action. This is why we must now make the decision to undertake civil disobedience, to show the School that we are not going to take it lying down.[112]

Reminiscent of the Berkeley protests, Crouch and other LSE students demanded to be treated as rational adults with the democratic rights of natural justice, participation in governance, and free speech. Faced with hostile authority, students felt that they had no choice but to express their dissent through direct action.

On Friday, 18 November, the Student Union passed a motion, deploring the disciplinary action against its president and calling for a boycott of lectures and classes on the following Monday, when the Board was due to meet.[113] Over the weekend, Union leaders thoroughly prepared for the boycott, making posters and organizing students to visit all lecture halls and classrooms to persuade other students to join the boycott. That Monday, students picketed all the entrances of the School and announced that 78 per cent of students had boycotted their classes. The Socialist Society, without the approval of the Student Union, also held a sit-in outside the room where Adelstein's disciplinary hearing was taking place. About sixty students participated, singing protest songs such as "We Shall Overcome" and a number of other songs they had learned from the American civil rights movement and CND marches.[114] Indicating their identification with the global student movement, they also made a banner reading "Berkeley 1964: LSE 1966: We'll bring this school to a halt too."[115] Late in the afternoon, the sit-in and boycott ended in victory. The Board announced that Adelstein would not be punished because he had acted in the belief that he was not disobeying a regulation of the School. At the end of the term, students won an additional victory when School authorities invited students to meet with the staff and the Director to discuss student participation. Although this resulted in no further progress on the issue, LSE students ended 1966 believing that their direct action had been effective.

In January, the Soc-Soc succeeded in getting the support of the Student Union and the Graduate Students' Association. Marshall Bloom, an American civil rights activist who had recently taken up postgraduate studies at the LSE and was elected president of the Graduate Students Association, organized the meeting and booked a large lecture room known as the Old Theatre, where Student Union meetings were always held, for the meeting on 31 January. Bloom was especially interested in discussing how the sit-in strategy used by the civil rights movement and the Berkeley FSM might be applied to the campaign against Adams.[116] One publicity poster, entitled "Stop Adams" asserted that the Adams issue was "symbolic of a host of problems including the place of the students in their college, and there is no better place to begin work for a different LSE than by opposing the appointment of Adams."[117] It went on to announce that they were prepared to take direct action to prevent him from becoming their Director. When someone put up additional posters including obscene and racist remarks attributed to Adams to advertise the meeting, the Director banned the meeting. The Soc-Soc portrayed this action as another betrayal of students' rights to free speech and assembly, and used it to draw more attention to their meeting. As a consequence, over 600 students turned up outside the Old Theatre for the banned meeting. The Troubles of the LSE then began in earnest.

While the national media portrayed the Troubles at the LSE as erupting suddenly out of nowhere and something unique to the ultra-radical LSE, it was actually years in the making and represented broader trends within the British student movement of the mid-sixties. Located at the center of "swinging" London, just a short walk from Trafalgar Square, LSE students had been in the thick of the 1956 Suez protest as well as the nuclear disarmament marches and sit-down protests. They had formed their own nuclear disarmament and anti-racism clubs years earlier, and their student activists had been involved in multiple other protests throughout the mid-sixties, providing LSE students with a solid foundation in organizing protest meetings and demonstrations long before the Troubles of 1967. LSE students, like their counterparts at many other universities around the country and the world, had been politely requesting student representation in university decision-making and other reforms to improve student conditions within the university for years, but they had met with resistance from the authorities, despite the fact that they had been promised reforms following the *Robbins Report* and the election of 1964. It was this resistance to reform and the disillusionment it caused that led LSE students to take direct action against their university administrators, setting in motion the events which led to the porter's death in the Old Theatre and the massive sit-ins which

followed. LSE may have been unique in the radicalism of its IS-led Socialist Society and the willingness of so many students to participate in direct
action against the university, but it was not nearly as as different from other
British universities as contemporary commentators suggested.

The original issues behind the LSE student protests, including student
rights and Rhodesia, were both key elements in the nation-wide student
movement of the period. Student activists in this period built upon the
foundations of a national student movement that was created out of the
New Left, the Campaign for Nuclear Disarmament, and the anti-apartheid
movement in the late fifties. Activism around these issues continued through
the mid-sixties, but students took on new moral issues such as Rhodesia,
the Vietnam War, and overseas student fees, and began to use new tactics, such as teach-ins and sit-ins, which were borrowed from the CND
and the American student movement. As students attempted to use university resources to support this activism, they were frustrated by university
authorities who limited their ability to effectively protest these issues. This
frustration, together with disciplinary actions taken against student activists and a national debate over university reform, led activists to take up
the issue of student rights as a way to gain the power to effectively protest
external issues and involve more students in protest activity.

The reframing of student rights as an issue of national importance was
crucial to the developments at the LSE and the student movement as a
whole. The *Robbins Report* and the election of 1964 had elevated issues
of higher education to national prominence. In that same year, Berkeley's
Free Speech Movement introduced the nation to a large student protest
movement which was successfully fighting for student rights using demonstration marches and sit-ins. This helped to reframe the issue of student
rights as a protest issue and made the press more aware of the problems of
higher education. The unjust disciplining of students in Glasgow in February of 1966, consequently, elicited an outcry from not only from students,
but also from the press and Parliament. These events set the stage for the
Troubles at LSE. Viewing student rights as a protest issue of national and
international importance, LSE students framed their protests within the
context of morality, democratic rights, and modernization. In this way,
they made their appeals using the political discourse of the day.

"Modernization" was a key concept underlying much political and social
discourse in the mid-sixties. Everyone agreed on the need to modernize
higher education, but students had their own views on how this should
be done, and used protest as a means of expressing their views when they
were ignored by university administrators. While many universities had
modernized technology and content, student-administrator relations and
facilities did not keep pace. This created a sense of frustration with the lack
of change amongst many students—a sense that their elders were not keeping up with their own rhetoric of reform and modernization. The *Robbins
Report* and election of 1964 had raised student expectations, and when

authorities failed to radically change universities, students perceived this as "relative deprivation."[118] This dissatisfaction with the university system festered and grew until it exploded in the Troubles at the LSE. When student activists were punished for transgressing outdated university regulations, this reservoir of anger and frustration was tapped, resulting in widespread participation in the sit-ins and boycotts. For the first time, a large-scale student demonstration was directed primarily at the university with the protest taking place within the university and expressing dissent against the university, as opposed to protests earlier in the decade which had taken place in Trafalgar Square and other locations outside the university around external issues. The Troubles of the LSE thus reveal a refocusing of the British student movement on the lack of modernization within the university system itself.

National discussions about modernizing higher education paralleled discussions in nations across Europe, Japan, and North America as their economies were similarly transformed by technology and global integration in the second half of the twentieth century. Student organizations in these countries similarly formed protest movements to contribute to debates over higher education. The British RSA, however, formed several years after the American and German SDS, and faced more difficulties in creating a strong, cohesive student organization. Unlike West Germany and the US, the British Communist Party influenced the RSA from the start, competing with New Left ideas for dominance within the student movement. Social movements, however, do not need central organizations to lead them, and the British student movement continued to grow despite the weakness of the RSA.

The British student movement also paralleled student movements in other countries in its relationship to the international New Left and discourse of dissent against the Cold War. Although the British student movement was distinct from the New Left, British socialist societies brought New Left and Marxist ideologies to the protests over Rhodesia, South Africa, Vietnam, and student rights. Socialist students framed these issues in terms of their broader struggle against imperialism, racism, and economic inequality, and while their ideologies remained unintelligible to most students, New Left and Marxist concepts crept into student discourse in the mid-sixties. The terms "powers that be," "democratic control," "alienation," and "liberation" derived directly from the discourse of the international New Left, and were brought to the British student movement via the second generation of the British New Left. The student movement thus drew from both international and national ideologies, applying them to specific local contexts, connecting wider political discourses to immediate local circumstances.

Despite its parallels and connections to global developments, the British student movement was clearly home-grown. The majority of activists were born and raised in Britain, and acted within a British tradition of rational debate, liberal reform, human rights, and political protest. Students especially drew upon a national discourse of morality as they made their case on the issues. The rhetoric of the New Left, CND, and the anti-apartheid campaigns, however, had led student activists to see these British traditions in a new light. These movements had planted the seed of participatory democracy in the nation, establishing the belief that in a democracy, citizens had a right to express their opinions through direct action and that these opinions should be considered in decision-making. This led students to demand a voice in decision-making in university governance.

Although the LSE protest had much in common with its counterparts elsewhere in the nation, it was much more successful in drawing media attention and student support than other British universities. Partly because of its location at the center of the nation's media, government, and fashion world, and partly because of its cosmopolitan student population and radical reputation, the LSE became the poster-child for the British student movement of the sixties. The media coverage of the Troubles at the LSE produced a national narrative of the British student movement, emphasizing the role of foreign students and ideas, and minimizing the actual issues raised by the students, thus creating an illusion of the LSE protest as an isolated, imitative and irrational out-pouring of youthful rebellion instigated by a minority of students. Similar to the West German and American news media, the British media thus helped students to publicize their protests, but also undermined their respective student movements by framing them as communist or foreigner inspired conspiracies against public order.[119] These media portrayals were inaccurate, but helped to create misperceptions about the student movements of the sixties that persist to this day. The image of a global student conspiracy, however, not only affected the British public perception, but also how students viewed themselves. Although some students had already begun to feel solidarity with students of other nations in the early sixties, the media framing of the LSE protest encouraged even more student activists to identify themselves as part of a global student movement.

While the student movement of the mid-sixties shared much in common with that of the first phase of the movement in the late fifties and early sixties, the second generation of activists differed in important ways. Like Stuart Hall, Tariq Ali came to Britain from overseas and brought with him a strong sense of outrage at imperialism and racism, which motivated his entrance into student activism. Unlike Hall and Sheila Rowbotham, however, Ali and his cohort of activists, including those born in Britain like Colin Crouch and David Fernbach, entered the university after the New Left, CND, and anti-apartheid movement had already laid the foundations for student activist organizations. They were thus already familiar with the use of direct action in confronting authorities. They were additionally inspired by powerful student movements in America and France, witnessing how other students used direct action to protest for university reforms and student rights. Expecting to enter into modernized democratic universities, they were deeply disappointed with the perceived conservatism of administrators and were less patient with paternalistic and authoritarian responses. As a result, they advocated the more dramatic tactics of the sit-in, boycott, and teach-in to draw attention to their protests and force authorities to give in to student demands.

Contrary to the media-generated image, the British student movement was a widespread, nation-wide movement consisting of overseas and home students who used New Left and mainstream British political discourse to frame their protests around the issues of student rights, racism, and the Vietnam War. Student activists were outraged at what they saw as the immoral and irrational actions of authorities in their universities, national government, and foreign governments. They used peaceful demonstration marches, pickets, boycotts, teach-ins, and sit-ins as tactics to publicize their outrage, expecting authorities to rationally listen to their opinions and react with reforms. Instead, authorities and the media ignored their demands and treated activists as children. This treatment angered radical and moderate students alike, and united both groups in protests to improve the treatment of all students. To students, therefore, their protests were rational and justified responses to the irrational, immoral, and unjust actions of authorities. Student perceptions of their movement thus directly contradicted the media-generated narrative. This contradiction would contribute to considerable confusion over the meaning and legacy of the British student movement which has lasted to this day.

3   1968, That Magical Year

It was an evening early in May 1968, that momentous month of that most magical year. The setting: rural Essex University. Two hundred students sat in the Senate Room of Wivenhoe House at the center of the new campus to hear a lecture given by Doctor D. T. Inch of Porton Down, the government's chemical and biological warfare center. The Essex chemistry society and department had invited Inch to speak on the properties of toxic chemicals and to recruit students to careers at Porton Down. Little did they or he know of the plans of the Essex Socialist Society. They had been busily involved in protests against the Vietnam War and the new Immigration Bill, and were already in trouble with university authorities for their protests against Enoch Powell earlier that semester. After hearing from a staff member about Inch's visit and his invention of some chemical weapons used in Vietnam, the Socialist Society had quickly and secretly planned the protest.

When Inch got up to speak, Socialist Society member David Triesman dramatically stood up. Consciously modeling himself after Bertrand Russell's War Crimes Tribunal for American actions in Vietnam, Triesman read aloud an indictment of the genocide that chemical weapons had inflicted upon Vietnamese peasants. Triesman compared Inch and Porton Down with Nazi scientists, saying, "The fact that Porton Down is not yet responsible for the deaths of millions of people seems to me to be little justification for the lack of prosecution of the potential murderers at Porton. The lessons of the last twenty-five years must surely have been learned by now."[1] After five minutes of Triesman's presentation, Inch began shouting back at him. Chemistry staff chimed in, accusing Triesman of abridging Inch's freedom of speech. Triesman responded that all he wanted was an open discussion. As Inch turned to leave the auditorium, another student surprised even Triesman by emptying a packet of mustard powder over Inch, shouting "ban mustard gas!" Enraged, Inch and Chemistry staff members rushed out into the corridor, but were followed and surrounded by a large group of students who promptly sat down and began asking Inch questions about his research. As Inch answered the questions, he and the students began to relax, but tensions escalated once again when the police (who had been called by worried staff at the beginning of the protest) arrived with their dogs. The police themselves seemed bewildered as to why they had been called and their dogs ran around loose, barking excitedly. [2] Students were shocked by the fact that the police had been called. As police pushed their way over seated demonstrators and surrounded Inch, angry students circled the police with linked arms. Chemistry staff and the police violently pushed the students out of the way and hustled Inch out to the police car. Students attracted to the commotion swelled the crowd surrounding the cars and angry arguments broke out between students and staff. One of the chemistry staff, apparently frustrated with the crowd of students, drove straight through them, nearly injuring several of them. [3]

The protest infuriated chemistry students and staff. The staff demanded that the protesters be expelled and threatened to resign from their positions en masse. Vice Chancellor Albert Sloman responded by summarily suspending Triesman, Peter Archard, and Raphael Halberstadt, arguing that he must defend freedom of speech at all costs. Archard had thrown the mustard powder, but Halberstadt was not even at the protest. His only offense was apparently the fact that he looked like Che Guevara. Triesman was shocked by the suspensions because he had been working very hard and was hoping to graduate that year. [4] Similar to the LSE in 1967, these suspensions then set off a round of new protests.

Student meetings to discuss their response began as soon as the suspension notifications went out on Friday 10 May. After briefly meeting at the foot of Keynes residential tower, 250 students marched to the Vice Chancellor's house to present a petition calling for the suspensions to be lifted. They discovered that Sloman was nowhere to be found, presented their petition to a frightened Mrs. Sloman, and left. That Saturday, the three suspended students went to London to meet with a lawyer to explore their legal options. When the students returned to campus on 12 May, over a thousand students and staff passed a motion deploring the Vice Chancellor's action and called upon him to explain his actions to the rest of the University. When the Vice Chancellor refused, the meeting discussed the possibility of direct action. Sociology lecturer Michael Freeman told the crowd that the suspensions were a breach of natural justice. Another young sociology lecturer, Paul Thompson proposed that "all routine teaching and functions at the university should be suspended," a Free University should meet until the suspensions were lifted, and a Student/Staff Committee of Enquiry should be created. [5] This proposal won the approval of the great majority of those at the meeting.

The Free University began the next morning and lasted for a week. This Free University was more of a continuous teach-in, where students and staff discussed chemical and germ warfare, the legality of the university authorities' action in suspending the three students, university reform, and the role of the press. [6] Notices that the university was now a "Liberated Zone" were posted all over the campus. That first evening, many of the staff attended an emergency assembly to listen to Paul Thompson's proposal. They approved it overwhelmingly. The next day, however, an emergency meeting of the formal Senate was called. This body consisted of academic staff representatives and was the supreme authority on student affairs and all academic matters. Students waited hopefully on the Senate response before taking any further action. When the Senate finally announced its verdict supporting the Vice Chancellor a few days later, students were angered and disappointed.

Finally that Thursday, over a week after the initial protest had occurred, the Vice Chancellor spoke to the assembled students to answer their questions. He refused to reconsider the suspensions, stressing his duties as the Vice Chancellor as the reason for this refusal. The student newspaper wrote that, "The question was always 'are you right?' and the answer always 'I am authority.'"[7] Sloman kept trying to persuade the staff and students that the University felt this or that as though he alone was the university, until Peter Wexler, a lecturer in Linguistics, stood up and said "Vice Chancellor, you do not understand. We *are* the University."[8] At the end of the meeting, students voted resoundingly to continue their Free University and occupation until the students were reinstated and the Senate was made more democratic.[9]

During the occupation, Essex students received support from a number of prominent dissenters, including Jean Paul Sartre and Bertrand Russell, as well as more than forty scientists who also wanted chemical weapons research stopped. Student delegations from universities across the nation arrived to give them advice and support.[10] At the meetings of the Free University, discussion shifted from chemical weapons to "the power structure of the University, the validity of the examination system, the nature and purpose of knowledge, [and] the concept of free speech."[11] In this way, the issues of student rights and educational reform quickly superseded the chemical weapons issue which had originated the first protest. Similar to the Troubles at the LSE, official resistance and reaction had once again turned activists' attention away from external issues to focus instead on their own lack of rights and power within the university.

Although the Free University and occupation were carried out peacefully and seriously, at other times, the protest resembled a carnival of sorts. Evenings were filled with music and dancing, vivid artwork and graffiti sprung up around campus, and television crews and even a film crew established themselves on campus to document the unfolding drama.[12] Finally, on Friday 17 May, the Senate and progressive staff indicated the three would be reinstated pending a full enquiry into the Porton Down protest. On Monday, when it appeared that Sloman and the rest of the university would go along with this resolution, students packed the Square at the center of the university to celebrate. They played music through the university loudspeakers and students danced in the fountains in victory. A chain of dancers encircled the pool as fireworks exploded and bonfires were set. The celebrations continued into the night. The next day, the campus returned to normal and students began studying for their final exams in earnest.[13]

After the sit-in and final examinations had ended, Essex activists continued to protest against Chemical and Biological Weapons (CBW) in other ways. More than 100 Essex students joined several hundred more protesters in an anti-CBW march to Whitehall in June 1968 and the student newspaper noted that the mainstream media was now giving intensive coverage to this issue. They additionally claimed a victory in government announcements seeking an international ban on CBW.[14]

Widespread media coverage of the Essex protests brought Triesman to the attention of student activists elsewhere in Europe and the United States that summer. Indeed, the United States National Student Association invited Triesman to America to speak to student activists there about the situation in Britain. Triesman visited Chicago during the infamous Democratic National Convention that August in which the police mercilessly attacked thousands of anti-war activists in the streets. Triesman himself was clubbed and sprayed with mace, and was astonished at this "naked show of force." He was impressed with Tom Hayden, the author of the *Port Huron Statement* and former leader of SDS, but was disappointed with the rest of the American student activists he met. He felt that compared to the British student movement, the American student movement was "utterly incoherent," with no clear political strategy or ideological awareness. After returning to England at the end of the summer, Triesman began a Ph.D. at Cambridge, but had to drop out because he was denied a grant due to his notoriety at Essex.[15]

In the months following the Essex sit-in, administrators and staff attempted to understand the incident in order to prevent further disruptions. The Chancellor of the university and a few members of the university's governing council blamed the incident on communist agitation as part of an international conspiracy.[16] After the university conducted a full inquiry, however, administrators and staff concluded that it had actually been caused by a breakdown in communications between students and administrators, and that the solution was to allow student representation on Senate committees.[17] In the months afterwards, Essex students won representation on most university committees and over fifty per cent representation on several which directly concerned student interests.[18] Even Sloman came out against *in loco parentis* rules, urging the recognition of students as adults who were free to live their own lives and the effective involvement of students in university government.[19] More so than student protests at most other universities that year, Essex students had won a clear victory.

The Essex protest of May 1968 was neither the largest, nor the longest-lasting student protest that year, but it did succeed in attracting an enormous amount of publicity, sympathy, and support, and it did hint at a number of important distinctive features of a new phase in the national student movement that year. First of all, it was the culmination of events which originated in the early sixties and it formed the basis for protests which would continue through the 1968–69 academic year. In this way, the magical year actually overlapped two academic years: 1967–68 and

1968–69. As such, both years must be analyzed in order to truly understand the events of 1968. Hundreds of protests occurred across the nation in these years on a wide range of issues, including student rights and university reforms, as well as opposition to the Vietnam War and racism. These were the same issues that had been at the heart of the student movement in the mid-sixties, but what made 1968 different from earlier years was the larger numbers of protest actions across the nation and the fact that most of these protests involved sit-ins and occupations of their universities. Inspired by the 1966–67 LSE protests and student movements elsewhere, students across the nation now adopted this technique in support of their diverse demands. A smaller minority of students adopted even more radical tactics, including shouting down speakers and obstruction, to force authorities to listen to them and attract publicity to their cause. These strategies not only reflected the increasingly confrontational nature of the student movement, but would also affect government and university officials' perceptions of the student movement. The British student movement came into its own in 1968 and was finally reckoned a force of considerable power.

THE CASE OF ESSEX UNIVERSITY

Similar to the LSE Troubles of 1967, the Essex protests of 1968 were a product of a unique confluence of local, national, and international elements. Even more so than many other universities, they were a product of the high expectations generated by the discourse of modernization and democratization which dominated in British society and politics in the fifties and early sixties. Essex University opened in 1964 as a result of the Macmillan and Wilson governments' recommendations that new universities be created to help fill the demand for more scientists and educated workers in post-industrial British society. This connection to the needs of industry was explicit from the beginning. Discussing the generous contributions of local industries to the university endowment fund, Chancellor R. A. Butler stated, "It is our desire to remain closely in touch with these industries, so that the university may serve them and so that they eventually profit from the activities of the university."[20] The founders of Essex intended the university to be on the cutting edge of higher education, utilizing new theories of education and experimenting with different course structures. Essex, unlike the older English universities, had common courses for all first-year students to "give the student a critical sense of the basis and limits of his own discipline, and of its place in the universe of knowledge."[21] Even more so than its counterparts, Essex University strove to teach all of its students to question their education and apply it to understanding the problems of the wider world.

In keeping with this emphasis on broad knowledge, Essex University strove to build a cosmopolitan atmosphere by inviting and hiring lecturers from all parts of the world, and enrolling students from other countries. By 1967 most members of the government department were French or American, the economics department was dominated by Americans and Canadians, and one-third of the staff in the literature department was American.[22] From its beginning, Essex University stressed the fact that it was an academic community in which the Chancellor, Vice Chancellor, Deans, Members of Court, staff, and students were equally important.[23] The first Vice Chancellor, Albert E. Sloman, emphasized the idea of "integration" in many of his speeches. By this term he meant that students and faculty would be integrated in the university, sharing the facilities and participating on university committees. Although the school was theoretically integrated, students only had a small minority representation on those committees which directly concerned student interests. Students had no direct role in making decisions for the university. Like other more traditional universities, the Vice Chancellor was the most powerful individual at the university, but the Senate, consisting of academic staff, was the supreme authority in academic matters, including student discipline. All non-academic matters were controlled by the University Council, which consisted of local businessmen and academics.[24]

Vice Chancellor Sloman also indirectly influenced the direction of activism among Essex students. He was a brilliant liberal educator who had promised that this new university would live up to the expectations set for it by the *Robbins Report*. He had envisioned a high-tech modern university, which would offer the best education to students of all classes. In a series of six national Reith lectures for the BBC in 1963, Sloman spoke about his high hopes for building a modern and liberal university, enrolling up to 20,000 students to help the nation accommodate its increasing demand for university-trained workers.[25] He told the nation of how his university would be a role model "self-governing academic community" where the curriculum would be relevant to the problems that concerned its students.[26] He promised a radically innovative university, while "preserving the essential nature of a university in the face of a double explosion of knowledge and of numbers."[27] These lectures helped to recruit a more radical staff and student body, interested in being part of this non-traditional university and great progressive experiment.[28]

In the mid-sixties, seventy per cent of Essex students came to Essex because of its new, non-traditional nature, and many students came in search of alternatives not only in education, but in society in general.[29] In 1964 Essex enrolled only 100 students, but that number jumped to 400 the next year, and reached 2,000 by 1974. Essex students operated their own student union from the start, and it was a formal part of the university structure equal to academic departments in staffing, funding, and building space. Students in the various departments of the university elected a Student Council who ran the union. At times the council acted without recommendations from the student body, but increasingly in the late

1960s it held general meetings in which all interested students could vote on political matters and determine union policy. The Essex student newspaper, *Wyvern*, began publishing in 1965 and quickly became a voice for its students on many controversial issues. The student body directly elected its editor, and the union and administration had no power to censor it.

As part of its non-traditional approach, Essex actively recruited students from non-traditional backgrounds, including working class and mature students, similar to David Triesman. Triesman arrived at Essex University in 1965–66, expecting it to be "ultra-modern" and progressive. Triesman was interested in politics all of his life, coming from a left-wing family, but he also loved football, and played semi-pro after school and while at university. He had taken a job as a journalist for a time before coming to Essex to study sociology. He had very high expectations of Essex, but when he arrived in 1965, he found Essex to be a poor excuse for a university. It consisted of the Wivenhoe Park building, a shabby old house which had been converted into a university center, with a dining room and administrative offices. This was surrounded by a number of temporary huts, which housed the library and some "extremely draughty seminar rooms." The two lecture theatres were located across a huge field of mud. Students were housed eight miles away in Colchester or in neighboring villages. [30]

In March 1965, the student newspaper revealed undergraduate's high hopes and expectations inspired by the Reith lectures, but admitted that students were having difficulty adapting to the situation on campus and had become "intensely self-conscious and introspective."[31] In November of that year, the newspaper reported stronger complaints: "Many have voiced their dissatisfaction at the noise and dirt, the long walks and endless queues, the hour-long journeys back to digs. . . . It's not as if things are getting any better either. . . . Essex is a record of mismanagement and incompetence. . . ."[32] Male undergraduates outnumbered females by a ratio of two to one, and male postgraduates outnumbered females eleven to one.[33] Only in 1966–67, did the university open on-campus lodgings in a tower block, located across another large field of sticky mud. The tower accommodated both male and female students and had no regulations on student's personal lives—something that pleased students but shocked many parents and those in the right-wing media.[34] Despite its modernist ethos, Essex University did not live up to Triesman's progressive expectations. He believed that its traditional decision-making hierarchy, as well as its physical environment "produced the circumstances in which radical progressive thinking spilled over into all sorts of other things."[35]

To participate in political activism, Triesman and other like-minded students, created some of the first student societies at Essex, including the popular Socialist Society, the Radical Student Alliance, and a Vietnam Solidarity Campaign Committee. He and other Essex Socialists dominated the Student Union. Triesman won a position on the executive committee of the student government in the spring of 1966.[36] Echoing New Left discourse, the student government president Dave Kendall wrote that the Union should strive to establish an "egalitarian society in University," defend the "right of students to control their own lives, individually and collectively," and protect student rights nationally and internationally.[37] Towards that end, they requested representation on the Senate, the most powerful governing structure at Essex. Throughout the remainder of that spring, student activists became increasingly disillusioned as authorities repeatedly denied their requests for increased representation.[38]

The resentment at their living and working conditions, and their lack of power in university decision-making led Essex students to be strong supporters of the Radical Student Alliance in 1967. As a founding member of the RSA, David Triesman was a leader in its overseas student campaign at Essex. Essex students peacefully demonstrated against the overseas fees increase at their university when Minister of Education Anthony Crosland spoke on campus in February of 1967.[39] Over 200 students additionally attended a teach-in and boycotted lectures and classes on the RSA national day of protest.[40] That afternoon, 150 then joined with students from nearby colleges in a protest march. At the urging of Triesman and RSA leader David Widgery, Essex students also voted to leave the NUS and join the RSA.[41] Essex students would re-join the NUS in a few years, but their Student Union's commitment to the RSA and leadership in direct action campaigns indicates the strength of its student movement in the mid-sixties. Although these student protests at Essex were overshadowed by the protests at the LSE at the time, they reveal how the unique physical environment of a university and its philosophical outlook could stimulate student activism.

THE GLOBAL SIXTY-EIGHT

The Essex protests were only one part of the global student protests of 1968, often seen as the most important year of the worldwide student movement of the Long Sixties. In Paris, Tokyo, Chicago, Mexico City, Berlin, and London, thousands of students fought police openly in the streets. In France and Japan, workers joined students in nation-wide general strikes of millions. It seemed as though the entire world was aflame in protests that year. These protests came as no surprise to student activists, but disturbed governments and shocked the wider public. Eager to feed widespread government and public curiosity, the international press provided a steady stream of analysis by student "leaders," academics, and social commentators. By the mid-point of 1968, they had already dubbed it "the year of the student." The high fever pitch of reporting on the global student movement added to Essex students' sense of being part of a much wider social movement which was powerfully shaping the world.

In Europe and the United States, New Left ideology lay at the heart of this intellectual dissent movement, critiquing both modern capitalism and Soviet communism, suggesting a way forward guided by a new form of socialism, and emphasizing the liberation of the individual through participatory democracy. Students and intellectuals could lead the way in this modern revolution by exposing the flaws of the system and uniting with workers in creating a new socialist system. As this ideology spread through academia, Cuban, Vietnamese, and other Third World revolutionaries gave them further hope that the binaries of the Cold War were indeed breaking down.[42] Students and intellectuals tried to support these movements and waited impatiently for a sign that the revolution would begin in their own countries.

That opening came in January of 1968 with the Tet Offensive in Vietnam. This week-long North Vietnamese offensive, though it failed to force the Americans out at the time, shattered the US government's argument that it was winning the war and demonstrated its inability to defeat a Third World liberation movement. The North Vietnamese called upon its supporters everywhere to help them win the war by bringing the war home to their own countries, to press their governments unrelentingly to intervene on behalf of the North Vietnamese and force the US out of Vietnam. Their pleas for global solidarity inspired student activists everywhere. As a result, student supporters of North Vietnamese victory threw themselves into protests with renewed hope and vigor in 1968, believing that their protests would indeed succeed in forcing the American government to withdraw.

To foster this global solidarity, the West German SDS sponsored an International Vietnam Congress in Berlin that February, bringing student activists together from across the world within one month of the Tet Offensive. In the main hall of the Congress hung a huge Vietnamese National Liberation Front (NLF) flag and a banner with Che Guevara's slogan, "The duty of a revolutionary is to make the revolution."[43] This event brought more than 6,000 students from all over Europe and the world to West Germany, where they heard speakers such as Tariq Ali and German student Rudi Dutschke speak of liberating zones in bourgeois society like Maoists in China's civil war and using the universities as "red bases" to train a revolutionary cadre to replace the ruling class.[44] The Congress culminated in a march of 20,000 through Berlin, the geographic epicenter of the Cold War. Ali remembers this Congress as "an important turning point for the Vietnam movement in Europe. It was the first real gathering of the clans and it reinforced our internationalism as well as the desire for a world without frontiers."[45] This Congress gave new life to the antiwar movements in Europe and infused them with New Left ideologies.

Dutschke was particularly important in this process. An East German refugee, SDS leader, and sociology student at the Free University of Berlin, he was inspired by the theories of C. Wright Mills, Herbert Marcuse, George Lukacs, Che Guevara, and Franz Fanon. Combining these theories, he promoted the theory of revolution through action. He argued that direct action, especially when it caused authoritarian repression, created a revolutionary consciousness among the activists: "revolutionizing the revolutionaries."[46] He wanted to bring revolutionary theory to the masses of students and workers around the world, but his activist career was cut short by an assassin who shot and crippled him a few months after the Congress. SDS blamed the right-wing Springer media as the inspiration for the attack. Students retaliated by smashing the windows of the Springer publishing house and 45,000 demonstrators in over twenty cities blocked the delivery of Springer papers, leaving two people dead and 400 injured. The West German Parliament then enacted emergency laws, effectively suppressing the movement. In the face of this defeat and mounting internal factionalism, the German SDS disintegrated by the end of 1968.[47]

French students reacted to the West German student movement with their own small movement at Nanterre University in March of 1968. Identifying themselves as part of the global New Left, a small group of radical activists there reinterpreted Marxist theory, emphasizing the alienation resulting from modern capitalism and the liberation of the individual from repressive capitalist culture. Influenced by Dutschke and led by Dany Cohn-Bendit, they argued that direct action against authorities would lead to repression, and that this experience would expose the repression and alienation of the system and thus mobilize a massive revolutionary movement.[48]

From Nanterre, small-scale student protests calling for university reform spread to the Sorbonne in Paris, where authorities took action against the protesters and the protests began to escalate in May of 1968. Students built barricades in the Latin Quarter of Paris on the night of 10–11 May, drawing mass media attention to the dramatic symbolism of their barricades. The Minister of the Interior ordered the police to remove the barricades the next morning and the ensuing arrests and police brutality were publicized across the world. At that point, students and labor unions across France called for a 24-hour general strike to protest this repression and demand reforms. After the 24-hour strike, over 7 million French students and workers spontaneously continued to strike against the authoritarian structures in universities and industry, demanding participatory democracy in universities and in industrial decision-making and management. President Charles de Gaulle called upon the nation to fight this "Communist" threat and held national elections in June. Millions responded to de Gaulle's speech and supported him in rejecting the demands of the protesters and dispersing the movement. Despite their failure to win over the voters or topple de Gaulle's regime, the tremendous worker support, huge demonstrations, and the sense of solidarity generated by the protests gave French student radicals and students around the world great hope that a student-led revolution was indeed possible.[49]

Students from all over Europe traveled to Paris that May to join in this revolution in the making. In this exciting atmosphere, New Leftist ideas blended with those of Situationists, anarchists, and the Marxist-Leninist Left, resulting in an outpouring of revolutionary theories, which students then carried back to their home countries. Situationism became especially popular that year. Begun by Guy Debord in 1957 as an anti-authoritarian movement in art and philosophy, Situationist International sought to create intense "situations, constructed encounters, and creatively lived moments" which would liberate individuals from the oppression and alienation of their environments, enabling them to transform cultural, political, economic, and social life. Attempting to interpret society in a non-capitalist way, Debord developed a "theory of the Spectacle," which asserted that capitalism created a "Society of the Spectacle," an unreal world where people are brainwashed into substituting material consumer-oriented things, such as television, computers, and technology for real experience. These things control our existence by creating new meanings for happiness and fulfillment, but they also separate people and alienate them. Countercultural and violent protests could expose the Spectacle, but capitalism would respond with "recuperation," or shifting ground to create new roles and meanings, reforming just enough to turn experimental and threatening life-styles into commodities which could be co-opted and controlled. Situationists sought to undermine capitalism by shunning its values and culture, provoking state repression to expose its true nature, and restructuring communities and environments. They were responsible for some of the most outrageous displays of provocation, vandalism, and creativity during the French May, and received considerable attention from the radical media. [50]

Nineteen sixty-eight was also an explosive year in the United States, where students developed alternative theories of revolution and escalated their protests against the Vietnam War and the university system, leading to increasingly violent confrontations with authorities. The most prominent protest to take place at a university that year was undoubtedly the Columbia University protest which began in the spring of 1968. Earlier that year Columbia's SDS chapter, led by the flamboyant Mark Rudd, joined with the student Afro-American Society to pressure the university to address student and community concerns over black poverty and the Vietnam War. Rudd, a leading agitator behind the demonstrations, wrote an infamous letter to university president, Grayson Kirk, which ended with this statement:

> There is only one thing left to say. It may sound nihilistic to you, since it is the opening shot in a war of liberation. I'll use the words of Leroi Jones, whom I'm sure you don't like a whole lot: "Up against the wall, motherfucker, this is a stick-up."[51]

After several months of demonstrations, Kirk banned indoor demonstrations and brought police in to arrest student protesters. In response to the arrests, students occupied several buildings on campus through April. Finally in May, the president sent in police to forcibly evict the students.[52] Some of the police brutally beat the students they evicted, hospitalizing 150. This brutality outraged many moderate students, who then came to the side of the protesters. After more massive demonstrations, Kirk and his vice president resigned and a new administration granted students all of their demands.[53] Although the Columbia protest was one of the most extreme protests in the US and not representative of the vast variety of peaceful, moderate activism sweeping the nation, because it received heavy media coverage, the Columbia revolt came to represent the American student movement to the rest of the world.

Most of the rest of the American student movement was preoccupied with continuing efforts to end the military draft and the war in Vietnam. Faced with a draft which threatened the lives of most students or their loved ones, this issue was particularly relevant and personal to this generation of students, especially as the death toll in Vietnam escalated dramatically that year. Even libertarian conservative students opposed the draft in those years. Students across the nation, in small local protests and huge national demonstrations 100,000 strong, pressured the government and presidential candidates to take their side on this issue. These protests reached a violent climax at the Democratic National Convention held in Chicago in August of 1968. Although only 10,000 protesters turned out, they and the Chicago police made a dramatic impact on the student movement and public perception of protest activism. For three days activists protested, and for three days the Chicago police beat, maced, and arrested them. In some cases the police attacked bystanders, residents, and news reporters. As the official *Walker Report* on the protests concluded, the events in Chicago amounted to a "police riot."[54] As the media televised the protests, blow-by-blow, the nation and world watched with mixed reactions. Although most adults sympathized with the police and condemned the violence they believed was provoked by the protesters, most students sympathized with the protesters.

Police brutality in these demonstrations and FBI harassment further discredited authorities in the eyes of many student activists. SDS leaders had known that the FBI had infiltrated their organization and by 1969 many SDS leaders had succumbed to paranoia, refusing to openly discuss their plans and suspecting everyone of spying for the FBI. Many leaders of the SDS and the New Left sincerely believed that America stood on the brink of an impending revolution and they sought the best way to support and facilitate that revolution. In their search for their place in the coming revolution, many turned to the non-Stalinist Marxism of Mao Zedong and Leon Trotsky. Instead of viewing racism and the war as flaws within a fundamentally good democratic system, SDS leadership now viewed their entire society as corrupted by American capitalism and imperialism. They increasingly advocated fighting for revolutionary socialism using any means necessary.[55]

Student protests elsewhere became even more powerful and deadly in 1968. The most violent protests occurred in Mexico and Japan that October. In Mexico City, students had been protesting for university reforms, but the Mexican government had a zero tolerance policy on demonstrations and shut down the Autonomous University to prevent it from becoming a center of protest in the upcoming Olympics celebration. Thousands of students assembled to protest this repression, but on 2 October, the military surrounded the peaceful protesters in the Plaza of the Three Cultures and shot into the crowd. The government refused to release the numbers killed, but estimates range in the hundreds, with thousands more arrested and wounded. In Japan, students at Tokyo University had been on strike since the beginning of 1968, demanding practical university reforms and that their government oppose US imperialism and admit its crimes during the Second World War. By October of 1968, they had formed a tentative alliance with young workers for a large protest in Tokyo. When the police moved in to stop the protest, the demonstration turned into a riot with pitched battles between thousands of protesters and police, and the destruction of police vehicles and train stations. Their protest lasted until Tokyo University was forcefully reopened in January of 1969. These violent protests revealed the extent to which students faced harsh repression and reacted with strategies ranging from extremist language to property destruction.[56]

Closer to home, students in Northern Ireland were building their own movement in 1968. Throughout most of the Long Sixties, they had lacked a strong student movement. Caught up in the politics of their region, and without a rebellious youth culture, the only dissent movement of the era that resonated with them was the African American civil rights movement. It was easy for Northern Irish students to draw comparisons between the segregation, discrimination, and police violence faced by African Americans and the situation faced by Northern Ireland's Catholic minority since the partitioning of Ireland in 1921 and the election of a Protestant Unionist government at Stormont. Outraged by police violence against peaceful protesters in a civil rights demonstration in Derry in October 1968, 3,000 students from Queen's University marched to Belfast City Hall. Stopped by the police, they returned to Queen's University and after a long discussion about what to do to stop the violence and blatant discrimination against Catholics, they decided to form a new student activist organization called the People's Democracy (PD).[57]

One founder of the PD, Eamonn McCann, later described the PD as "a loose organization without formal membership and with an incoherent ideology comprising middle-class liberalism, Aldermaston pacifism and a Sorbonne-inspired belief in spontaneity. At its core was a small group of determined left-wingers."[58] While attending Queen's University (the only large non-sectarian university in Northern Ireland) in the mid-sixties, McCann had frequently travelled to London and become immersed in the culture and discourse of the transnational New Left. Like other student leftists in the rest of Europe and America, McCann supported the black struggle in the US, the workers' struggle, and the Vietnam guerrilla fighters. He hoped that leftists could somehow unite Protestant and Catholic workers to create a Socialist Republic in Northern Ireland.[59] The most famous of PD's leaders, however, was Bernadette Devlin (later McAliskey). She felt that the PD was not a typical student movement. Although it was composed mostly of students and met at the university, it was not active on issues only involving students, such as university reform and student rights. Instead, it identified with the community of Northern Ireland and the civil rights movement, rather than with the global student movement.[60]

Like other global dissent movements, however, the PD planned to use non-violent direct action to draw attention to their cause and provoke the government into a reaction which might bring the majority of the population over to their side. Their first demonstration, a march to City Hall for 16 October was permitted by worried police and was a great success with over 1,500 students taking part. The next week, the PD had an even more surprisingly successful protest when seventy of them occupied the Northern Ireland Parliament building in support of the United Nations Declaration of Human Rights Day and even held a teach-in there when the House refused to discuss the issue of Human Rights. This was the only time when students in Europe occupied a parliamentary building, a remarkable accomplishment for such a young and small movement.[61]

Surprisingly, English students paid little attention to their counterparts' in Northern Ireland, Japan, and Mexico in 1968. A few student unions passed motions of solidarity with them, but took little other action on the issue. It is understandable that English students would know less about the movements in Japan and Mexico and therefore feel less solidarity with them, but Northern Ireland was a part of the United Kingdom and governed by Britain's own Parliament. Although it would have made sense if British students had united with the PD in a massive show of solidarity, English students focused on their own student movement and the French student movement in 1968 instead. Perhaps it was the lack of communication between the Northern Irish students and those in England. Indeed the student movements in Northern Ireland did little to forge an alliance with students elsewhere because they were much more focused on forging alliances with adult organizations within their borders.

British students were much more connected to the 1968 student movements in Europe and America. Many traveled to these regions, witnessing and participating in the protests first-hand. A large contingent of British students traveled to Paris for the French May and were greatly influenced by the experience. Many British student radicals, enthralled by the spectacle of this powerful student movement, joined in the revolutionary debates there and returned home with a strong sense of solidarity with student activists everywhere. These veterans of the French May often formed the core of extremely active student agitators. Indeed, a number of Essex students ventured to Paris to work in the hospitals and at the barricades. When they returned to Britain they raised money for food and medical supplies for the striking French students. Hull students also expressed their solidarity with French students and likened the situation in France to that of England. Two hundred LSE students held an all-night vigil proclaiming their solidarity with the French protesters. In this way, the ideas and tactics of the French student movement became integrated with the British student movement.[62]

Trevor Pateman, a third-year undergraduate at Oxford University that year, read about the events in the newspapers and recalled that it had a great liberating effect upon British students: "we all became at once revolutionaries. . . . The French eruption extended everyone's belief in the possibilities of change. . . . Contestations such as those at LSE and those in which we ourselves participated had made us believe that some things could be changed, by direct action but without violence; now the French were seriously suggesting that everything could be changed."[63] By confirming the legitimacy and power of student protest, the French May thus emboldened British students already active in their own movement. The French student movement also exposed British students to an incredible range of radical theories and tactics, from Communist to anarchist, Trotskyist, Maoist, and Situationist. Another Oxford undergraduate, Hilary Wainwright, recalled that the French May "introduced the idea of student worker alliances and maybe also gave us a sense of our own importance."[64] These twin concepts, of a student-worker alliance and the power of student protest, would dramatically shape the British student movement into the early seventies. Within this global context, the seemingly minor incidents at Essex became magnified in importance as one more sign that the global student revolution had come to Britain.

BRITAIN'S 1968

Although the Essex student movement was interconnected with student movements in other countries, it evolved within specific national and local contexts, and thus retained a uniquely British outlook. Most relevant to the Essex protests and the wider British student movement was the influence of the LSE protests of 1966–67 and of the British New Left and Stalinist, Leninist, and Trotskyist organizations. These gave student activists a blue-print for expanding their movement, strategies for winning their campaigns, and hope in the power of student protest.

The Troubles at LSE in 1966–67 had the most immediate impact on British students. For Trevor Pateman, the LSE affair revealed the ineptitude of university administrators and the power of united students. In 1971, he recalled that LSE bosses:

> displayed quite remarkable dishonesty and ineptitude and did so very visibly. [This] shifted a whole generation of liberals leftwards, literally overnight. . . . Perhaps because we were young and certainly because we had been put through years of schooling in Christian and liberal virtues, we were very moralistic, and the recognition achieved through

the events at LSE that so many teachers and administrators were unprincipled men was a tremendous blow and of great significance in the future.[65]

Pateman and students from all over Britain had visited the LSE during its Troubles, were inspired, and learned valuable lessons about what to do and what not to do in protests at their own universities the following year.

The editors of the *New Left Review* were especially interested in the LSE protests and published a special edition on student power in June of 1967. This edition was widely read by many socialist students who not only contributed to the articles, but responded to them in subsequent issues. One of the lead articles, "Student Power: What is to be Done?" analyzed the LSE protests and proposed a strategy for the student movement. Authored by postgraduate students, the essay argued that the LSE protests heralded the beginnings of a collective identity of students in their role as students and that "the British student, belatedly, has become part of the international typology of militant student action."[66] It posited that this new student consciousness was caused by structural changes in the British university system since 1954, which had resulted in overcrowding and a lack of funding not only for accommodating this growth but also for student grants. It went on to argue that students were not only oppressed economically by the state and their parents who controlled them financially, but they were also oppressed by "the suffocating weight of dead and conformist departments." These factors, together with public condemnation of students had "fortified the students' consciousness of their corporate identity."[67] The essay proposed seven practical forms that the student movement should take as its future strategy, including student control over university funds, the destruction of the *in loco parentis* system, student control over the content of education, and a massive grant increase.[68] In articles such as these, the second generation of the New Left overtly reached out to the student movement and attempted to guide it with its own structuralist and Marcusean ideology. It would profoundly shape the British student movement in the late sixties, just as it had earlier in the era.

Organizations of the "Old" Left—the Communist Party, International Socialists (IS), Maoists, and the International Marxist Group (IMG)—also realized the potential power of the student movement in 1968 and increased their efforts to shape it in support of their own strategies and goals. They recognized the appeal of the New Left theories of participatory democracy and of the importance they put on student activism, but vehemently disagreed with many New Left theories and each other about the role of the student in the coming socialist revolution. International Socialists, Maoists, and the IMG were especially popular among student radicals in 1968 and 1969 because they had not only rejected Soviet Communism and American capitalism, but they seemed to be the most extreme of all leftists in their willingness to use any means necessary to foment revolution. Similar to

American students, many British radicals had given up the strategy of non-violence as ineffective in forcing real change.

International Socialists were especially vocal in their criticism of New Left theories. For example, Martin Shaw, then an LSE student and member of IS, wrote to the *NLR*, arguing against the idea that students should focus only on the university system and that they should instead be "committed to aiding the socialist movement outside the University (for socialism is not and can never be a movement of the intellectuals)."[69] This emphasis on developing a socialist revolution outside the universities and focusing on the working class was the hallmark of the IS position on the student movement throughout the era. By the late 1960s, Peter Sedgwick (former student leftist at Oxford University and now a don at Oxford) was a leading theorist and recruiter for the IS. IS students typically leafleted nearby factories, wore short hair, and dressed conservatively to better relate to workers. Through their seriousness of purpose and tremendous activity in support of multiple socialist causes, the IS was able to build a following of up to 3,000 students, staff, and workers by 1970.

While much smaller, the International Marxist Group, was another Trotskyist group that actively recruited students in the late sixties. Its leading theorist at that time was economist Ernest Mandel. He argued that the global student revolt was actually the "vanguard" of the revolution against capitalism because it confronted the contradictions of capitalism: the raised expectations, bureaucracy, alienation, powerlessness, and frustration with bourgeois culture. Similar to Herbert Marcuse, Mandel believed that students were the best potential revolutionaries because they had become conscious of "the contradictions, injustices, and barbarities of contemporary capitalism."[70] The working class, the traditional leader of the revolution, could not begin it because workers' unions were "bureaucratized and long since co-opted into bourgeois society."[71] By struggling against capitalism and imperialism in a variety of ways, the student movement could expose the working class to the injustices of the system and thus radicalize them. In this way, Mandel and other theorists in the late sixties encouraged student revolutionaries by convincing them that not only was revolution possible in Britain, but the students themselves could lead it.

Mandel attracted the admiration of Tariq Ali, who had become Britain's most famous (former) student revolutionary. Partly because of his admiration of Mandel, Ali joined the IMG in 1968.[72] To provide a voice for the British dissent movements, Ali and a number of other prominent young socialists founded an alternative newspaper called *The Black Dwarf* in May of 1968. Inspired by the French May and the uprisings of students around the world at the time, Ali and other writers for *The Black Dwarf* analyzed the British student protests and put them within the wider context of global dissent movements. They explained New Left and Old Left theories, and applied them to contemporary events, helping a new generation of young people to see the value of radical socialist thought. The 15 October

1968 issue, for example, was dedicated to coverage of the student movement. Leaders of student protests, such as David Triesman, David Fernbach, and Tom Fawthrop, wrote articles explaining the student protests at their respective universities and giving suggestions for how other students could learn from their experiences. They discussed strategy and theory, and generally tried to expand the British student movement.[73]

Another 1968 issue of *Black Dwarf* was devoted to Che Guevara. Che was the natural hero of leftist student movements all over the world. As a young international revolutionary who actually helped to make a successful revolution and selflessly tried to help others succeed in their revolutions, he was already popular with student leftists when his assassination in October of 1967 propelled him to the status of martyr. Che was a hero to Ali because not only had he helped lead a successful revolution in Cuba, but he left the safety of Havana to resume the struggle elsewhere, harmonizing theory and practice.[74] Organizations like *The Black Dwarf* contributed to this cult of Che, giving away free posters and adding to the thousands of posters already on the walls of student bedrooms across the nation in the late sixties and early seventies. Although it had a small readership, *The Black Dwarf* became integral to helping socialist students in universities across the nation to understand their own movement and its relationship to other dissent movements around the world, providing them with a blend of New and Old Left ideology, images, and rhetoric which infused the student movement in 1968 and 1969.

Through his position at *The Black Dwarf*, as well as through hundreds of speeches, pamphlets, and other writings, Ali also supported and expanded on Mandel's theories, spreading them to a student audience. Ali accused the Labour Party and Parliament of limiting the power of workers' organizations, cutting workers' living standards, crusading to save British capitalism, and supporting American brutality in Vietnam. Since no major political party offered true socialism and parliamentary dissent was useless, Ali concluded that extra-parliamentary dissent would inevitably increase. He predicted that this dissent would mobilize primarily around opposition to the Vietnam War because this was the primary symbol of the immorality of Western imperialism. He claimed that anti-war opposition would eventually lead to an anti-capitalist revolutionary movement because it exposed the evils of capitalism and made students see that only socialism could end the war, racism, and social inequalities.[75]

Even the Communist Party benefited from the increasing popularity of dissent in 1968. It was able to recruit students by emphasizing that all socialists needed to cooperate to form a united front within the student movement. It even adapted some New Left rhetoric in support of CP goals. For example, it claimed that the CP sought to force Parliament to establish socialism, to end exploitation at home and abroad, and to allow people to be decision-makers at all levels. It asserted, "People will be released from the need to be cogs in a machine. They will do that which makes them human: develop their minds and contribute to the good of society."[76] Although the CP did see an increase in numbers of student members from approximately 400 in 1965 to 500 in 1968, most activists disliked the CP because of its bureaucratic and hierarchical structure, and subservience to the disreputable Soviet Union.[77] The CP, however, would continue its campaign to lead the student movement, but would focus on leading national organizations, including the Radical Students Alliance and the National Union of Students.

In the expectant climate of the late sixties, when revolutionaries jockeyed for leading positions in the coming revolution, the divisions between various Old and New Left groups magnified existing divisions within the student movement. Each left-wing group sought to recruit members from student activists and lead the British student movement to socialist revolution. While New Left advocates wrote off the Marxist-Leninist Left because of its failure to lead a revolution in Britain, the Leninist Left criticized the New Left for its adventurism and lack of theory. Leninist groups believed that only the working class could carry out a socialist revolution, and that only a well-disciplined, centrally-controlled revolutionary party could lead the revolutionary movement. All other struggles against oppression were considered secondary and subordinate to the struggle of the working class.

Marxist-Leninist groups, however, were also deeply divided. Because Leninism does not accept a plurality of revolutionary parties, only one of these groups could lead the revolution. This common belief led each group to compete for membership and power, and to focus considerable energy towards undermining and destroying the other revolutionary groups. Writing in 1968, for example, Glasgow University's Trotskyite Marxist Society president James Craighead and secretary Leslie Jardine accused the Communist Party of being "neither revolutionary nor Marxist. . . . When the British Revolution begins, they will ALL be on the other side of the barricades, Independent Socialists and Tories alike. When Socialism is established, they will be executed as traitors and counter-revolutionaries."[78] They were also critical of student rights activism, asserting that student power which is allied with anarchist and Stalinist groups "can only be seen as sabotage, deliberately fostered by the capitalist press."[79] Willie Thompson joined the Communist Party precisely because he believed that they were more willing to work together with other ideological groups towards common goals.[80] David Triesman, who would join the CP in 1969 for the same reason, was also intent on overcoming the factionalism which he saw as deadly to the student movement. He was particularly resentful of Leninists, Trotskyists, and Maoists, who he perceived as not only wrong-headed, but truly harmful to the student movement because of their divisiveness. [81] The dozens of tiny groups of leftist activists infused the British student movement with ideological vitality, but the animosity which they felt for each other presented a major obstacle to achieving a strong, unified movement for change.[82]

THE DIALECTICS OF LIBERATION
AND THE ANTI-UNIVERSITY

The diverse British Left briefly met with an emerging counterculture in the Dialectics of Liberation Congress at the Roundhouse in London in July 1967. This was "an Intellectual Be-In," a blending of the political and the counter-cultural, a two-week long conference and carnival, with French, American, and British left intellectuals and artists performing and exhorting the audience to join in the movement of change sweeping the world.[83] Organized by four psychiatrists from the anti-psychiatry movement, which blamed the dysfunctional social structure for mental illness, the conference aimed "to create a genuine revolutionary consciousness by fusing ideology and action on the levels of the individual and of mass society."[84] Speakers ranged from Herbert Marcuse to Allen Ginsberg, Stokely Carmichael, Ernest Mandel, and alternative psychiatrist R.D. Laing. They explored the roots of violence in society by analyzing repression, personal alienation, and the student revolt. Similar to Dutschke and the Situationists, Carmichael advocated the strategy of provoking liberal authorities until they reacted with violence, thus exposing the corruption of the system and radicalizing far more supporters for the cause.[85] This idea for the creative use of provocation and strategic violence would spread throughout the global student movement and influence some within the British student movement.

With his thick glasses, white thinning hair, and strong German accent, Marcuse was the oldest speaker there, but he also made a strong impression on many of those in attendance. In his speech on "Liberation from the Affluent Society," he explained that he was seeking liberation from a repressive and false system toward "progress and freedom on the historical scale."[86] He asserted that the intelligentsia was ideally positioned to lead this liberation movement by using their positions within universities to indoctrinate students in freedom, generating an "instinctual need for a life without fear, without brutality, and without stupidity."[87] David Widgery, a student activist in London, attended Marcuse's lecture and recalled:

> He was brilliant, so delicate and fragile and precise. It was the authentic voice of a recovered Marxism, a lineage that was being reconnected. It was astonishing. There he was—along with other middle-aged and quite old people— saying what I actually felt . . . We felt very isolated, marginal, crazy, an embarrassment to our parents and the authorities— and then we'd see old Marcuse beaming out at his audience as though we were his spiritual children.[88]

Speaker after speaker likewise exhorted the audience to get involved in transforming their world, including them in lively discussions and modeling participatory democracy in the organization of the Congress itself.

Following the Dialectics of Liberation Congress, participants tried to continue the conversation in a permanent institution, the Anti-university. Veterans of the Free University of New York, the London Free School, and leading anti-psychiatrists formed a committee and wrote a manifesto for this "anti-institution," proclaiming:

> We must destroy the bastardised meanings of 'student', 'teacher', and 'course' in order to regain the original meaning of teacher—one who passes on the tradition; student—one who learns how to learn; and course—the meeting where this takes place. At the Anti-university many of the original and radical artists, activists and intellectuals of London as well as Europe, America and the third world will have a place to meet among themselves and others to discuss their ideas and work.[89]

They hoped that it would become a center of radical politics, joining the intelligentsia with the working class in struggling for a liberated society. The Anti-university opened in February 1968 in a building rented from the Russell Foundation. It attracted an influx of intellectuals and radicals from around the nation and the world, including Tariq Ali, Juliet Mitchell, and Theodore Roszak. Although it failed to interest the working class, it did attract a large influx of British, German, American, and Austrian students, many of whom lived in the rooms (which lacked toilets) and cleaned them in exchange for free classes. It also attracted intense media interest, which made a spectacle of the classes. Ultimately, the Anti-university devolved into a continuous anarchic argument and was abandoned within six months of its birth.[90]

Though short-lived, the Dialectics of Liberation Congress and the Anti-university it spawned were important in revealing the relationship between the counterculture and the political activists in the student movement. They infused the student movement with liberationist rhetoric and brought it ever further into the international counterculture developing in 1967 and 1968. Although middle and working class youth could participate in the counterculture on a surface level, wear longer hair, smoke the occasional joint, listen to rock n' roll, and read an underground newspaper, few could afford the high cost of living the hippie lifestyle. The drugs, rock concerts, even hippie clothing and beads all priced many young people, and especially students living on a meager grant, out of the counterculture. Indeed, photos of student protesters from 1968 show that most were clean-shaven, wore suits and had short hair, far from any hippie stereotype. The counterculture likewise had little interest in student political activism. The underground newspaper *International Times* reflected this attitude in its coverage of the continuing LSE struggle in March of 1969: "gloomy political masturbation that has been boring us all for a so long . . . the official student left reveals its amazing boringness, its bureaucratic nervousness, its Sunday-paper emptiness . . . a drawing-room charade of internal LSE politics for which *IT* readers will be justified in feeling the greatest contempt."[91] Perhaps countercultural lifestyle choices may have made some students more inclined to demand more personal freedom from university regulations and contribute to some students believing that they were being persecuted by the Establishment, but they had little other relationship to the student movement.

THE RISE OF THE RSSF

At the same time the Dialectics of Liberation Congress was fostering alternative perspectives at the Roundhouse, student leaders from across the country were meeting at the LSE to form a new revolutionary socialist student group. Inspiration from the global and national student movements of the spring of 1968, together with disillusionment with the Radical Student Alliance, were important factors in the formation of this new Revolutionary Socialist Student Federation (RSSF). By 1968, even RSA founder David Triesman thought that the RSA was too focused on the NUS and was not doing enough to lead the student movement in its Vietnam activism and other political issues.[92] It had failed to politicize the NUS or coordinate the student movement, and was crippled by left-wing disagreements. At its last convention in January 1968, various left-wing groups disagreed over the future direction of the RSA and attacked each other mercilessly, blaming each other for the failure of their goals. Amidst dwindling support and infighting, the RSA formally disbanded in November 1968. After students gave up on the RSA, they joined other socialist students in forming the RSSF to lead the student movement.

Leaders of the second generation of the New Left organized the first meeting of the RSSF. Tariq Ali and Robin Blackburn had been arguing throughout 1967–68 that British students needed an organization more like that of the American and German SDS, which explicitly challenged political and university authorities. They invited David Triesman and a number of other well-known participants in various student protests to the *New Left Review* offices in May of 1968 and agreed upon some points to be discussed with RSA groups and Socialist Societies at all of the universities in an attempt to convince them to join in a formation meeting at the LSE that June. This idea received widespread support after the events in West Germany, France, and Britain that spring, which had generated an enormous amount of enthusiasm for an organization to unite British students and make them a leading force behind a socialist revolution.[93]

To draw media attention to the upcoming conference and get input from famous student revolutionaries, the conference planners joined with the BBC to host an international teach-in at the LSE on students and revolution. Between 1,500 and 2,000 students participated in the televised teach-in, including a number of prominent student radicals from France,

America, and Germany, such as Dany Cohn-Bendit, a representative from the Columbia University branch of SDS in America, and British radicals who had gone to the continent that May.[94] At the RSSF teach-in and conference, a contingent of about 200 International Socialists competed with Maoist, New Left, and Communist Party students over the direction of the new student organization. The majority refused to allow the organized and disciplined group of CP delegates to take over the direction of this new organization. Acknowledging this defeat, the CP called on its members to leave the RSSF. With the CP gone, the primary battle was between IS and New Left students.

Both the IS and New Left subscribed to a "red base theory." Derived from Régis Debray's ideas on guerrilla strategies, this theory urged the creation of bases of student revolutionaries at every university in order to agitate and radicalize the student body first, so that it could then become the vanguard a working class revolution.[95] David Fernbach supported the red base theory, believing that Marxism could replace bourgeois liberalism as the dominant ideology among students and that student power over courses, exams, and college facilities could be used to materially assist a socialist revolution.[96] The two groups disagreed, however, over who would lead the revolution. The IS argued that revolutionary workers would lead the revolution, while the New Left believed that the British working class was non-revolutionary and that students should lead the revolution by exposing and destroying capitalism and authoritarianism in education. These disagreements may seem minor in retrospect, but at the time, they caused paralyzing divisions within the RSSF.

Each faction coordinated its student representatives to present a united position as they discussed a manifesto for the RSSF. Fifty students from Essex attended and formed a strong New Left block to prevent the RSSF from being dominated by the Marxist-Leninist Left. The Essex students emphasized the difference between the British and French working classes. Calling the British working class deferential and bordering on reactionary, an Essex pamphlet asserted that the student occupations and sit-ins were "beyond the epistemological framework of the working class and thereby rejected. By adopting what have been successful techniques in other countries the student movement in Britain by not being sufficiently British runs the risk of isolation and reaction."[97] The author stated that since the British working class would not automatically ally with students, the student movement must contact the working class and articulate common demands. In the end, however, the competing factions formed an uneasy alliance around their common desire for a socialist revolution and the RSSF was born.

Although the RSSF shared the RSA's tendency towards factionalism, it was more radical than the RSA and addressed a wider range of socialist issues which were not directly related to problems in the universities. Whereas the RSA manifesto emphasized students and education, the RSSF manifesto focused on how students could help bring about a socialist revolution. Reflecting the influence of the IS, the manifesto stated that the RSSF "commits itself to the revolutionary overthrow of capitalism and imperialism and its replacement by workers' power, and bases itself on the recognition that the only social class in industrial countries capable of making the revolution is the working class." [98] The new organization opposed all forms of discrimination, imperialism, capitalism, and fascism. Revealing the strength of New Left theories, it asserted that modern capitalism has made the "intellectual element increasingly crucial to the development of the economy and society" and therefore a vital revolutionary ally of the proletariat. Claiming that existing political parties and trade unions could not bring about revolutionary socialism, it argued that "new, participatory mass-based organizations are required to overthrow capitalism." Guided by these common beliefs, the manifesto's specific "Action Program" for universities for 1968 included democratic access to higher education and mass democracy in student unions as the first stage towards politicizing students to build support for revolution. [99]

At its peak in 1968–69, the RSSF had contacts at 100 universities and colleges across the country, and a formal membership list of 1,100. They supported a wide range of issues in their discussions and actions, including university and examination reform, workers' strikes, the Palestinian struggle, Irish civil rights, women's liberation, racial equality, and Czechoslovakian liberation. [100] Their largest action came in the spring of 1969, when they held a national day of action in support of LSE students who had been punished for a recent protest against the university. This was the single largest coordinated action within the student movement up to that point, with occupations, demonstrations, and other protests at Oxford, Cambridge, Essex, Manchester, Warwick, Glasgow, Strathclyde, Newcastle, Sussex, and eight other universities. [101]

Similar to the New Left, the RSSF emphasized participatory democracy. The Oxford RSSF explained that the aim of their revolution was "quite simple—to set up a democratic university." [102] They stressed that towards this end, their organization "should reflect the participatory democracy and minimal bureaucracy which we advocate for the university as a whole." [103] This ideology, while extremely appealing to many anti-authoritarian students, posed some important challenges for the RSSF and the wider student movement from the start. The most important problems were that in rejecting bureaucracy, hierarchy, and elected representatives as leaders, the RSSF had no single vision to articulate to the wider world and especially to the press, and it had no way to resolve deep-seated disagreements between different factions. Attempting to use consensus decision-making with a group of 200 people from a variety of entrenched ideological positions simply could not work, especially when they were not trained in this type of decision-making and many had extensive experience with organizational hierarchy, bureaucracy, and representative democracy instead. As meetings broke down into unresolvable arguments and chaos, and as their message repeatedly was garbled or lost even amongst students, the disciplined hierarchy of the Old Left organizations became ever more appealing.

The RSSF would particularly struggle to gain the sustained support of the majority of less radical students. Moderate students joined with revolutionary students on many marches, sit-ins, and demonstrations, and could be counted on to support the RSSF if they were victimized by authorities, but they were outspoken in their disagreements with revolutionary students. Moderates objected to injustice, racism, class inequalities, and imperialist excesses in Third World countries on moral grounds, but believed that their government and country were essentially good and only needed to be reformed. They especially criticized the tendency of many revolutionary students to advocate violent methods to disrupt the system. For example, one Essex sociology student, Jenny Bingham, wrote an article in November 1968 criticizing the Essex "extreme left" for their "intolerance and their closed-mindedness."[104] Bingham agreed with students controlling their own lives, increasing political participation, and protesting violence and repression in society, but disagreed with the far left on the means to change things. She asserted that left-wing students must stop silencing those who disagreed with them by branding them "bourgeois/liberal/reactionary/reformist" and find new tactics to gain the support of the majority of students.

Revolutionary students, however, were often far more organized than the reformers and frequently imposed their will on student unions and organizations. For example, during an LSE protest in October 1968, Socialist Society students affiliated with the RSSF packed the meetings, shouted down speakers who offered alternative tactics, and manipulated union rules to suit their ends.[105] Some of their opponents attempted to do the same, but LSE's Socialist Society contained some very dedicated activists who took their fight for control of the Union more seriously than other students. The majority of students consistently refused to elect revolutionary students to the union leadership, so union meetings normally pitted a moderate majority on the Union Executive Council against radicals in the audience. Because General Meetings could dictate union policies and majority ruled at these meetings, radicals could pack meetings and force the Union Executive to do their bidding. Union Executives who objected to these radical policies then resigned in protest. As a consequence, the rate of resignations on the LSE Union Executive was extremely high, leaving the union in organizational disarray throughout the rest of the Long Sixties. The Socialist Left succeeded in manipulating the LSE Union, but at a high cost to the Union's effectiveness.[106]

Despite its success in spreading socialist theory to pockets of activists across the nation and sometimes taking control of student unions, the RSSF continued to be divided by sectarian in-fighting. The New Left, Maoists, Trotskyists, anarchists, libertarians, and independents within it constantly argued over issues, tactics, and goals for the organization. At the November

1968 RSSF conference, actual fist-fights broke out among the student delegates. Those who could shout the loudest often led the way at the expense of the unity of the organization. Many well-meaning student activists grew disheartened by these displays of machismo, theoretical elitism, and exclusionism, and rejected RSSF leaders who ignored the concerns of grass-roots activists. Perhaps it is unrealistic to expect that students would ever be ideologically unified, but more awareness of the problem of factionalism and willingness to compromise could have helped to lessen the negative impact it had on the organization. In a situation remarkably similar to that of the American SDS, Maoists in London formed their own separate RSSF in 1969, while the IS and the others remained in control over the national organization. By the end of 1969 the RSSF had a total of only 200 members, and in 1970 it ceased to exist.[107]

The Socialist Left's efforts to organize students were thus a mixed blessing for the British student movement. Socialists offered student organizations their time, important energy, organizational skills, and contacts with political organizations that could provide considerable resources for the student movement. They helped to organize student activists into the RSSF and provided goals, theories, and tactics for the student movement. Through heavy recruiting efforts, they drew many activists into socialist politics and introduced them to a variety of radical theories. Their recruiting efforts and attempts to politicize the issues, however, alienated many activists who were less devoted to a socialist revolution. In some cases socialist and non-socialist students turned the focus of their efforts away from the original issues towards competing with each other over the direction of the student movement. As a consequence of this divisiveness, the RSSF remained a small group of highly dedicated activists, who ultimately failed to lead the student movement.

While the RSA and RSSF failed to truly lead the British student movement, the RSA's efforts to politicize the NUS were ultimately successful. In April of 1969, the Liverpool NUS Conference voted to amend Clause Three of the NUS Constitution to include all matters relating to students and education. This would allow it to take a stand and organize direct actions around any issue of concern to students.[108] This shift in the NUS also resulted from the withdrawal of a number of university student unions from NUS membership in reaction to the 1967 discovery that its international affiliate organization, the International Student Council (ISC), was funded by the CIA. The American underground newspaper, *Ramparts*, originally broke the news that the two foundations that financed the ISC and exerted considerable control over its projects were CIA fronts for combating the influence of the communist International Union of Students. Since the RSA had been calling for a withdrawal from the ISC and the formation of a new international student organization, the scandal seemed to vindicate the RSA and embarrass the NUS executive.[109] As the conservative forces within the NUS weakened, the forces of the Broad Left, now led by

Jack Straw, an activist in the student movement at Leeds University, used the ISC scandal, the popularity of the RSSF, and escalating student protests to justify the NUS taking more of a lead in the student protests sweeping the nation. After several attempts, he was finally successful in winning the presidency of the NUS in April 1969 and getting the NUS to dissociate from the ISC. Although he and his leftist executive would not take office until October of 1969, the events of 1968, together with the dedication of the RSA and the Broad Left, would finally succeed in making the NUS the new leader of the British student movement in the seventies.

Throughout 1968, however, no national organization would lead the student movement. Hundreds of student protests occurred at universities across the nation in the 1967–68 and 1968–69 academic years, but most of these were locally organized and not coordinated by any outside body. The majority of protests retained a commitment to non-violence, a traditional middle-class sense of morality, justice, and fairness, and a concern for a respectable appearance so that they would be taken seriously. Pockets of RSSF activists, however, took more dramatic actions in the hopes of provoking authorities and escalating the protests to eventually spark some sort of larger revolution. As a result of these actions, the student movement thus gained a reputation for being more violent and revolutionary than it actually was.

THE VIETNAM SOLIDARITY CAMPAIGN

One issue that united all students in 1968 was the Vietnam War. Despite repeated pleas from left-wing organizations and polls showing that the majority of Britons opposed US intervention in Vietnam, the Wilson government had maintained its uneasy support of the US position in Vietnam. Britain committed no material support for the war or combat troops, but its weapons researchers and manufacturers were deeply complicit in supporting the US war effort. This fact, together with the seeming injustice, immorality, and brutality of this war, deeply offended many Briton's moral sensibilities, leading many to support the anti-war movement in the late sixties. Although this movement began in earnest in 1965, it grew exponentially in 1967 and 1968 as it became more organized, international anti-war coordination increased, and war casualties and destruction escalated.

The most successful organization in the British Vietnam War movement in terms of recruiting widespread student support was the Vietnam Solidarity Committee (VSC) and the most important person in the VSC was Tariq Ali. Ali had turned his full attention to the Vietnam War after leaving Oxford in 1966 and was quickly recruited by the Bertrand Russell Peace Foundation. It had begun planning a war crimes tribunal (based on the Nuremburg trials) to put the US government on trial for its actions in Vietnam. Ali's activism attracted their attention and they recruited him to travel to Vietnam to collect data in 1967. Neutral Sweden agreed to host the war crimes tribunal and made a big celebration of it. Jean-Paul Sartre presided over the tribunal, which included Isaac Deutscher, Simone de Beauvoir, David Dellinger, and Stokely Carmichael. Russell and Sartre viewed the tribunal as a moral intervention to expose an immoral war. It was indeed successful in that it was reported all around the world and inspired more people to speak out against the war.[110]

The harrowing experience of traveling around North Vietnam, enduring bombing raids, and seeing the incredible damage done to the civilian population and the great confidence of the Vietnamese people and leaders, made Ali even more committed to the fight against American involvement in Vietnam. As he recalled, "It was a searing experience. I'd never had any doubt that the US was the main enemy, but now it was stamped on me for life. It wasn't demagogy when I said one should stay on there and fight. I didn't want to come back."[111] He took to heart Premier Pham Van Dong's plea for Ali to help create a worldwide solidarity movement instead. When he returned from Vietnam, he wrote extensively about his experiences for the *Tribune* and *New Statesman*, and was deluged with invitations to speak at universities across the country. As he traveled the country that year, he sensed a rapid change in the mood on campuses, which he believed was caused by disenchantment with the Labour government and the international examples of the Cuban and Vietnamese revolutions. He joined the International Socialists that year because they overtly expressed solidarity with the North Vietnamese and sought their victory in the war. His most important activity of this period, however, was to join the Russell Foundation's Vietnam Solidarity Campaign (VSC).[112]

Directors of the Bertrand Russell Peace Foundation, Ken Coates and American Ralph Schoenman, founded the VSC in 1966 as the first explicitly pro-National Liberation Front organization in Britain. It was ostensibly non-sectarian, but the International Marxist Group and International Socialists held a strong influence over it. VSC members were young and many were students, but the organization was not explicitly oriented toward or led by students. The VSC, however, was important in exposing student activists to an interpretation of the Vietnam War that differed from the mainstream media and involving them in confrontational protests which radicalized many students.[113]

The VSC held demonstrations in London in October of 1967 and March of 1968, which attracted 10,000 and 25,000 respectively. The first demonstration was larger than either the police or the organizers had anticipated, and a few hundred protesters broke away from the largely peaceful march to attack the American embassy in Grosvenor Square. Police were barely able to turn back the surging crowd and arrested several dozen protesters. Among the crowd that day were twenty-five students from Essex University. That week Essex students held a "Vietnam Week" to educate others about the war and to raise money for the Red Cross in Vietnam.[114] Essex students and staff were also among those who attacked the American Embassy and battled with police. Their experiences with police and violence in this demonstration made a deep impression on many activists. Police arrested Rick Coates, who was the president of the Essex Socialist Society and a third-year sociology student. He called his advisor, Charles Posner, who had also participated in the demonstration, to bail him out of jail, but police allegedly ejected Posner from the jail. Posner then contacted the Council for Civil Liberties, and Coates was finally allowed to post bail.[115] The student reporter asserted, "All those from Essex who were involved in Sunday's events agreed that the militancy of the demonstration and the brutality of the police was unprecedented in their experience."[116] This incident radicalized Coates and other Essex activists and they became increasingly hostile to government authorities.

Both the police and the students came prepared for even more violence in the March 1968 VSC protest. In Trafalgar Square, the VSC protest looked just like the Suez demonstration, with prominent speakers including actress Vanessa Redgrave, addressing a crowd of young people holding flags, banners, and posters. When the march arrived at Grosvenor Square near the American embassy, however, fights erupted between the protesters and the police. Unlike the Suez and CND marchers, VSC protesters disobeyed police orders to maintain tidy lines and obey the traffic signals. Angered at this disrespect and disorder, the police began to truncheon the unruly protesters and the protesters fought back, grabbing the reins of the police horses and mobbing officers they could isolate. A journalist for *International Times*, Horace Ove observed:

> It was incredible. Grosvenor Square was packed; it was the first time I saw young people in this country, mostly middle-class, really angry, really come out into the streets and really stand up to the police, really fighting back. . . . When the police started to charge with their horses and really lay into people and beat the shit out of them there was one girl that was shouting and screaming back to them and about five police really laid into her and really kicked her about on the ground and then they pulled back. And then the crowd surrounded one police that did not get away and they really laid into him and beat him to the ground.[117]

David Widgery was there and "couldn't believe his eyes. 'Instead of doing the English thing of nudging the police a couple of times and then moving on, people were actually pushing through the police and running for the embassy steps' . . ."[118] Protesters fought with police for several hours afterwards.

Tariq Ali recalls that most of those in the crowd were students, with a small number of young workers.[119] LSE student Rachel Dyne remembers the March 1968 VSC march as "one of the happiest moments of my life. . . . We took over the whole street as though we could do what we liked, it echoed to the chanting. I felt we were a real force, part of an international movement that could change the course of events on a worldwide scale."[120] Both of these demonstrations infused the anti-war and student movements with a new sense of the power of protest as well as a more defiant attitude towards the police.

The media had a field day covering what they perceived as the violent "hooliganism" of the protesters, completely siding with the police.[121] The media had been criticizing Vietnam demonstrations almost from the start. Writing about an earlier Grosvenor Square anti-war march, the *Observer* reported that "these student demonstrations are not serious political movements pursuing real aims: they are more like a highbrow version of football hooliganism."[122] As the VSC began to plan another large protest for October of 1968, the media used the March 1968 protest to whip up public fears of chaos and disorder in the streets of London. The protests in Britain and the rest of the world that spring and summer intensified public fears of the potential power of massive dissent movements, creating a moral panic not only about the VSC protests, but about the student movement as well. As the media prepared for the October 1968 protest, it interviewed some of the most radical dissidents who spoke of using violence to provoke the authorities and thus expose the repressive power of the state. Many papers warned of the violence to come, but other papers treated it condescendingly, arguing that these were not revolutionaries, just misguided and foolish young people letting off steam. Both sides agreed that the authorities should come down hard on any violence or hooliganism.[123] Although polls continued to show that the majority of Britons opposed the war in Vietnam, many also called for the banning of protests. For example, one survey in September 1968 indicated that while 66 per cent of Britons disapproved of British support for American policy, 56 per cent wanted to ban political demonstrations.[124] Because of this media-generated panic, Tariq Ali was barraged with daily death threats and had to constantly reassure the public that their next demonstration would be completely non-violent.[125]

Government authorities reacted to the rumors of violence with a strong determination to avoid a repeat of the August 1968 Chicago demonstration. One right-wing MP Tom Iremonger blamed the protests on foreign agitators, claiming that "the British people are fed up with being trampled underfoot by foreign scum."[126] Whereas some Labour and Tory MPs wanted to ban the march and deport Tariq Ali, who was by then a British citizen, others urged tolerance of the dissenters, claiming that banning the march would only outrage the protesters and give them public sympathy. Technically, there was no law against protest demonstrations, but there was no law specifically guaranteeing protesters the right to march either. It was agreed, however, that the police could employ any number of laws restricting the behavior of the protesters, ranging from "riotous assembly" to "insulting behavior" and "obstruction."[127] The Wilson government, though it made no public announcement of its policy on the protests, decided to use the Special Branch and the police to control the demonstration. Similar to the FBI's actions in America, the Special Branch monitored VSC actions and plans through infiltration, tapping its phone lines, and opening its mail. Scotland Yard also harassed the VSC by raiding its offices. [128] The police knew that only a minority of the protesters wanted violence to provoke repression and radicalize others. To thwart these plans, they were determined to ignore provocation and maintain order at all costs. Toward this end, law enforcement authorities ensured that the police would appear respectable in their normal unarmed uniforms, be well fed and rested, and above all maintain their discipline. [129]

The vast majority of participants also wanted an orderly nonviolent demonstration. The Ad Hoc Committee, which organized the demonstration, had considered the use of violent confrontation to draw public attention to the seriousness of the issue and provoke repression by the authorities, thereby exposing the coercive nature of their capitalist government. Tariq Ali and others on the Committee, however, decided against this tactic because they too feared a situation similar to the Chicago Democratic Convention in which protesters were blamed for police violence used against them. They also felt that protesters would be unprepared to defend themselves against the more powerful government forces. Instead of a violent confrontation with the authorities, the Ad Hoc Committee planned a peaceful rally for those of all political backgrounds to express public solidarity with the NLF. In the wake of the Tet Offensive, they believed that a simple but massive show of support for the Vietcong would bolster the confidence of the NLF and weaken that of the United States. Tariq Ali attempted to counteract press reports and rumors of violence by touring the country that autumn explaining the VSC's nonviolent intentions to university students and trade unions.

Partly because of this strategy and the extra publicity, the march was a huge success in terms of numbers of participants. Over 100,000 participants, including trade unions and people of all political backgrounds, joined in this protest. While half of the participants were students, people of all ages joined. Three-quarters of the demonstrators obeyed the directions of the organizers and police and peacefully marched to Hyde Park, but a contingent left the main body to attack the US embassy. This group of protesters sought violent confrontation and police repression similar to what had happened in the French May to provoke a student and worker revolution. For several hours the protesters taunted police and attempted to break through the lines of officers who stood with linked arms protecting the embassy. One of the protesters later wrote of the theatrical nature of the confrontation and how the police had impressed him:

> The bobbies knew how to absorb charges, how to disintegrate and retreat, how to reform and how to charge. They were a rugby scrum at its best. . . . It was really a most embarrassing rout for the Anarchists. . . . They [the police] consistently used less force than was used

against them and they depended greatly on their deportment, appearance and uniforms. They were not dressed for battle or even riot. They were indestructible symbols of public order.[130]

After a few hours of futile maneuvering, most of the protesters abandoned the embassy. The next day, the media attributed the low level of violence to the excellent conduct of the police.[131]

The protesters, however, had mixed feelings about this massive demonstration. Many participants felt that the march had been a success: it had remained peaceful for the most part, received extensive media coverage, and the anti-war and radical speakers had a chance to reach hundreds of thousands of people. Many revolutionary students, however, were dissatisfied with the march and felt it had been a complete failure. RSSF students had hoped to expose the repression of the capitalist establishment if the police violently dispersed the demonstration, but they believed that the police had outwitted the organizers of the event. By showing their tolerance of protesters, the police had reaffirmed the belief that the British police were the best in the world and that British society was in fact a tolerant society.[132] Essex student Robin Jenkins pointed out that even huge protest demonstrations would not lead to revolutionary change unless they exposed contradictions in society, made alliances with the working class, and divided the opposition. Putting it succinctly, he asserted: "The British class structure is not going to be fractured by a trite plagiarisation [sic] of Paris 1968."[133] Paradoxically, the October '68 VSC march was both the high point of the VSC movement and the beginning of its end, as supporters began to doubt the power of peaceful demonstrations.

Because it coalesced in such an out-pouring of dissent, the VSC demonstrations inspired a wide variety of local-level protests against the Vietnam War at many universities across the nation in 1967–68 and 1968–69. These protests took many different forms in different places across the nation in these years. Those mentioned by national newspapers include Sheffield, Birmingham, Liverpool, Glasgow, the LSE, Cambridge, and Sussex. For example, twenty University Glasgow students in the Student Christian Movement participated in the national fast for peace in Vietnam in October of 1967 and held a picket at the center of Glasgow to publicize their protest of the war.[134] Sussex University protests, on the other hand, were more dramatic. In February of 1968, they splashed a press liaison officer from the American embassy with red paint as he left their teach-in on Vietnam. A month later, 600 students and 40 staff members held a 72-hour fast and 500 others burned an American flag in another demonstration.[135]

The case of Cambridge University's protest against the Labour Party's foreign policy was especially important in reframing student protests as "violent." In March of 1968, nearly 1,000 Cambridge students came out to protest a speech given by Defense Minister Denis Healey. As he attempted to leave, they surrounded his car and lay down in front of it to prevent him from leaving. As students threw themselves in front of Healey's car, the police tossed them into the gutter, injuring many. This enraged the already agitated crowd and they began banging on the car and rocking it. In the end, the police successfully beat off the students, arresting five in the process. The incident made all of the major papers the next day. The *Daily Telegraph* led the way in sensationalizing the event, declaring that "utter violence broke loose" and accusing students of "vicious rioting."[136] A few days later, Healey called violent student demonstrations "a threat to the British people and the whole system we honor."[137] Even the House of Commons discussed the demonstration. MP Kenneth Lewis commented "we have in the past been used to having student protests that were nonviolent, we enjoyed them, and hope the students did too. We are not enjoying them anymore. They are getting a little out of hand."[138] After the Cambridge protest, the press expected violence at every student protest, thus framing student protest as potentially violent and a threat to the nation. Together with the press coverage of the VSC protests, the Cambridge protest of 1968 helped to shift the public perception of the student from a young person "prone to healthy excess into that of a dangerous subversive."[139]

Despite the outpouring of support for the VSC campaigns in 1968 and widespread smaller protests, only a small minority of students devoted much of their time to protests around this issue because of their distance from the conflict and their lack of influence on the US government. Hull student David Barrow concluded that Vietnam protests were futile because "it is for the US government and the US government alone to realize that [it] can no longer continue to intervene in other country's conflicts."[140] Partly because of the global student protests against the war, as well as long-standing resentment against American bullying, the majority of the British population opposed the war by the late sixties. In 1969 the Trades Union Congress came out against the war and held a mass lobby of Parliament in 1969. The Labour and Liberal parties, prominent church leaders, and all the organizations of the Left condemned the Vietnam War by the end of the sixties.[141] Despite this widespread opposition, the Wilson government made no indications that it would publicly break with the United States, and the US government continued to largely ignore international opposition. As a result, the anti-war movement declined dramatically after 1968. Only 4,000 attended the Vietnam Solidarity Campaign's national demonstration in March 1969 and only 1,600 attended a November 1969 protest against the My Lai massacre.[142] The VSC demonstrations may have been the most famous protests of the Long Sixties and there is no doubt that the Vietnam War was an important issue within the British student movement, but by no means was it the only or even the most important issue even at the high point of the VSC protests in 1968.

THE NATIONAL DEBATE OVER RACE AND IMMIGRATION

More important within the student movement that year was the issue of racial discrimination both within Britain and abroad. Demonstrations against apartheid in South Africa took place at the LSE, and Glasgow, Liverpool and Birmingham Universities, but most anti-racism protests in 1968 focused on race relations and immigration inside Britain. Although students had been fighting home-grown racism since the fifties, this fight intensified greatly in 1968 as the nation debated the problems of racism and immigration in Parliament and the media. The new attention to these problems arose when the Kenyan government began to deport its Asian citizens, who held British Commonwealth passports and were requesting entry into Britain. Although the 1962 Immigration Act had severely limited this sort of immigration, the refugee status of these new immigrants forced the Wilson government to make a decision on whether to admit them or deny them based upon the restrictions put down in the 1962 Act.

Bowing to considerable pressure from the trade unions and conservatives, the Wilson government quickly pushed through the Commonwealth Immigration Act in March 1968, extending the same limits on immigration to the Kenyans as were imposed on all other Commonwealth immigrants. The very next month, perhaps to balance the perceived racism of this immigration act, the Wilson government proposed a Race Relations Bill, banning racial discrimination in employment, housing, and commercial services, and establishing the means to handle complaints of racial discrimination and incitement to racial hatred. As Fred Lindop asserts, however, both the immigration and race relations acts were inherently racist in that they "assumed that the presence of black people in a predominantly white country constituted a problem which could only be resolved by limiting numbers and reducing the social and cultural visibility of blacks by 'integration.'"[143] Both also reflected widespread views that the key to racial harmony and preserving Britain's heritage of tolerance and democracy was to restrict immigration from culturally and racially different nations.

As Parliament and the press debated these bills, a number of Conservative MPs, including Patrick Wall and Enoch Powell, traveled the country speaking to groups about the importance of restricting "colored" immigration and protecting the rights of Britain's white majority. Wall had long defended Britain's colonial record in "civilizing" Africans and had supported white rule in South Africa and Rhodesia as a bulwark against the "virus" of communism. In short, his views were opposite to those held by most student activists. Although there were a number of protests against Wall, the most publicized was the Leeds University protest of May 1968. The Leeds Conservative Association had invited Wall to speak at their Union and 400 students turned up to protest. There was little coordination of the protest and some students acted out angrily against Wall and his wife Sheila. After heckling Wall, they followed the couple to the refectory and lay down around them to obstruct their entry. As the couple attempted to pick their way through the demonstrators, Mrs. Wall alleged that a student kicked her and she fell. The *Daily Mail* added that the MP was "spat at as he wrestled in the mob."[144] Regardless of the validity of these allegations, the Leeds protest hints at the new willingness of some student activists to take more confrontational measures to get their point across.

Anti-racism activism, however, occasionally had a farcical side, as in the case of a Hull University student disruption of a 1969 speech by Wall on immigration and race. Protest organizers Tom Fawthrop and Christine Sheppard could not find a "coloured girl" to present flowers to Wall, so Sheppard darkened her face and performed in front of cameras before the meeting. Fawthrop, "bearded and miniskirted," performed for the crowd until he realized that the television cameras had not been allowed into the meeting. A student reporter commented, "We should not be surprised if in future guest speakers of any eminence decline to travel 240 miles to be ridiculed by a gaggle of hooligans who between them have not the competence to run a whelk stall on the Anlaby Road."[145] These students may have taken their activism very seriously, but actions such as these did little to convince the public of their sincerity.

Even more so than Wall, Enoch Powell made himself a pariah to student activists in 1968. Powell argued that immigrants competed with Britain's white working class for housing and jobs, and that the new Race Relations Bill would give the immigrants an unfair advantage over whites, effectively discriminating against white Britons. He asserted that continued immigration and attempts to equalize treatment for racial minorities would inevitably lead to racial violence of the sort faced by America with its race riots. In an oft-quoted speech, he quoted Virgil: "Like the Roman, I seem to see 'the River Tiber foaming with much blood'."[146] Edward Heath removed him from the opposition shadow cabinet for this comment, but Powell had considerable support among the British public. Later that year, one Gallup poll found that 74 per cent agreed with him.[147] When the Commons voted to approve the Race Relations Bill, more than a thousand dock-workers protested it and supported Powell with a demonstration and wild-cat strikes. While the trade union leaders continued to support the Wilson government, the rank-and-file workers were becoming disaffected from the Labour government. Some workers appreciated Powell defending their rights, while others opposed what they perceived to be an attack on Powell's freedom of speech. For whatever reason, many workers clearly supported Powell.

Although right-wing students often approved of Powell's views and Conservative Societies across the nation invited him to speak at their universities, many students were appalled with his racism and the apparent racism of his working-class supporters. Left-wing student groups especially opposed Powell's views and were eager to make their dissent and opposition to racism known throughout the nation and the world. As Powell travelled around the nation's universities to speak about these issues, he faced crowds of angry students ready to use any means necessary to stop him from using their university to spread his perceived racism. Students protested Powell at the LSE, Essex, Exeter, Cardiff, Sheffield, Oxford, and a number of other universities in 1968 and 1969. In many places, students heckled Powell until his audience could no longer hear him speak, while in other places they picketed the speaking venue, attempting to prevent Powell from speaking and his audience from attending. These protests reveal that protest strategies had evolved considerably since the mid-sixties, reflecting the new militancy of the RSSF and the global student movement.

When the LSE Conservative Society invited Powell as a guest speaker in April 1968, the Union wrote a letter to Powell requesting that he not come because his appearance would "greatly offend the coloured students and those who detest racism."[148] In May of 1968, the Union also helped to organize a class boycott as a "symbol of our deep commitment to complete racial integration and abhorrence of the racialist views of Mr. Enoch Powell."[149] They urged all students to instead join a May Day demonstration against racism. Although the original purpose of the trade union sponsored May Day demonstration was to support workers issues, such as the Amalgamated Engineering Union's pay and holiday increase grievance, the student marchers' anti-Powell slogans drowned out the issues central to the march. About 4,000 dock-workers, however, were there demonstrating in favor of Powell's efforts to curb immigration. The *Guardian* commented:

> Office workers watching the May Day march on their lunch break were almost universally hostile to the student contingent. Every comment overheard during the two-hour walk was a more or less forceful variation of "go on you students, never done a . . . day's work in your lives."[150]

Powell's popularity among the dock-workers shocked the LSE Socialist Society, who saw working class racism as a result of capitalism pitting workers against each other. They blamed themselves for not reaching out to the working class in order to explain their opposition to racism and resolved to work harder to establish contacts with the working class. With the support of the student union, they organized a one-day teach-in on racism at the LSE to educate students and workers on the issue.[151]

At Oxford University, students and dons held a demonstration during a March 1968 lecture given by Home Secretary James Callaghan, author of the Immigration Bill. Although the protest was quiet and peaceful, and even Callaghan saw no problem with it, the mainstream press portrayed the protesters as "hooligans." This greatly upset the students, who sent a letter of complaint to the Press Council.[152] Ruskin College, Oxford's trade union institute, organized an extremely successful march on May Day 1968, protesting Powell's views through the streets of Oxford, with several thousand students and community members in attendance.[153] When Powell came to Oxford to give a lecture on behalf of the Oxford Conservative Association several months later, 800 demonstrators blocked his entrance and he had to be secretly moved into the lecture hall. When this was found out, the protesters attacked a police cordon protecting the entrance of the lecture hall, resulting in thirty-one arrests.[154]

Not all students, however, were angered by Enoch Powell's views on immigration and racism. A small but vocal group of Glasgow University students formed an affiliate of the fascist British National Front in April 1968 to support "patriotic" politicians who favored a "ban on Afro-Asian immigration, a resumption of trade with Rhodesia and South Africa, the restoration of capital and corporal punishment, and a foreign policy of opposition both to Communism and US economic domination."[155] The group had a small membership, but created an immediate stir by asking Rhodesia Prime Minister Ian Douglas Smith to run for the rectorial election the next year.[156] Smith declined the invitation on the basis that the British government refused to recognize the Rhodesian government and probably would not allow him to attend.

This group of students, which included Ross McKay, the conservative editor of the student newspaper and later president of the Student Representative Council, presented a strong opposition to left-wing student activists, constantly criticized student protests at other universities, and mounted counter-protests to those held in Glasgow. Calling student protest against Powell "disgraceful," McKay stated, "Any such behavior should be regarded as intolerable in a civilized academic community and those responsible be ejected summarily from the privileged position given them thanks to the subsidies taken in taxes from the citizens of the society they are determined to subvert."[157] In May 1968, the group of forty students staged a pro-Powell demonstration just two days after an anti-Powell march of 400 students.[158] Conservative student protests, however, were extremely rare. As conservatives, many of these students would have viewed demonstrations and marches as vulgar tools of their enemies and would not want to associate with the wider student movement which was perceived as leftist or anarchist. At most, conservative students harassed student protesters or held small counter-protests to express their opposition to the leftist student movement.

The case of Essex reveals how students were divided over Powell and how protests around these issues set the stage for the massive sit-ins later in the year. In February 1968, the Colchester Conservative Association invited Powell to speak at their meeting, and about a dozen Essex students attended to protest his "racialist" views. This protest, however, was much more provocative than protests elsewhere. Second year sociology student Andrew Pring set off a "fizzing bomb" on a table near the podium where Powell was speaking; David Triesman shouted "racist sod" as Powell tried to defend his views on immigration; and another student set off the building's fire alarms. Student Union president Colin Rogers organized a chain of students across the roadway to prevent Powell from leaving. Postgraduate student Peter Archard heckled Powell and allegedly threw an iron pipe at the car which drove Powell from the meeting. Soon afterwards, university officials began disciplinary proceedings against these students and three others for their involvement in the Powell protest.[159] Essex officials claimed that they wanted to deal with the matter in university courts rather than handing it over to the criminal courts because they wanted to protect the future careers of the students involved.[160] Student activists, on the other hand, felt that the university disciplinary procedures were arbitrary and did not reflect "natural" laws of justice, such as the assumption of innocence until proven guilty, the right to a defense and witnesses, and the necessity of evidence to prove a case. They demanded that the matter be turned over to police courts because at least there their rights would be protected.[161]

This round of protests, however, quickly ended when university faculty members convinced the administration to drop the charges and the protesters encountered a strong backlash from other students as well as faculty, administrators, and the outside public. Many Essex students wrote to the student newspaper to criticize the actions against Powell. Although most opposed Powell's views, they felt that the protesters had committed senseless criminal acts and should be punished. Student newspaper editor Shaun Leslie claimed that the protesting students were unrepresentative of the majority of students and that they were hypocritical when they demanded power to the people but excluded students and journalists from their meetings.[162] He further asserted,

> Their actions are deplorable. . . . Contrary to what the demonstrators and their supporters may think, most students do not want to be known as members of an institution with a reputation for violence and a blatant lack of self-control and capacity for reasoned argument. The University should take a firm line with those who are responsible for bringing the University's name into disrepute.[163]

This incident convinced activists like Triesman that they must do more to gain the support of the student majority in future protests.

Triesman and many other Essex activists participated in the March 1968 VSC demonstration and were strongly affected by events in Europe that spring. As a result, Triesman wrote an article the next month defending the selective use of violence to achieve political goals.[164] Using the example of Warsaw and Prague students, he asserted that in some cases student violence is the only way to fight against an Establishment that uses violence to suppress revolt but condemns student and worker violence. He declared that even if their tactics and protests did not achieve their ultimate goals, the feeling of community that student actions created was important and "at least we are not just sitting back and watching events go by."[165] Triesman defended the attack on the American embassy in London, stating that the mounted police caused the violence when they charged at the students. He also defended the disruption of the speeches of Enoch Powell and others like him, arguing that "These men are talking 'violence' . . . and because of their audiences, they are inducing a great deal more violence than any ten students who rock their cars, or throw paint at them. . . . The rational response to these men is to stop them . . ."[166] Reflecting the influence of Situationist thought prevalent in continental Europe that year, he asserted that free speech in Britains only intended to protect the Establishment, and all those who challenge their power are blocked by Establishment media which distorted their criticisms and refused them equal access. In his view, the only alternative left to dissenters was to raise their voices "above the polite whisper which marks the pleasantry of tea-time England, and every so often you break some china."[167]

Indeed, hundreds of peaceful student protests across the nation earlier in the sixties were largely ignored by the press and thus had little impact on the government or wider society. Confrontation and physical provocation, while un-British and offensive to many, forced the authorities to respond and inevitably drew media attention. The Porton Down protest and sit-in of May 1968 were simply the logical application of Triesman's argument and the culmination of student discontent stretching back to the early years of the university.

UNIVERSITY REFORM

Moderate and radical activists agreed that the system of higher education should be democratized and modernized as the *Robbins Report* had recommended. In activists' minds, however, democratization also entailed reforms to make the entire structure of higher education more democratic, including student representation in university decision-making. Most British universities in the late sixties allowed only minority student participation on low-level committees and were making slow progress in their modernization attempts. Because this issue appealed to students of all political beliefs, it interested activists at nearly every university in Britain in the late sixties. Activists who were more concerned with broad political and moral issues, such as capitalism and racism, realized that universities could be their most important tool in these struggles. If students had control over their own universities, they could not only empower themselves, but they could use their university's resources to fight racism and militarism at home and abroad. The issue of student representation, therefore, had the potential to unite revolutionaries, moderates, and conservatives.

At the national level, the RSSF and NUS devoted the majority of their time and energy to the university reform and student rights issue. The RSSF national office publicized these issues and mobilized support and solidarity for striking students, but they were never able to coordinate an effective movement around these issues. They consistently tried to use university reform as a starting point for getting the student movement to see that the real problem was actually capitalism and that socialism was the only real solution. The majority of activists, however, only sought to democratize the university through small reforms as they had been promised, and when authorities made concessions toward this end they ceased to support further disruptions of the university. Even though the RSSF failed to convince the majority of students that their revolutionary theories were applicable to the university reform issue, RSSF students were often the most dedicated of activists on this issue and did succeed in using it to transmit revolutionary socialist rhetoric to a wider segment of the student movement.

While the RSSF worked at the grassroots level to influence the student movement, the NUS worked at the top levels with university administrators and student union representatives to reform universities without widespread disruption. It put forward ten common demands of the student movement, including "real equality in what is . . . an undemocratically governed system of higher education. . . . Effective student presence on all relevant college committees," staff and student control of discipline, freedom of speech, student control of their own organizations, relevant academic courses, abolition of all paternalistic and outdated rules based on *in loco parentis*, and radical reform of assessment.[168] The ten NUS demands formed the basis of NUS negotiations with the Committee of Vice Chancellors and Principals of the Universities of the United Kingdom over the summer of 1968. At the outset of the negotiations, the Vice Chancellors stated that "we utterly condemn, and will resist, attempts by extremist groups to obstruct or disrupt the life of the universities. Such activities destroy freedom of speech and the freedom to learn, and we believe that they are entirely unacceptable to the overwhelming majority of members of the university."[169] In October, the Vice Chancellors and the NUS issued a joint statement in which they agreed on the need for further student participation in university governance, research into reforming examinations, fair disciplinary procedures, and freedom of speech on campuses. The Vice Chancellors, however, disagreed with the students' demand for representation on Councils and Senates because these dealt with private issues such as exam results and academic appointments and promotions. The NUS viewed the statement as a major victory for student rights, but realized that the agreement did not bind university administrators to its suggestions and vowed to continue to work for the implementation of the statement at every university in the country.[170]

As a result of the initiatives of the RSSF and the NUS, and the slow pace of change, student rights and educational reform were by far the most common demands of the student movement in 1968. Students at Regent Street Polytechnic, Holborn College of Law and Commerce, Aston, Leicester, York, Manchester, Oxford, and Cambridge universities all agitated for reforms centering around increased student representation and control within their universities. Students at Birmingham's Aston University tried to force their university authorities to accept student representation by holding a sit-in in the administration block. Authorities responded by setting up a committee to examine the possibility of student representation and other reforms. At the University of Leicester, students also sat-in to force administrators to accept their proposals for student representation on certain major committees in the university. The sit-in ended when university officials agreed to allow some student representation. In response to moderate student requests for representation, authorities at York, Manchester, and Oxford universities agreed to investigate the relationship between their respective authorities, staff, and students. In June of 1968, 100 undergraduates at Cambridge demonstrated for equal and democratic student-staff control of curricula and communalization of college life. In nearly all of these cases, university authorities ultimately conceded moderate reforms, allowing minority student representation on committees which would most benefit from student input.[171]

The specific target of these protests varied according to university-specific circumstances, but similar tactics and the common theme of democratization united them. One important tactic used by a number of highly-publicized protests in these years was that of the sit-in. This tactic was first used in the late fifties by British pacifists, but after LSE students adopted the sit-in as part of their protests in 1966-67, students at other universities were quick to adopt it for their own protests. Sit-ins required students to occupy part of the university continuously and involved considerably more planning and dedication than simply showing up at a demonstration or heckling a speaker. Unless students took shifts in the sit-in, they would have to forego showering and sleep on hard floors, or not sleep at all for as long as the sit-in lasted. Someone would have to supply them with food and drink, and all these activities would require coordination. They thus required much more time and dedication than other forms of protest and indicate the importance of the university reform issue within the student movement. More so than demonstration marches or pickets, they also represented a direct challenge to the authorities, who normally controlled university facilities, and as such demonstrate the increasingly confrontational nature of student rights protests in 1968.

Some of the most significant sit-ins in 1968 took place at Aston University in January, Leicester in February, Essex, Hull and Hornsey in May, Leeds in June, Birmingham in November, and Bristol in December. Although all were interesting in their own ways and resulted from specific local circumstances, all centered on the issues of student representation and university reform. The Hull, Hornsey, and LSE occupations, however, stand out for several reasons and warrant some in-depth discussion.

THE HULL UNIVERSITY CLEARWAYS CAMPAIGN

Located in the northeast of England, Hull University's sit-in was the culmination of a year-long student rights campaign. Since October of 1967, the

Hull Student Union had been requesting a number of university reforms, including reform of the examination system in consultation with students and staff; staff-student committees to consider questions of assessment, syllabus and teaching techniques; the elimination of *in loco parentis* rules; democratic student control of student facilities; and direct student representation on all administrative bodies of the university.[172] Under pressure from the Socialist Society, the Student Union created the "Clearways Campaign" to mobilize student activism in support of the demands in May of 1968. They threatened direct action if their demands were not met within ten days. When the University Senate took no action, the students occupied the university for five and a half days.[173]

The Hull occupation ended when the Student Council compromised with the authorities, accepting their offer of equal representation on governing structures which were parallel to the current bodies. While the students failed to achieve all of their goals, the conflict had an important effect on many of them. One student wrote in the university's newspaper *Torchlight*:

> Even the most smugly non-active people have been forced to question not only the immediate parochial issue concerning themselves but the validity and purpose of the entire educational system of which society has inevitably made them a part. . . . Students are in fact not behaving irresponsibly. On the contrary they are at last attempting to claim some sort of responsibility for themselves, to prove that they are not just examination machines but are capable of rational enquiry and of issuing a direct challenge to established values. . . . Whatever else the campaign has achieved it has at least shown the authorities that students at Hull, like students elsewhere, are capable of re-examining their society, as theoretically at least education is supposed to encourage us to do.[174]

Reminiscent of Berkeley's Free Speech Movement, Hull students defended their action as a defense of the ideal of the university as a place which encouraged free inquiry and responsibility among students. The Clearways Campaign thus reveals the how the British student movement explored a wide range of reforms to improve the quality of higher education and gain more from their educations.

THE HORNSEY AFFAIR

The issue of reforming higher education was also taken up by students in dozens of art colleges in 1968. Student grievances in the art colleges, however, differed considerably from those of university students. As part of Labour's "binary program" for higher education, sixty-eight colleges of technology, art, and commerce would merge into thirty new polytechnics, losing their independence and identity. Art college students, staff, and administrators all opposed this plan, but Local Education Authorities went forward with it in 1967–68. Hornsey Art College was to be incorporated into the Faculty of Art and Design in Middlesex Polytechnic, but was particularly under-funded and mismanaged. It consisted of a series of temporary annexes spread out across North London, with a main college in Crouch End. There were no student common rooms or places for tutorials and few workshop spaces, yet the Haringey LEA, which was dominated by conservatives, refused to increase funding despite the continued pleas of Hornsey's principal, Harold Shelton. Shelton himself, however, governed the university as a dictator, rarely consulting staff or students. By the spring of 1968, Hornsey was ripe for revolt.[175]

When repeated attempts to improve their situation were rejected, the Hornsey Student Union met in early May of 1968 to plan a seminar for the end of May to discuss the structure of the college, and develop reform proposals to democratize the college's academic structure and secure recognition of student rights. As Kim Howells, Tom Nairn, and other students planned the seminar, the student protests in Paris and throughout Britain unfolded, transforming their vision from a mere seminar into a sit-in, more along the lines of those occurring at the LSE, Leicester, Hull, and Essex. They invited a number of radical students and staff to speak to them on a variety of issues related to higher education and art. The demands for the sit-in would now be control of union funds, a sabbatical year for their student union president, and student participation in university governance and course content.[176]

The sit-in began on 28 May and was planned to end the next day. Most participants rejected the overtly political speeches, but were intensely interested in continuing their discussions about art education, so they decided to continue the sit-in until their demands were met. The more they discussed art education, the more they objected to the proposed inclusion of their colleges within local polytechnics and the new requirement that they take general studies in order to obtain a four-year diploma in art and design. On Friday 31 May, the Board of Governors agreed to some of their initial demands for the president's sabbatical and some future student participation, but by then, the student protesters had a new list of demands, including the elimination of entry qualifications and more flexibility in the requirements of art education. As students continued their sit-in, now named "Crouch End Commune," they became more excited about all of the issues it raised. Small seminars met, often led by staff from other universities, and these seminars made proposals for general meetings, which in turn posed more questions for the seminars to discuss.[177] One student claimed that "we have learnt more in the last three weeks than in the last three years."[178] Eventually, their demands came to include the total reform of Hornsey's educational structure to cultivate the individual and become a "working model for a fundamental re-organization of the educational system . . ."[179] Similar to elsewhere, the Hornsey sit-in began with very limited demands, but in the process of extensive discussions analyzing the issues, students concluded that the entire system of higher education needed reform.

Although the administration and the local education councilors initially showed some sympathy for some of the demands, their patience quickly wore thin when students added their new demands to the list. When negotiations broke down on 4 July, the governors closed the college and surrounded it with security guards and dogs. The students barricaded themselves in at Crouch End, but they were well-organized, bringing in food and supplies throughout and even sharing sandwiches and tea with the sympathetic security guards. Although the student-staff committee finally reached a tentative agreement with the governors and principal Shelton on 8 July, the administration closed the college from 12 July until November, claiming that the sit-in had delayed admissions and that all students would have to reapply for admission. Before it reopened, the administration excluded student leaders of the protests, sacked staff who participated in the sit-in seminars, and fortified the main college with security alarms and steel bars.[180] In the end, Horney's administration succeeded in defeating the reform efforts of its students and staff, and in punishing those involved in the sit-in.

The Hornsey affair, however, did inspire other art students to form their own protests, and thirty other art colleges went on strike that year. It also led to a nation-wide reassessment of art education. In the midst of the sit-in in July of 1968, Hornsey students and staff organized a national conference on art and design education at the Roundhouse in London. This conference founded a national movement to promote their art education reform, called the Movement for Rethinking Art and Design Education (MORADE). The art college students, however, were quick to dissociate themselves from the RSSF. They stressed that MORADE was not political; rather it sought specific art education reforms such the abolition of verbal and written entrance qualifications for art colleges and that art colleges be funded directly by the UGC like the universities.[181] MORADE did succeed in getting the government to convene a committee under the chairmanship of Sir William Coldstream to review the whole system of art education. The report, *The Structure of Art and Design Education in the Further Education Sector* (1970), however, made only small changes to the system and even those were rejected by the incoming Conservative government.[182] Hornsey was a spectacular example of how art colleges joined in the student movement to reform higher education in 1968, but were ultimately defeated by conservative forces in the college administration, Local Education Authority, and government.

THE LSE GATES INCIDENT

University reform and student rights protests took a different course at the LSE in 1968. As a consequence of the "Troubles" of 1966–67, LSE officials had accepted student representation on committees that directly affected students. By November 1968 the number of student representatives on some committees had increased by fifty per cent, but students still had no representation on the most powerful bodies, the Academic Board and the Admissions Committee. The Student Union, under pressure from RSSF and IS students in the Socialist Society, continued to press for the complete restructuring of the university and parity of student numbers on all university committees.[183] This reform effort provided the back drop for the "gates incident."

The gates protest focused on the issue of security gates. The LSE administration installed security gates in late 1968 after 800 students had occupied the LSE to use it for housing during the October 1968 VSC demonstration. Socialist students, who were protesting the Director's refusal to sever the university's ties with South African and Rhodesian firms with a sit-in in the senior common room, encountered these locked gates when they attempted to enter the administrative building in January 1969. They interpreted the gates as an unwarranted attempt to prevent them from free access to the university. In a general meeting of the Student Union, radical students used the tactics of shouting down opponents and repeated votes to get the Union to pass their motion to tear down the gates. The Union Council considered this inappropriate since it was a criminal offense and held another vote to use negotiations to remove the gates. Students sympathetic to the Socialist Society once again voted to tear down the gates and immediately implemented the motion. Two New Left lecturers, Nick Bateson and Robin Blackburn, accompanied the students and participated in the removal of the gates.[184] Marxist student Rachel Dyne, participated in the attack on the gates and recalls: "It was a euphoric feeling, I felt a great sense of power. We were doing something authentic, we resented the gates, felt they were transforming the place more or less into a prison. Taking them down was a way of challenging authority."[185] This dramatic gesture not only succeeded in expressing student feelings, it also accomplished the RSSF's goal of provoking a repressive response.

The gates incident, while seemingly minor in hind-sight, escalated into a highly-publicized and sensationalized contest of wills between the administration and the students throughout the spring of 1969. The Court of Governors responded to the removal of the gates by closing the university until 17 February and announced its intention to prosecute all staff and students involved in the removal of the gates. It did, however, offer a conciliatory gesture by allowing student representation on the Building Committee and the General Purposes Committee in the future. The Student Council Executives resigned on January 27 in objection to what they thought was the illegal action of removing the gates and were replaced by a more radical committee. The new Student Council accepted the increased student representation, but demanded that all disciplinary action against staff and students be monitored by an outside independent tribunal. The administration ignored these demands, filed criminal charges against several students, and dismissed Blackburn and Bateson. Throughout March, April, and May, students boycotted classes and occupied buildings over the issue of the "victimization" of students and faculty who had acted under the directives of a Union meeting.[186]

During these three months, students escalated their attempts to get the authorities to relent in their victimization of the staff and students, occasionally devolving into frustrated vandalism. In one occupation of university buildings, students spray-painted walls and trashed faculty offices, but IS students cleaned up the mess, not wishing to discredit their serious protest. American student Paul Hoch, who had emerged as a leader in the protests, symbolically and carefully took down a portrait of Lord Robbins during one occupation: "The portrait symbolized authority to many of the academics there. So I moved it about two feet off the wall and put it on the floor. Within a second I was grabbed by about five people—it was almost as though I'd shot the Queen! Academics were erupting from their seats, yelling and screaming."[187] LSE authorities then pressed criminal charges against Hoch for moving the picture, which was promptly laughed out of court.

The strike received support from a surprisingly broad range of students and staff at LSE and across the nation. By 2 May, a Strike Newsletter was reporting 100 per cent success in preventing students from crossing the picket lines surrounding the school. The LSE Student Union, now in the hands of radicals, called for the support of the staff for their strike and staff-student meetings to consider the radical revision of examinations and democratic control over all future appointments and dismissals. Twenty lecturers joined the student strike and seventy staff members signed a statement condemning the school administrators' actions. Students from around the country sent letters of support to the LSE strikers. RSSF groups at Cambridge, Oxford, and Manchester tore down their university gates. Cambridge, Essex, Warwick, Glasgow, Strathclyde, and eight other universities all held sit-ins in support of LSE students. This flurry of activity reveals the strong sense of solidarity in the student movement and the importance of university reform not only to LSE students, but also to British students everywhere.

The LSE strike initially gave student radicals hope that they could force the administrators to reform the entire university, but by the end of the term, the administration offered no further concessions and the strike ended when students left for the summer. That July, however, the Court of Governors finally allowed student representation on a larger number of university committees, including six students on the Court itself. Despite the initial resistance of school authorities and mass exodus of students in the face of summer vacation, the LSE student movement ultimately achieved its primary goal of greater student representation in school government.[188]

The sit-ins of 1968 reveal the importance of university reform issues within the student movement. Despite the accusations of their critics, students did not want to destroy their universities, but rather wanted them to live up to the ideal of the university as a rational, democratic institution of higher learning. Students suggested specific reforms and made their case eloquently with great seriousness and dedication. While the sit-ins had a tremendous impact on participants and won some important victories, they failed to achieve their highest goal—the complete reform of the higher education system.

Clearly the British student movement had become a powerful force in 1968, not only successfully challenging the power structures within their universities, but also in forcing government and university authorities to take it more seriously. As the Essex protests indicate, the student movement became more confrontational and more focused on university-specific issues than in earlier years. Similar to the earlier periods of the Long Sixties, however, it continued to concentrate on the issues of militarism, racism, and university reforms, and to be shaped by national and global influences. Nationally, it was shaped by the rhetoric and ideologies of the New Left and various socialist groups, as well as national debates over education, immigration, and the Vietnam War. The British student movement also expressed solidarity with student movements in other nations, interacting with counterparts in Germany, France, and the United States, and drawing strength from the perception of a powerful global student movement forcing the world to change. British students attempted to use their universities as bases for expressing their political dissent, but when university authorities reacted with tough disciplinary actions, students turned their protests toward demanding more freedom and power within the university itself. This powerful combination of moral, legal, and practical issues resulted in some of the most widespread and longest-lasting university occupations of the era. Nineteen sixty-eight was indeed a magical year for the student movement in Britain as well as in the rest of the world.

The 1968 protests at Essex University reveal how local, national, and global issues combined, resulting in prolonged sit-ins at many universities that year. Essex students expected their university be more democratic and modern because of its unique mission as voiced by its Vice Chancellor. When students encountered rigid hierarchy in university decision-making, therefore, they demanded increased equality within the university structure by allowing more student representation on all of its governing bodies. At the same time, Essex students were involved in the national movement against racism, the Vietnam Solidarity Campaign, and the confrontational French student movement. These experiences inspired them to bring anti-war activism to their own campus and to organize the initial protest against the Porton Down scientist who was seen as complicit in helping the US in the Vietnam War. When university officials arbitrarily punished students for this protest, the student movement at Essex mobilized in earnest to reiterate its demands for more democracy within the university decision-making structure.

This was virtually the same pattern as the protest at the LSE in 1967. In both cases, small protests around external issues led university authorities to punish activists, which then caused more students to participate in larger, more confrontational occupations against "victimization" and in support of student rights and representation. Both groups of students had expected their respective universities to be models of modernization and radicalism, but both were sorely disappointed by the perceived conservatism of their respective administrations. In both cases, socialist student societies were able to translate student disillusionment within a socialist framework and convince others of the need to take direct action. National student organizations came to the aid of both protests. While the RSA coordinated support for the LSE in 1967, the RSSF coordinated support for Essex in 1968. Because of this support, as well as a flurry of communication between student protesters, both LSE and Essex activists felt solidarity with students at other British universities as well as with students in other countries. They both consequently saw their own local protests as part of wider national and global student movements.

The major difference between the LSE Troubles of 1967 and the Essex protests of 1968 was the fact that the LSE was the single most prominent student occupation of 1967, while the Essex protests occurred within the context of prolonged, intense occupations and confrontations occurring at universities across the nation and world that year. As a consequence, Essex students felt more empowered by and connected to a stronger student movement than students in previous years. The longest-lasting occupations of 1968 occurred at the LSE and art colleges such as Hornsey, but protests around the issues of student rights, racism, and the Vietnam War were more widespread that year than in any year prior to 1968. The main causes of this dramatic escalation in protest activity were the inspiration of the LSE protests and the student movements in France and America, the strength of the Vietnam Solidarity Campaign, the national debates over immigration, racism, and higher education reform, and the increasing strength of socialist students, especially those in the newly formed RSSF.

Opposition to the Vietnam War may have temporarily united British students with their counterparts elsewhere in the world, but this issue was always secondary to others in the largest British student protests. The VSC marches of 1967 and 1968 were sensational, enormous in size, and inspirational, but in the end, students did not sponsor them, and students only consisted of about half of the participants, so they can hardly be called student protests. In this way, the VSC protests were similar to the Aldermaston marches and the Suez demonstration in the late fifties and early sixties: they may have inspired local student activism, but they did not directly result in occupations and other large-scale activism at universities. The Vietnam issue was definitely an important part of the British student movement and many student activists, especially those on the Left, were concerned about this issue for a variety of reasons, but it hardly made sense for most students to protest this issue at British universities. After all, most administrators and staff agreed that US intervention in Vietnam was a bad idea, and even if they disagreed with students, British universities could not affect US decisions in Vietnam. Even the British government felt that its hands were tied in terms of advising the US in its operation of that war. It was a great moral issue to unite the global student generation of 1968, but it was not a central focus of the British student movement.

Far more important to the British student movement in 1968 was the issue of university reform. British students had been told that modernizing their university system was of the highest national importance. When they encountered outdated hierarchical structures and disciplinary regulations, they thus felt justified in demanding reform. The NUS, together with the RSA and the RSSF all supported this effort, as did the majority of the student population. The RSA and even more so, the RSSF and most of the local socialist student societies may have used this issue merely to attract more students to the socialist cause, but it is evident that each of these organizations did indeed prioritize university and student rights issues. All saw university reform as an issue that could truly unite the student population in direct action because it seemed to be such a rational and practical demand. Even the government and university authorities could not help but approve of students' desire to improve the system of higher education, though they may have disagreed with the students' methods and specific demands. Within the national discourse of modernization, therefore, university reform was seen as the most practical thing for students to demand.

Another difference between the protests of 1968 and those of earlier periods was the unusually active role played by university staff. In most cases, a minority of faculty were sympathetic and supportive of student activism, providing legal advice as well as encouraging deeper analysis of the issues. Most often it was younger staff, often influenced by the New Left, who prodded their students into thinking more deeply about the wider social, economic, and political system. At the LSE and Essex, young faculty such as Robin Blackburn, Michael Freeman, and Paul Thompson played an active role in leading the protests and negotiating with the administration and rest of the staff. Perhaps this was because at these two universities in particular, young staff were recruited in the belief that they would help to make their respective institutions role models of progress and modernization. They themselves were frustrated with the perceived conservatism of the rest of the staff and particularly the administration. Those staff that actively supported the student movement often faced the worst consequences in the aftermath of protests. The sacking of Robin Blackburn and Nick Bateson at the LSE, Dick Atkinson at Birmingham University, and dozens of staff at art colleges sent a strong warning to staff and students that administrators would use every tool at their disposal to retain control over the universities. This is not to detract from the most important role played by students themselves in thinking and discussing the issues, as well as strategizing and organizing the protests, but university staff did in fact facilitate the protests of 1968.

University administrators were primarily concerned about activists besmirching the university's reputation and disrupting its normal functions. They often called in police for prolonged or destructive occupations, but this action was legally questionable. Protesters were not technically trespassing or breaking laws if they were enrolled students and used their occupations to learn in teach-ins or free university settings. After all, this was the purpose of education and the ideal of active learning. Only if students damaged facilities or attacked persons, which rarely happened, could the police legitimately intervene. In terms of public demonstrations, students claimed a legal right to use public places for protest, something that the government hesitated to deny because of Britain's traditions of political freedom. As long as the marchers obeyed the signals and commands of police, they could take no legal action. However, if marchers disobeyed traffic signals or the police, or even made threats to do so, they could be arrested for a variety of offences. Police did take what action they could to limit the effects of protests on the lives of non-protesters in a variety of ways. There is little evidence of extensive police or Special Branch attention to local socialist societies and activists, but they did closely monitor Tariq Ali and the VSC, fearing that they might become more violent and disruptive like their counterparts in Germany, Japan, and America. Unlike these other countries, however, the British government almost never banned protests and did not pre-emptively arrest VSC leaders. This restraint did indeed help to reduce the violence of British protests in comparison to other countries, and prevent them from escalating into larger, more violent protests like those in the French May or Chicago Democratic Convention.

Protests in France and America in the spring of 1968 led to much debate over revolutionary theory among socialist students and intellectuals and attempts to create a revolutionary student movement in Britain. In Britain, the RSSF briefly became the primary activist organization of the student movement, but it fractured amidst ideological disagreements. The RSSF, however, was successful in getting revolutionary socialist and New Left rhetoric introduced to the wider student movement through their considerable influence over local Socialist Societies that were at the heart of most local protests in this period. Influenced by the New Left, socialist students demanded equal student participation on important university decision-making bodies, student control over university finances and curriculum, and a complete reform of the system of higher education as a first step towards making their nation more supportive of socialism. Through student newspapers and participation on strike committees and student unions, RSSF supporters in Socialist Societies succeeded in making their ideology and strategies well-known to the student movement. Socialist students, however, vehemently disagreed with each other. While the New Left continued to play an important role in encouraging student activism and providing it with ideological and rhetorical strategies, "Old Left" organizations such as the Communist Party, International Socialists, and the International Marxist Group made a determined effort to attract student activists and direct the student movement towards their own goals of working-class power and socialist revolution. These ideological differences strengthened the student movement's theoretical grounding, but weakened its ability to present a united front in many protests.

Similar to students at Columbia, Chicago, and Paris, British socialist students tried to make the student movement more provocative and confrontational in 1968 as well. Learning from Carmichael, Dutschke, and Debord, radical students argued that unless they provoked the authorities with extreme behavior, they would be ignored by both the authorities and the press, and their protest would fail. Provocation not only forced authorities to react, it often succeeded in recruiting more participants to the movement by getting free publicity in the press as well as gaining sympathy. Another reason for the shift in strategy was the apparent failure of more moderate, polite protests to win any significant victories for the movement. While authorities agreed to make relatively minor concessions, such as allowing minority student representation on low-level university committees, socialist students wanted more from their government and universities and they refused to accept these minor reforms. These radical students were willing to be more confrontational—to shout down or throw paint or mustard powder at speakers they perceived as immoral—to force authorities to take them more seriously.

Although these provocative strategies did indeed attract more attention from both the authorities and the press, this attention was overwhelmingly negative. These new strategies seemed to confirm popular stereotypes of the student movement as disrespectful, immature and irrationally violent, and made it easier to label it as criminal and therefore more easily repress it. Provocative strategies also widened the divisions within the student movement between those who still wanted to take the moral high ground and maintain a respectable appearance, and those who were willing to sacrifice this identity in the hopes of finally forcing the authorities to make the desired changes. Moderate, non-socialist students still dominated on most campuses, with individual socialist student societies typically numbering less than 100 members. National revolutionary socialist organizations ranged in membership from forty in the IMG to over a thousand in the Communist Party.[189] Perhaps another 1,000 students, who did not officially join a radical organization but were very interested in social, economic, and political theory, would have read radical theories, understood them, and been able to apply them to their own personal and university contexts. Most students, however, had neither the time nor the inclination to become highly knowledgeable about revolutionary theories. They encountered these ideas through leaflets at demonstrations, or through speeches and discussions, but these would necessarily amount to only a surface knowledge of the theories—enough to help them to grasp the complexity of the systems they dealt with and the depth of the problems, and perhaps even to convince them that student-led socialism was the solution to their problems, but not enough to make them devoted disciples of New or Old Left theories. Socialist students did make their ideologies known to the student body, but failed to gain the strong support they needed from their colleagues and there were ominous signs of a mounting backlash against their provocative strategies on the horizon.

The British student movement of 1968 was clearly much more complex than was portrayed in the mass media of the period or in the scholarly literature published afterwards. It was similar to its counterparts in other countries in many ways, including some massive national demonstration marches and widespread university occupations. It was, however, less violent and more focused on university reform because of its unique national context. British students interacted extensively with the global student movement, but they were always more concerned about expressing moral and political dissent in ways that spoke to their unique national context. They appealed to reason and widely accepted discourses of modernization and democratization, typically requesting modest, practical reforms. Far from the media-generated image of the British student movement as imitative, immature, and foreign-led, it was a rational and practical response to the local, national, and global contexts of the time. Nineteen-sixty-eight was magical, not in that it was just entertainment or an illusion, but rather in that all of these forces came together in an outpouring of earnest student dissent never before seen in the British Isles.

4   The Transformation of the Student Movement

Shortly after 8 p.m. on Wednesday 11 February 1970, Edward Palmer Thompson received a phone call from one of his students. A founder of the first New Left, Thompson had taken a position as a Reader in the Centre for the Study of Social History at Warwick University in 1965 to teach non-traditional students in an innovative program. Thompson's popularity with history students had skyrocketed with his ground-breaking *The Making of the English Working Class* (1963). With his piercing blue eyes and wild shock of prematurely graying hair, Thompson's passion, fairness, and willingness to listen and learn from students had quickly made him a favorite amongst Warwick's left-leaning students. Thompson, however, had never had much hope in the student movement. He was offended at the thought of students ordering staff and administrators to do their will, but he had always treated students with respect and expected the same of them. He was surprised, therefore, to receive a telephone call from a student activist who was in the process of occupying the university Registry office.[1]

The student sounded agitated. His comrades had been bored and had begun looking for something to read in an unlocked file drawer. They had found a file marked "Student-University Relations" and began reading. They soon came across a confidential letter from Gilbert Hunt, the Manager of Rootes Motors and chair of Warwick University's Building Committee, to Warwick's Vice Chancellor Jack Butterworth. Apparently, Hunt had asked an employee to spy on a meeting of the Coventry Labour Party that was addressed by David Montgomery, a visiting lecturer in Thompson's Social History Center. The spy had made some derogatory comments about Montgomery and the small audience, which included a Warwick student and several employees of Rootes Motors. He had concluded that there was not enough evidence in the discussion to prosecute Montgomery under the 1919 Aliens Restriction Act. Since Montgomery had come to Warwick at Thompson's invitation, the student felt that Thompson would want to know about this letter. Thompson was indeed alarmed and angered at what sounded like a case of an employer spying and keeping secret political files on his workers. This letter seemed to be proof of the collusion between Warwick University administrators and local industrialists in deceitful, if not illegal, activities. He rushed over to the Registry and asked the students for the letter so that he could reproduce and distribute it to the staff the next day. Thus began the Warwick files affair, the most prominent student protest of 1970.[2]

The original occupation at Warwick had actually begun as a simple demand for a building where staff, students, and the surrounding community could socialize together. Students felt that this would build community feeling at Warwick which was sorely lacking. Students had been petitioning the Building Committee for three years with no results. When four student representatives met with the Building Committee on 2 February 1970, its chairman Gilbert Hunt told them that "he was offended by the wording of the motion, which reminded him of the type of demands put forward by the unions at Rootes in Coventry."[3] He sent them away so that his committee could discuss the demands in private. That evening, the Student Union executive decided to hold a twenty-four hour sit-in to show them that the students were serious in their demands, but the Socialist Society felt that they should wait on the decision of the Building Committee. At a Union meeting the next day, 400 students voted overwhelmingly in favor of a sit-in. That sit-in was extremely well-organized and orderly. Three hundred students went to the Registry, ordered food from a wholesaler in Coventry, sent out a press statement, established a security committee, and sat down in empty carpeted offices. Secretarial staff and administrators continued to work uninterrupted and left at the end of the day. Students left exactly twenty-four hours after they began the sit-in, even cleaning the building before they left.

If the Building Committee had made even minor concessions, perhaps the conflict would have ended then, but like so many other university protests in the Long Sixties the administration instead provoked an escalation of protest. Six days after the sit-in, the administration charged eight of the nine members of the sit-in committee with disorderly conduct for breaking into the Registry. Four of these students were not even there when the break-in occurred. On 11 February, the Building Committee announced that it would not grant the students' wish for a new building, but that the University would not proceed with prosecuting the eight students. At a meeting later that day, the Student Union decided to reoccupy the Registry indefinitely in support of their building demands. This time, they asked the secretarial staff to leave with their offices unlocked, so that students could sleep on their warm, carpeted floors. The Assistant Vice Chancellor then met with three members of the Sit-In Committee and told them that he would leave all of the offices open as long as they agreed that no damage would occur. They readily accepted this offer and settled in for the sit-in. As some of the students began leaving for lectures, others replaced them. All was relatively unexciting until the files were discovered.[4]

After the files were found, however, the entire nature of the protest changed. Students were stunned and angry, and quickly decided to make a full search of all of the files to see if there was further evidence of political spying on students and staff. They would uphold their agreement with the Assistant Vice Chancellor by being careful not to damage anything and to put all of the materials back in the right files in the right locations. As dozens of students systematically plumbed through the files, they photocopied relevant evidence and replaced the originals, carefully protecting personal information. All night and over the next days, "assiduously they read page after page of correspondence, reports, minutes."[5] Anna Davin, a mature student in the history program, recalls that this research exposed the bureaucracy that they had already mistrusted.[6] Biting personal comments on everything from student looks, to their political behavior, and their mental health poured forth from their school teachers, university staff, and administrators, painting a new picture of the entire educational system more sinister than any of the students had ever imagined.[7]

When the staff read the documents that Thompson had distributed, many of them were also deeply offended and angered by the information that their employer had kept in their own personal files. The French Department was the first to react by coming out on strike against the keeping of political files on staff and students. Then students and staff in other departments held meetings to discuss their course of action. As Thompson recalled, "The atmosphere in these joint staff-student meetings was intense; motions were passed calling on the University to destroy its political files, to institute a public inquiry—some even called on Vice Chancellor Butterworth to resign."[8] Over a thousand staff and students all met together for the first time on 12 February to discuss the issue and decide on a course of action. More documents were read to the crowd. Thompson called on "the academic community to reassert themselves, and warned of the dangers of an indiscriminate wave of repression emanating from the Administration."[9] The meeting then voted to end the sit-in and reconsider their tactics. The students at the Registry, however, wanted to continue the sit-in. At another large meeting outside the Registry in the snow, a narrow majority extended the occupation until the next day, when the protesters finished their search of the files and left the building at 9 a.m.

Meanwhile, the administration had been busily denying the allegations of political spying, and repeated its claim that it kept no political files on students and staff. When it heard that students were planning to publish many of the documents they found in the files, they went to the magistrate and succeeded in getting an injunction against them, ordering the students to leave the Registry by 9 a.m. on 13 February, surrender the files and all copies, and restrain themselves from disclosing their contents. At 11:30 p.m. on 12 February, while the students were finishing their occupation of the Registry, administrators announced the injunction over a loud-hailer outside the building, and handed out copies of the injunction to all the students. From the administration's perspective, students had no right to break into confidential files and violate the privacy of the staff, students, and administrators. The administration felt it had an obligation to retain all communications with the university, especially letters of recommendation from former teachers and dons, as well as the comments and requests of the university's industrial benefactors. To them, the injunction seemed a fair and logical legal response.

To students and staff, however, the injunction was just one more piece of evidence against the administration, seemingly another attempt to cover up the existence of the political files. Another meeting of 1,200 students and staff on 13 February called for what they thought was the most sensible solution: an independent public inquiry into the whole administration of the university. Although a subsequent ad-hoc staff meeting did not support the call for a public inquiry, it opposed the keeping of political records. After an all-day meeting the next day, the Senate (which was chaired by the Vice Chancellor and included representatives of the various sections of the university) issued a statement supporting the injunction and disciplinary action against the students, but invited the University's Chancellor Viscount Radcliffe to conduct an inquiry into the political files issue.[10]

Meanwhile, over the weekend several students had secretly made a twenty-page dossier of some of the political files and distributed copies of the dossier to all the staff and students, as well as a number of newspapers around the country. Davin was one of the few activists who had a car, so she drove a group of students to London to have the photocopying done there in secret, and then drove around to deliver the dossiers to newspapers by hand. She recalls that they "had a great sense of being on the run and people pursuing us which was a lot of fun. Kind of spy story stuff."[11] She later asserted:

> We wanted people to know what was going on and that we weren't just irresponsible students. They were real issues that we were rightly angry about, and we could prove them and we therefore didn't want to submit to the injunction because then we couldn't prove them. So it was partly defending ourselves, and partly fuelling the campaign to get rid of Butterworth which we saw as the only way of making real change.[12]

This sense of defending themselves against hostile and repressive authorities would continue to fuel the students and staff at Warwick for months afterwards.

By the time the students and staff arrived at another huge meeting on Monday, everyone had seen the dossier. At that meeting the entire Senate arrived and finally met face-to-face with the irate academic community. Despite the Senate's explanations, students and staff remained unconvinced and several departments called for the Vice Chancellor's suspension. The next day, Radcliffe began his investigation by asking for evidence from staff and students. Although they appreciated this first step, they distrusted Radcliffe's insistence on maintaining the complete secrecy of his proceedings.

Students and staff continued to call for Butterworth's resignation, an end to political spying on staff and students, a public investigation into the administration of the University, and their original demand—a new community building.[13]

The scandal of the Warwick political files was broadcast to the nation as one newspaper after another began publishing parts of the dossier and discussing the events. Students at other universities invited Warwick's activists to speak to them about issues surrounding the political files. In March, Warwick students began a mass lobby of Parliament to draw government attention to their case. Fifty Labour and Liberal MPs responded by supporting a motion calling for a public inquiry into the matter. Students and staff additionally began working on a new democratic charter for the University, totally restructuring its decision-making system and reasserting the "ideals of academic excellence and the pursuit of knowledge" over the interference and needs of business.[14]

Radcliffe's report was released in May. Although it exonerated the Vice Chancellor, it proposed changing the structure of the University's government and destroying all non-academic material in student and staff files. Dissatisfied, the university again assembled in June to call for Butterworth's resignation. At the end of the term, students occupied the Student Union building and held an Open University. For one week, they held public lectures and seminars to discuss the issues of higher education reform, labor rights, student rights, political repression, and all sorts of other related topics. The protest ended at that point, but many students and staff remained unhappy with the outcome. Butterworth remained, E. P. Thompson resigned, and the students moved on with their lives. In retrospect, this protest may seem to be "much ado about nothing," but at the time it had a tremendous impact on the student movement and reflected the climate of backlash which was emerging at the end of the sixties.

THE LOCAL CONTEXT OF THE WARWICK FILES PROTESTS

The background history of Warwick University is essential to understanding students' reactions to the political files as well as the wider significance of their protest. Warwick was the product of the Second World War like no other university in the country. The beautiful medieval town of Coventry had been almost completely destroyed during the war and as it rebuilt in the years afterwards, the citizens of Coventry wanted a university as a symbol of their community spirit and pride. Coventry City Council worked long and hard to get the funding for the university and was rewarded when the Macmillan government began investing in the expansion of the university system. To convince the County Council of Warwickshire to help fund the university, Coventry agreed to call their new institution Warwick University. Once the University Grants Committee awarded them the funding, it appointed an Academic Planning Board for the new university, effectively eliminating Coventry Council control. This Board then appointed J. B. Butterworth to be the Vice Chancellor and he largely determined the form that the university would take. Similar to Vice Chancellor Sloman at Essex, Butterworth envisioned a large University with up to 25,000 students, which would be cutting edge in its contributions to industrial technology and business. He therefore began working closely with local industrial leaders not only to shape the university according to their needs, but also to secure additional funding. Despite the wishes of Coventry Council, Butterworth and his advisors decided on a location three miles outside the city and had no plans to ever make it integrated within that city's community.[15]

The first 450 students arrived at Warwick University in 1965. The only part of the university that was built at this point was the East Side, which housed a library and a few buildings, with no provision for student housing. Over the next few years, new buildings went up, but many of these were more than a half-mile's walk away, spread out to accommodate future expansion. By 1970, the student population had grown to 1,800 with about 800 living in university housing.[16] Anna Davin arrived at Warwick in 1965 and remembers it as a small, but close-knit community. Building sites continued to go up throughout the late sixties, but the buildings were "fairly ugly." Down a path from the administration buildings through some woods was the Students' Union in Rootes Hall. It was the main meeting space for students, with a cafeteria and bar, but it was very modern and plain, so they called it "the airport lounge."[17] As the university grew more spread out, it became more alienating and isolated from the Coventry community.

Davin would continue on as a student at Warwick University from 1965 through the political files protests in the spring of 1970 and as such, joins E. P. Thompson as an excellent eyewitness to the long-term context of those protests. Davin was twenty-five when she arrived at Warwick and was already the wife of one of Warwick's math lecturers, Luke Hodgkin, and mother of three small children. She had gone on CND marches and was a Labour supporter, but Hodgkin was a supporter of the New Left. Davin remembers the history department as particularly progressive, partly as a result of staff like Thompson, but also partly because it had a strong exchange program with American universities. All of Warwick's forty history students would go to universities in the US for the first term of their second year, and forty American students would take their place at Warwick University. Berkeley and Wisconsin had additional exchange programs with the history department, sending two students each for a whole year, in exchange for six British students for one term. Davin recalls that many American students joined the Warwick Socialist Society and that "in political terms they did have an important influence on us."[18]

Davin became the secretary of the Socialist Society in her second year and in addition to the Americans, she felt that Thompson's graduate students and history undergraduates were particularly important in it. When an International

Socialist clique took it over the next year, however, she disagreed with their strategy of focusing on leafleting factory gates to radicalize workers. She felt that as outsiders, students could never be very effective in relating to workers. Other students in the group associated with the Communist Party and the International Marxist Group also disagreed with the IS leadership.[19] Although they discussed issues of university reform, racism, and the Vietnam War, they remained divided and took no significant protest action.

Warwick's Student Union, however, would lead the way towards supporting the wider student movement. In January 1969, the Student Union voted to occupy the library to express solidarity with the ongoing LSE student occupation. Vice Chancellor Butterworth visited the offupcation to find out why so many students were joining it and he was allowed to mingle around talking to various students until 11 p.m., when students asked him to leave so that they could start their meeting. He was "very cross," but left nonetheless. After twenty-four hours, they "tidied it all up" and left the building.[20] As this was the only significant protest prior to the political files incident, obviously the high proportion of leftists on staff and high proportion of American students did not in itself lead to student protest at Warwick.

The long-term local causes of the 1970 protest were instead the overall atmosphere of promises broken, of expectations denied, and of mistrust between students and the administration. Students had been told that their university would be a model of progress and integration with the local community of Coventry, but they discovered that the University had no adequate facilities for students, staff, and community interactions, only had good relations with industrial owners, and had virtually no contact with the rest of the community in Coventry. This long-term dissatisfaction was the cause of the original sit-in demanding the building of the long-delayed social facilities. If no files had been read, perhaps this issue would have remained the focal point of the Warwick student movement, but the discovery of political files triggered a student reaction that was based more upon the immediate national and international climate of 1969 and 1970. Repression of student movements around the world, a right-wing backlash amongst British politicians, media and public, and a consequent sense of persecution within the British student movement led Warwick students to immediately interpret the files within a broader framework of repression and to conclude that the files proved that this political repression was in fact real, and a serious moral and legal problem.

The secret files protest at Warwick touched off a wave of similar protests at universities across the nation in 1970. These protests were distinct from the protests of earlier years in that they were much more coordinated and united around similar issues. For the first time, a newly politicized National Union of Students played a major role in fomenting and coordinating this wave of protests, using its connections with student unions and funding to support the political files protests across the nation that year. The NUS also reflected the student movement's continued evolution away from New Left tactics and ideology towards those of the Stalinist and Trotskyist Left. A minority of radical students continued to use the strategy of provocation developed in 1968, while others began to invest more energy into forging an alliance with the working class. Those in the movement continued to perceive themselves as taking the moral high road, but were increasingly willing to defy court injunctions and use civil disobedience to attain their goals. The Warwick files protest, together with hundreds of small and large protests across the nation in 1969–70 illustrate the continued strength of Britain's student movement after 1968 and reveal useful perspective on the changes taking place across the nation and within the national and trans-national student movement.

THE AFTERMATH OF 1968

Although many scholars of the sixties highlight 1968 as the zenith of student movements in the sixties, the 1969–70 academic year actually saw an increase in student activism in many countries, sometimes as a direct result of the events of 1968. In reaction to the sense of crisis provoked by the massive protests of 1968, many governments began a concerted attack against radical student groups and leading protesters, harassing, imprisoning, and expelling them from universities. In Britain, Conservative politicians and social commentators called for a crackdown on protesters and student disruptions. This global and national backlash would make the Warwick political files seem to be part of this larger political attack on the student movement, fueling student distrust of authorities and forcing staff to take sides.

In the United States, public reaction against the student protests of 1968 contributed to the election of Republican Richard Nixon on the platform of restoring "law and order" to a nation wracked by student and race riots. Nixon not only unleashed a full-scale assault on New Left organizations, including the SDS, but also widened the war in Southeast Asia to achieve "peace with honor." This led to an increased sense of persecution and isolation amongst most student activists in the SDS and a dramatic increase in student protest against the war. In this climate, the already fractured SDS permanently split and descended into chaos and, in some cases, revolutionary violence. One faction attempted to forge an alliance with the working class by supporting labor strikes, but most labor unions had no interest in supporting the student movement, which it felt was unpatriotic and communist-inspired. Another smaller faction, called Weatherman, gave up their student careers, formed revolutionary collectives of three to four members, and went underground to use symbolic violence to provoke a socialist revolution. Both factions, which were far removed from the majority of student activists in local chapters across the nation, quickly lost any student support they once had and disappeared in the next few years.[21]

The United States National Student Association (NSA) stepped into the leadership vacuum and attempted to coordinate the national student movement through its connections to local student associations. Although the NSA had become politicized by leftists in its leadership in 1968, it was never as radical as the SDS. Progressive NSA leaders, however, forged ahead with a program of leading student activism against the draft, harsh drug laws, and paternalistic university regulations, and in support of student power, black power, and women's rights.[22] Their largest action was the coordination of student protests against the invasion of Cambodia and the National Guard murder of four students at Kent State University in April and May of 1970. An estimated four million students at 1,300 universities and colleges (44 per cent of the nation's total) protested the war in Southeast Asia and the murder of their fellow students, closing many universities in the process.[23] This represented an enormous escalation of anti-war protest from 1968–69, when only 10.8 per cent of American campuses reported anti-war actions.[24] Similar to 1968, the mass media spread its own narrative of an American student movement under attack and in decline to the rest of the world, feeding students' sense of global persecution.

The student movements in Japan and continental Europe generally reflected the trends of the American student movement. These student movements fragmented after their high points in 1968–69, but continued to participate in reform efforts, including women's liberation and workers' rights. Italian and French students especially focused on building student support for workers' actions, which sought participatory democracy in their work-places. Drawing on nineteenth-century syndicalist and utopian socialist ideas about self-management in the work force and to a smaller extent on the New Left's emphasis on personal liberation, workers strikes in Europe and the US escalated dramatically at the end of the decade. Worker unrest thus contributed to the sense of global crisis as the sixties drew to a close.[25]

While some students took up new issues, such as feminism and workers' rights, small numbers of French, German, Italian, and Japanese students, turned away from mainstream student activism, dropped out of their universities, and descended into the world of international terrorism in their continued attempt to provoke revolutionary change. The *Nouvelle Resistance Populaire* in France, the Baader-Meinhof Gang (also called the Red Army Faction) in West Germany, the Italian Red Brigade, and the Japanese Red Army were the equivalents of the American Weatherman, and they too were completely divorced from the bulk of student activists and the working class they sought to lead. In 1969–70, however, they would contribute to a growing global sense of crisis and a right-wing backlash.[26]

The British student movement similarly changed directions in the aftermath of 1968 as it faced a national political climate of increased polarization between the forces of liberalism and reform and those of reaction and fear. Negative media framing of the student movement, together with a growing public outcry against student protests, pressured the Wilson government and university administrators to crack down on the student movement. The government and universities, however, seemed to only appease students in 1969 and 1970. This factor, together with escalating wild-cat workers' strikes and economic troubles, opened the door for Conservatives led by Edward Heath to mount a strong attack against the Labour government, culminating in a Conservative victory in the 1970 General Election. The student movement then became the center point of a heated national debate over the limits of "permissive" reforms and the legitimacy of student protest. This debate would have a dramatic impact upon the course the student movement over the next five years, helping to create the climate of repression and mistrust which fed the Warwick political files protest of 1970.

Essential to this climate of fear, repression, and mistrust was the mass media coverage of the student protests of 1968. The media was a double-edged sword for the British student movement. Students actively sought to use to the press to publicize their protests, not only to have a larger impact on the public and pressure the government, but also to attract larger numbers of participants, but the press presented a misleading image of the British student movement. Similar to the press in the United States and West Germany, the British press portrayed the student movement as led by a minority of foreign or subversive radicals, focusing on the most radical and sensational aspects of the protests, rather than assessing the movement as a whole. The national media generally either trivialized or demonized protesters. They were "just a pack of students" and thus so privileged as to make any unity with the working class inconceivable, or they were "vicious reds, undermining Queen, country, democracy and anything else that morning's leader chose to include."[27]

This negative stereotyping of the student movement was nothing new. As Tony Aldgate's study of press coverage of hunger marches and fascist demonstrations in the 1930s indicates, the British media had always framed protest movements as an issue of law and order, of hooligan dissenters versus the calm and courageous defenders of law and order.[28] There are a number of reasons for this. Firstly, social movements are notoriously diverse, especially when they have no central organization to speak for the movement as a whole. The diversity and lack of organization within the student movement made it more difficult for journalists and later scholars to make generalizations about the movement as a whole. It was, therefore, easier to just select interesting participants to interview who could confirm whatever story journalists wanted to tell. Like many decentralized social movements, the student movement as a whole had no designated leaders. Most student protesters rarely had the time or inclination to formally elect leaders. Indeed, many New Leftist activists insisted on remaining leaderless in support of the participatory democracy ideal, which emphasized consensual decision-making as opposed to representative democracy. Student leaders, however, emerged regardless of this intent, whether through out-spoken students taking the initiative or through journalists selecting students to act as representatives for their movement. Partially because of the lack of organization and true leaders or representatives of the student movement, therefore, student perspectives appeared in media as contradictory, extreme, and confusing. Out of this jumble of information, the issues and demands could be easily obscured or misunderstood.

Stuart Hall explored political motives as the reasons why journalists and university and government authorities increasingly chose to depict student protesters as "criminals" after 1968, rather than as a diverse political and social reform movement. In his study of the moral panic of the early 1970s, *Policing the Crisis* (1978), Hall argued that the press and state intentionally reframed the political issues posed by the student movement as a non-political problem of hooliganism.[29] By labeling student protesters as "hooligans," they in effect criminalized student activists and depoliticized their movement. This discredited the student movement, justified taking legal action against protesters, led to increasing arrests, and effectively neutralized a movement that was growing in strength and threatening those in power. Hall concluded that 1968 was a "year of remarkable cataclysm," not because of any particular protest action, but because it was the year that the state began to fight back against the student movement in earnest and the press created the beginnings of a moral panic which would eventually sweep the forces of reaction and authoritarianism into power in the 1970s.[30]

Evidence of the public backlash which began that moral panic is readily available in the mainstream newspapers of 1968 and 1969. Already in March of 1968, a *Sunday Telegraph* editorial claimed that the general adult reaction to the student protests was "one of almost vindictive hostility . . . the waste of public money, the insult to the name of education, the ingratitude, the cheek, the damnable distraction of all this politics."[31] A 1968 gallop poll indicated that only fifteen per cent of the working class sympathized with student grievances about the universities.[32] Following the protests of 1968, an editorial in a local North London newspaper, the *Wood Green, Southgate and Palmers Green Weekly Herald* illustrated another common reaction to the student movements:

> . . . a bunch of crackpots, here in Haringey, or in Grosvenor Square, or Paris, or Berlin, or Mexico, can never overthrow an established system . . . They may dislike having to conform to a system in which they are required to study, and follow set programs, and take examinations or their equivalents; and acknowledge that in doing so they are through the indulgence of others, preparing themselves for a lifetime of learning . . . The system is ours. We are the ordinary people, the nine-to-five, Monday-to-Friday-semi-detached, suburban wage-earners, who are the system. We are not victims of it. We are not slaves to it. We are it,

and we like it. Does any bunch of twopenny-halfpenny kids think they can turn us upside down? They'll learn.[33]

One can understand how this perception of students as irrationally rebellious kids might be a natural reaction of older tax-payers, who had little understanding of or sympathy for the protests and thus reacted negatively to the student movement. Perhaps adults would have viewed students this way even if they knew first-hand why students were protesting, but the repeated negative stereotypes created and perpetuated in the media must have played at least some role in creating this reaction, not only by ignoring the real issues behind the protests, but also in sensationalizing their most offensive elements.

By 1968 most student activists were at least wary of news reporters from the mainstream "Establishment" press, and some radicals barred them from their meetings. Discussing reports that David Triesman was the mastermind behind the Essex revolt, Essex student Louise Lemkov asserted that "through the creation of such myths, the idea of an hierarchy is perpetuated. If the mass-media is faced with a movement which is not overtly hierarchical, reporters attempt to weed out the 'prominent figures,' then allot them the role of leaders." By focusing on leaders, the press overlooked the most important aspects of the protest movements and neglected meaningful discussion of the problems raised by dissident groups. Lemkov concluded that because it reduced the significance of protest, "the mass media is the enemy of protest."[34] Other Essex students were also sensitive to the biased news coverage of events at their university. In 1968 and 1969, their student newspaper repeatedly condemned national press coverage of Essex students for its distorted image of their university as full of radicals and drug-takers.[35]

The latter issue hints at how the media and public image of students was increasingly conjoined with that of youth in general, lumping working class football hooliganism and the middle and upper class hippie counterculture together with the student movement in the late sixties. Many youth were indeed swept-up by the blossoming counterculture of the late sixties. This counterculture was heavily influenced by transatlantic clothing, music, and lifestyle fashions. Similar to the United States, 1969 was a fantastic year for large-scale music festivals in Britain. While Americans attended Woodstock and other music festivals, British youth packed the free rock shows put on by Pink Floyd, Blind Faith, and the Rolling Stones in Hyde Park, and the massive Isle of Wight festivals. The counterculture's more commercial aspects, including fashion and music, were absorbed into mainstream culture after 1968 and its alternative meanings were largely lost. Psychedelic artwork appeared in mainstream and student newspapers, while major department stores began selling clothes based on hippie fashions. Recreational drug use and rock music spread to the wider population, beyond the boundaries of the youth culture. Many students reflected these larger cultural trends, but despite the popularity of countercultural fashions and the ideology of personal liberation, countercultural issues were rarely even mentioned in the student protests.

The growth of the counterculture, however, did spur a national debate which linked the counterculture and student movement with youth culture and permissiveness in general. Conservative social critics, such as Mary Whitehouse and her National Viewers' and Listeners Association, grew increasingly vocal in their dissent against the pervasive influence of the counterculture and what they saw as the corrosive permissiveness undermining the moral fiber of the nation. They had long opposed Labour's liberal social reforms and argued that, together with the invasion of cultural influences from America, they had inspired a wave of permissiveness amongst the nation's youth which had led to increasing crime rates, drug use, sexual promiscuity, and violence in student protests. Although a small minority, social conservatives received an increasingly sympathetic audience from a public which was already alarmed by the escalating student protests and the increased coverage of violent crimes such as the 1969 trial of the notorious Kray brothers.[36]

Escalating tensions in North Ireland seemed to confirm that the nation was under attack and that Labour was either unwilling or unable to defend it. Over the spring and summer of 1969, the peaceful civil rights protests there had developed into sectarian riots with Catholic communities raising the barricades against their Protestant neighbors and their police. The Wilson government felt forced to send in British troops to quell the violence, but the situation continued to deteriorate. The conflict defied the simplistic analysis of the RSSF and other socialist groups, leaving British students uncertain as to how to react. A number of student unions and the RSSF declared their support for non-violent Catholic protesters, but did little more. Northern Irish students in the People's Democracy continued to try to unite the working class in support of a non-sectarian government, but they could not stop the escalating sectarian violence. Bernadette Devlin did her best, even winning a seat in Parliament and manning the barricades in the Irish communities, but she was convicted of incitement to riot in 1969 and began six months of prison in June 1970, effectively removing her from the movement for a time and destroying her hopes of finishing her university degree.[37] The Northern Ireland question would plague the United Kingdom for decades, but in early 1970, it seemed as though new government strategies were necessary to stop the violence before it engulfed the nation.

Contributing greatly to the public's growing sense of crisis at the end of the sixties were the bomb explosions that began in earnest in 1969. The first wave of bomb explosions was directed against the Bank of Spain and its affiliates in London and Liverpool in February and March of that year. A Spanish anarchist group, the International First of May Group, claimed responsibility for these bombs, but soon afterwards, this bombing campaign blended in the public mind with other attacks, including the fire-bombing of Duncan Sandys' home, the Ulster Office in Saville Row, and the American embassy.[38] When no group claimed responsibility for the latter bomb attacks, the press speculated wildly, often implying that somehow the student movement was responsible for these attacks. The next year, the police would blame the Angry Brigade for these attacks and the press would directly link them to the student movement, but in 1969–70, these bombings contributed to a growing public panic over disorder and violence.

In the midst of this national debate over the meaning of these violent attacks and the student protests of 1968, dozens of articles and books were published dissecting the student movement in Britain and elsewhere. Students, educators, administrators, the New Left, and the Old Left all joined journalists, social critics, and politicians in discerning the true meaning of the student movement and its implications for the nation. Students and the Left unsurprisingly came out in support of the student movement, while administrators and staff were divided over what to do about student protests.

Conservative staff largely reflected the views expressed by critics of the student movement in the press and government. One of the most outspoken conservative critics of the student movement was Oxford history Fellow Max Beloff. He published several essays on the student movement in the late sixties and early seventies, and was frequently quoted in press coverage. He believed that students were unfit to make decisions for themselves, much less their universities or society. He compared students who shouted down speakers and let ideology overtake academic freedom to Nazis and fascists. He argued that universities must stop student rebels at all costs: "what the university authorities need is an injection of nerve, and unswerving support from those who pay the bill."[39] Most academics agreed that extremist students who disrupted the functioning of the university were intolerable and dangerous, but many supported student demands for representation in university decision-making.

Conservative former minister of education Edward Boyle, for example, was sympathetic to idealistic students who tried to apply "what they have been taught about justice, about fair play, or about the principles of Christian behavior" in their demands, and he supported student consultation on university decisions which affected them. But he also asserted that "what is intolerable is when a small minority within a university try to disrupt the ordered life of a staff-student community," and called them destructive anarchists who must be stopped.[40] Similar to government authorities, university staff and administrators were used to holding considerable authority over students. They would naturally feel at least some discomfort when students challenged this authority, either politely when they requested representation on university committees, or rudely when they sat down in their offices and physically asserted control over university spaces.

Liberal and moderate students reflected this mixed view of the student movement. The liberal perspective on the student movement was best expressed in a series of essays in *Anarchy and Culture: The Problem of the Contemporary Culture* (1969). Geoffrey Martin, an ex-president of the NUS, presented this perspective in his essay, "Organizational forms and styles of protest." He argued that the issues of the student movement were very real and important. Idealistic students had mounted a number of campaigns to reform their universities and create a more just, peaceful world over the past several years, but had been consistently frustrated by their failure to enact any real changes. This had led some to turn to more extremist groups and tactics, bordering on anarchy. He explained that extremist students took control of the student movement by creating mistrust between students and staff by establishing unattainable negotiating objectives, demanding immediate, uncompromising success, and disrupting or bypassing student unions. He argued that the voices of moderation, those who abided by parliamentary rules as well as the dictates of elected chairmen, were silenced by revolutionaries who demanded the removal of all authorities and remnants of bureaucracy, including parliamentary democracy. He strongly urged Vice Chancellors and the Government to support moderate students' plans for reforms and take the initiative themselves to further reform all existing government, university, and trade union systems before the extremists and their enemies further polarized the universities and nation.[41]

Leftists, on the other hand, applauded the revolutionary turn of the student movement. Tariq Ali edited a collection of essays written by himself, Ernest Mandel, Tom Fawthrop, and others entitled *New Revolutionaries: Left Opposition* (1969). Ali's essay put the British movement within an international context, but argued that it was primarily a response to the failure of the Labour government to bring about socialism. He urged all extra-parliamentary opposition to unite in steering the movement in a socialist direction.[42] Tom Fawthrop's contribution, "Towards an Extra-Parliamentary Opposition," asserted that the social-democratic parties of Europe, including the Labour Party, were elitist and isolated from their bases of mass support. He wrote that the new student movement had "realized that further progress along the path of socialism means throwing aside the rotting corpse of social democracy, upon which the vultures of Fabianism, careerism and orthodox communism are still sustaining themselves. These . . . are to be thrown on the rubbish-heap as the last of the 'reformists.'"[43] Fawthrop concluded that since "collective democratic control over all the managerial functions of the society" was the common goal of students and workers, it could form the basis for a future worker-student alliance[44]

The second generation of the New Left reiterated this argument for a worker-student alliance in *Student Power: Problems, Diagnosis, Actions* (1970). The two stalwarts of the *New Left Review*, Alexander Cockburn and Robin Blackburn, edited and contributed to this collection of essays. Cockburn argued that although the immediate goal of student power was to control the structure and content of higher education, the ultimate aim of the student movement was to forge a revolutionary alliance with working class forces.[45] David Adelstein's essay blamed the Labour government's binary system of higher education and the education system's subservience to the needs of industry for creating a deeply flawed and undemocratic system, which lay at the root of student dissent.[46] In another contribution, David Widgery concluded:

> . . . it is clear that out of the ideological wreckage of social-democracy and Stalinism, a new student revolutionary perspective is emerging— international, extra-parliamentary and returning militant politics to the street. These students have seen through the fancy dress of modern capitalism and found the irrational violence and the hopelessness which is its core. They have seen their community of interest with the working class—a community which should concern us as much as it should frighten those who rule us. There is a spectre haunting Europe and its banners read, in Berlin and Warsaw and Paris and London: 'Today the Students, Tomorrow the Workers!'[47]

This statement, in a nutshell, summarizes the views of the Left at the end of the decade: its high hopes for an increasingly radical student movement and for an eventual student-worker alliance to lead a socialist revolution.

Criticized and pressured by the student movement and the Left for its lack of socialism and attacked by the media and social conservatives of all classes for its permissiveness towards students, criminals, and immorality, Harold Wilson's Labour government struggled to please all sides. Although he never gave the student movement direct credit for any of his government's decisions, Wilson did in fact act on many student demands in the late sixties. For example, students demanded that the government take a strong stand against racism, and it did with the Race Relations Act of 1968. Students demanded increased democratization of access to higher education and increased funding, and the Wilson government had overseen the largest expansion of the university system in the nation's history. The number of full-time students in universities had risen from 140,000 when Wilson took office to 200,000 in 1969. Government expenditure on education had exceeded defense spending for the first time in the history of the country, reaching nearly five per cent of the GDP.[48] Students demanded a voice in university and national government, and the Wilson government lowered the age of majority and legal voting age from 21 to 18, and supported student representation in university committees in 1969. These were all clear signs that the student movement had begun to directly influence national politics.

The most significant of Wilson's reforms that directly affected university students came in 1968 in the midst of the widespread student protests. As a result of pressure from the NUS and a number of polls of young people indicating their desire to be treated as adults, the Wilson government had created the Latey Commission in the mid-sixties to study what legal steps on the age of majority should be taken in light what they saw as the changing nature of the nation's youth. The Commission met extensively with representatives of the NUS, who urged it to recommend ending *in loco parentis* regulations, as well as lowering the voting age and age of majority. The *Latey Report* (1967) supported all of these suggestions.[49] After a year's debate, the House of Commons implemented its recommendations by passing the Family Law Reform and the Representation of the People Acts which lowered the age of majority and the voting age from 21 to 18. Once the bills gained Royal Assent in 1969, students could finally claim the rights of adulthood and formally participate in their national government. These acts finally put the last nail in the coffin of *in loco parentis* regulations at most universities and provided a stronger legal basis for student rights in other areas as well. As a result, the Wilson government strengthened and emboldened the student movement which rightly saw these acts as victories for their movement.[50]

The massive uprising of the student movement in 1968 in Britain and elsewhere in the world also attracted the concern of both houses of Parliament in the late sixties. By arousing public and media fears of social disorder, the student movement essentially forced their government to take them seriously. The House of Lords consequently held a special debate on student disorders in June of 1968.[51] Later the same year, the House of Commons established the Select Committee on Education to study student protest in Britain. Throughout 1968 and 1969 this Committee travelled to various universities, interviewing student representatives, staff, and administrators. In some cases, students protested the presence of the Committee, seeing it as "living evidence of the growing interference in the affairs of the university by the monolith of state capitalism."[52] In several universities, students disrupted the Committee's proceedings and harassed its members. These actions drew a bitter reaction from Edward Short, Secretary for Education. He condemned "the tiny minority of students who were trying to disrupt university life" and called them "a new brand of anarchists—some Marxists, some 'brand x' revolutionaries for whom there was as yet no name. They were wreckers whose weapons were character assassination, intimidation, and, more recently, physical violence."[53] The resulting *Report from the Select Committee on Education and Science Session 1968–69: Student Relations* (1969), condemned radical student political actions, but asserted that most students were voicing real grievances against unjust and outdated university policies and facilities. It supported the demands of moderate activists for an end to *in loco parentis,* and improved facilities, teaching, courses, and student participation.[54] The student movement thus won another important victory from the government.

These moves, however, did little to endear the Labour government to the working class. Already disgruntled with Wilson for the Race Relations Act of 1968, working class voters grew increasingly unhappy with union leadership and its support of Wilson's economic policies. To keep the nation's economy growing and appease industrial owners, Wilson had asked the union leadership to avoid strikes when at all possible. Between 1967 and 1969, however, the rate of wildcat strikes increased dramatically. Even though real wages were rising faster than inflation and union leaders refused to strike, floor-level shop stewards increasingly took up workers' complaints and led these strikes over a variety of issues, from pay raises to working conditions. Wilson's Secretary of State for Employment Barbara Castle responded with a White Paper entitled *In Place of Strife* (1969). This proposed that the government mediate disputes between workers and employers, that the agreements they reached would be binding on both parties, and that both were subject to fines for breaches of the agreements or strike action without mediation. Even more than the Race Relations Act, this White Paper split the Labour Party, alienating the unions and many working class voters. Wilson dropped his support of the paper, but the damage was done.

Conservative politicians quickly exploited the split between workers and the Labour Party, as well as the public reaction against the student movement. They began their attack in a series of "Black Papers" on education published in 1969 and 1970. These asserted that Labour's progressive and egalitarian expansion of higher education had lowered educational standards and allowed mediocre, lazy students to gain entrance to universities where they caused trouble because they wanted less work and less studying.[55] This line of argument completely ignored the real issues of the protests and wrongly implied that student activists were the least capable students who did not belong in university in the first place. Politicians and university authorities, however, utilized these themes to support their own agendas and attack the student movement.

Conservative Party leaders met at a Conference in Selsdon in January of 1970 to strategize their next campaign against the Wilson government. Borrowing ideas from Richard Nixon, Edward Heath and his advisors took up the theme of "law and order" to gain the support of the "silent majority" of the public which was concerned about crime rates, permissiveness, and student protests. Tory leaders promised to stop the "interference with the liberty of people going about their ordinary business by demonstrating minorities" by clamping down on protesters through the use of conspiracy charges and the law of trespass. By March, Heath was including workers strikes along with the student rebellion as the most important threats to the nation. In April, Enoch Powell joined in the attack, calling the teachers' strike a threat to "the fabric of law and order" and warning that students were destroying universities, terrorizing cities, and bringing down governments. The climate of crisis in the aftermath of 1968 and this "law and order" campaign, together with the troubles of the Wilson government, resulted in a surprise victory for the Conservatives in the General Election of June 1970. This election and the rising backlash against student protests would have profound consequences for the student movement and formed the backdrop for the Warwick political files protest.[56]

The paradoxical effects of 1968, including the victories gained by the student movement as well as the growing conservative backlash, led student activists to develop new perspectives on their activism and new strategies with a growing sense of persecution, anger and frustration. Students responded to the national and international climate of crisis and confrontation by escalating their demands for educational reform and an end to apartheid in South Africa, as well as adopting new issues and strategies for their protests. The 1969–70 academic year was thus a turning point not only for British politics, but for the fate of the student movement which was intimately connected to currents in national politics and culture.

THE TRANSFORMATION OF ORGANIZATIONS, ISSUES, AND TACTICS

The National Union of Students played a prominent role in the transformation of the student movement in 1969–70. It had been politicized by the Radical Students Alliance and had recently replaced the Revolutionary Socialist Student Federation as the national organization of the student activist movement. At the beginning of the 1969–70 academic year, both the NUS and RSSF were poised to lead the student movement in a more coordinated effort to achieve their different goals. Both organizations agreed on the need to transform the university system, as well as on their opposition to the Vietnam War and other instances of international injustice, but differed on the specifics and appropriate tactics. As a revolutionary organization, the RSSF was of course more radical in its demands for dramatic, revolutionary changes using the equally dramatic tactics of occupation and obstruction. While the NUS had been politicized in April of 1969 and would now begin to take stands on political issues of concern to most students, it would continue to focus primarily on university reforms in its actions. With member unions at most universities and colleges throughout the nation, the NUS had a much larger formal membership, but in reality, could only mobilize as many supporters as its constituent unions could attract. Thus, its influence was stronger at those universities with student unions which had the support of activists and the student body. Neither organization, however, was able to control or direct the whole student movement, which continued to consist of hundreds of largely autonomous actions.

The NUS focused most of its efforts on university reform along the lines of their "Ten-Point Programme for Educational Reform."[57] Its Campus Reform Campaign coordinated student activism around the specific issues of student participation, union autonomy, discipline, and student voter registration.[58] Despite legislation granting students the right to vote and adult status, and the Vice Chancellors council's official approval of student participation in university decision-making, most universities only allowed student representation on committees which had no power over university finances, curriculum, and other important decisions. The number of universities with student membership on their university councils had risen from only one in 1960 to seventeen by 1970, but even at these universities, student members were a small minority on the councils and remained virtually powerless.[59] The NUS and local student unions, therefore, continued to push for parity of student representation on all university decision-making committees.

Jack Straw, then President of the NUS, traveled the nation and published a number of pamphlets that year, demanding real student participation in university governance as an essential component of a democracy. He explained that democratizing the universities was important because the autocratic nature of education and work, in which people were not allowed to participate in the decisions that affected them, caused widespread political apathy. Straw concluded that democratically governed educational institutions were essential to creating a truly democratic society.[60] His call for student representation on university governing bodies appealed to student leaders across the political spectrum. In October 1969, the Federation of Conservative Students came out in support of this goal and of the freedom of students to sit-in, provided they did not violate the rights of others.[61] This hints at how far the culture of protest and participatory democracy had spread as a result of 1968.

While the NUS grew increasingly active in the student movement, the RSSF disintegrated as an organization. Though fatally crippled by its inability to get its membership to agree on much of anything, the RSSF continued to push for educational reform, an end to the Vietnam War, and a student-worker alliance, as well as a host of new issues raised in its 1969 conferences, including support for the civil rights movement in Ireland and the women's liberation movement, and opposition to the Greek dictatorship. Its formal membership continued to disappear throughout the year, however, and it held its last meeting in 1970. Its agenda, however, was taken up by the NUS and student unions across the nation that year in a number of autonomous actions. By taking the lead in coordinating the national student movement and encouraging activism on the local level, the NUS largely replaced the RSSF as the organizational engine of the student movement after 1970.

As socialist students won control over the NUS and the rest of the student movement, they reoriented it towards socialist goals, including building an alliance with the working class. The Communist Party and International Socialists had always insisted that students could only be an ancillary to a worker-led revolution and had consistently tried to align the student movement with the working class. Few socialist students believed that students could create a revolution on their own; they knew that they were too few in numbers and had too little influence to topple

Britain's relatively stable liberal state. Only by allying with the working class could students truly help to bring about socialist change. This argument seemed to be confirmed by the success of the student-worker strikes which had stunned the world in the French May. Then a research fellow at Cambridge, Paul Ginsborg believed that the events of 1968 showed that "students by themselves would never get anywhere. Secondly, that the contribution of student activism, intelligence, humor, and organizational ability had to go into the workers' movement in some way."[62] The problem was that there was little evidence that British workers wanted an alliance with student activists in 1968. In fact, just as students were protesting against Enoch Powell, workers were protesting in support of him. Repeated opinion polls in the late sixties likewise consistently showed that student protesters had little support amongst workers. A British student-worker alliance thus seemed unrealistic in 1968.

When wild-cat strikes escalated in Britain in 1969, however, far-left students saw new hope for a student-worker alliance on the scale of France and Italy. Learning from their failure to gain the support of workers in their confrontation with anti-immigrant dock workers in 1968, socialist students took great pains to express support for workers in industrial struggles. In the 1969 May Day strike against the *In Place of Strife* White Paper, many students across Britain declared their solidarity with the workers and joined them in the strike. The LSE Student Union passed a resolution calling on all students to march with the workers on May Day to link their common struggle "against the same bosses," and about 200 LSE students heeded their call. Socialist students at Oxford, Glasgow, Strathclyde, and Hull universities similarly participated in workers' actions that year.[63]

While socialist students made some progress towards a worker-student alliance in this period, their opposition to right-wing regimes in other nations attracted much more media attention. The most famous of these actions was undoubtedly the Cambridge "Garden House Riot" of February 1970. The Cambridge protest was unusual in several ways. Firstly, it was one of the few large-scale British protests directed solely against the brutal military regime in Greece. A right-wing military coup had taken place there in 1967 and received considerable international condemnation. As part of the new regime's campaign to boost its image and economy, the Greek Tourist Office in London worked with Cambridge travel agents to put on a "Greek Week" in Cambridge, the highlight of which would be a dinner at the Garden House Hotel on 13 February. Cambridge University students and dons organized a picket of the Garden House dinner to draw attention to the plight of Greek exiles. The organizers were pleased with a turnout of 400 protesters, who peacefully gathered to picket the event, listen to music from a dissident Greek composer, and hear a speech from a Greek exile. Despite the freezing temperatures, the crowd was good-natured until someone sprayed them with a fire hose. At this, the protesters rushed back and in the melee, they broke through some French windows into the dinner party. At that point, students scuffled with the diners, overturning tables and breaking glass in the process. The police then rushed in with their dogs, arresting six students, and dispersing the rest.[64]

The incident itself was rather typical of protests in this period, but its aftermath was unusual for the severity of the reprisal against the protesters. The police requested that university proctors compile a list of names of all those involved, and they complied by providing the names of more than sixty students and several dons involved in various protests that year. The Director of Prosecutions then filed suit against fifteen of them, twelve of whom were members of the Socialist Society. One of the dons charged in the riots was well-known New Leftist Bob Rowthorn, but his charges were dismissed at a committal hearing in May. All of the students plead not guilty to the charges of riotous assembly, malicious damage, and carrying offensive weapons. While seven of the fifteen were acquitted due to lack of evidence, the remaining eight were convicted of various charges and given the most severe sentences for student protesters to date. Six were sentenced to prison terms ranging from nine to eighteen months, and the two overseas students were recommended for deportation. The press and public universally condemned the students, and university relations with townspeople were soured for a decade afterwards. The Garden House Riot was thus in some ways a turning point for the student movement, when police and authorities began using the legal system to stop student protests and the press and public became much more hostile towards any student actions which disrupted the everyday lives of residents outside of the universities.[65]

Another protest that angered the nation and demonstrated the more confrontational tactics used by some students at the end of the sixties took place at Oxford University later that spring. Foreign Secretary Michael Stewart came to speak at a debate at the Oxford Union on the morality of the Indochina war just days after the US invaded Cambodia. Socialist student Christopher Hitchens, in one of his final acts of protest as a student at Oxford, made a speech at the Union in opposition to the guest speaker, but instead of sitting down and allowing his rebuttal as was expected, he "loudly insulted the government's guest of honor, deserted the other guests, and went to sit with, and shout with, the mob. At a given signal when Stewart rose to speak, a phalanx also rose and simply and repetitively yelled the one word 'murderer' in his face. . . . At another signal, a noose was uncurled from the gallery and fell dangling within inches of the wretched foreign secretary's head."[66] Then they all marched away. For the first time in the Union's history, the House voted to adjourn on account of riot. Hitchens felt that since Stewart's views were well-known, their shouting and outburst was a just response to the outrage of the Cambodian invasion. The press, however, responded by hotly condemning the student protest, calling it "one of the nastiest political phenomena that Britain has experienced in this century."[67] To many, when Britain's most prestigious institutions succumbed to the student rebellion, the time had come for stronger action. Despite the fact that most Britons opposed the Vietnam War and many opposed the Greek dictatorship, these kinds of protests were unacceptable to the mainstream public and press at the end of the sixties, and thus only served to vent student emotions and add to the building backlash against the student movement.

SECRET POLITICAL FILES

The transformation of the British student movement, together with the mounting public backlash against student protest led many university administrators to take new steps to prevent disruptions at their own universities. As part of this effort, many administrators began to keep files on prominent student activists so that they would have evidence to present in disciplinary hearings or court hearings if these students committed violent or illegal actions. These files contained secondary school headmasters' comments about the political orientation and personalities of their students, information about student political affiliations, articles they published, speeches they made, and protest actions in which they participated. While administrators may have viewed this as simple record-keeping, in the context of the Conservative attack on student protesters, these files appeared to indicate that university administrations were indeed colluding with the political enemies of the student movement, and thus making this a highly controversial issue in 1970.

As a result of the political climate that year, the exposure of the Warwick political files had a dramatic impact on the rest of the student movement. Students at universities all over the country responded to the Warwick files case by demanding that their own administrators prove that no similar files existed at their universities. Calling the Warwick files "the most corrosive indictment ever made of the running of a British university," Essex student Mike Prior pointed out that Warwick was not a special case, just a spectacular case of university betrayal.[68] When administrators at most universities refused to open their files, students invaded their offices and searched the files themselves. Administrators then retaliated by having students arrested for trespassing and theft. Break-ins and thefts of political files occurred at Essex, Hull, London, Glasgow, Edinburgh, Manchester, Liverpool, and Oxford Universities that year.[69] Similar to Warwick, students at many of these universities attempted to publish letters taken from the official files to provide evidence of the secret dealings of the authorities, but at each university the authorities censored the publication of the letters through threat of discipline and court injunctions.[70]

At several universities, political files spawned large-scale student strikes similar to Warwick. The largest strike outside of Warwick on this issue occurred at Oxford University on the heels of the Warwick protests. As a result of the protests of 1968, Oxford University administrators had created the Hart Committee to study staff-student relations and how to prevent further disturbances. It had recommended the creation of joint student-staff committees from the Council on down.[71] In the discussions afterwards, the University additionally considered a new disciplinary statute that would ban disruptions and expel disruptors. Student activists considered this latter proposal as a repressive reaction to their protests and were already talking about how they might oppose it when news of the Warwick incident broke. Their Student Representative Council met with administrators to ask them to deny the existence of political files at Oxford, but the administrators refused. At a meeting the next day, the Student Council voted to present their demands against the keeping of political files and the repressive statutes to the administration. When they arrived at the administrative building, however, they found it locked and guarded by police, with the administrators refusing to speak with them. About 500 students then forced open the gates and began an occupation of the Delegates room. Their sit-in lasted until 2 March and involved up to 1,200 students in teach-ins, dances, marches, and petitions. At the conclusion of the occupation, a final mass meeting of students voted to form a Campaign for a Democratic University to "work towards transforming Oxford into an open, democratic and free institution."[72] This would lead to Oxford's largest, most spectacular protests three years later.[73]

The 1970 political files protests at Warwick University thus provided an important spark for similar protests across the nation that spring. They alerted all students to the potential threat of political files being used to control and discipline student protesters. Students had already mistrusted university administrators because of the disciplinary charges leveled against student activists from the beginning of the Long Sixties, but the political files seemed to indicate that official duplicity went much deeper. The repression of student movements elsewhere led many students to frame the keeping of secret files as a sign of this repression coming to Britain as well. In another era, these files might have been seen as logical and necessary to the functioning of the university, but because of the increased sensitivity to repression at the end of the sixties, British students quite understandably perceived them as a threat to their political freedom.

ANTI-APARTHEID ACTIONS

While the political files protests were the most widespread form of activism in 1970, the student movement's anti-apartheid campaign expanded in 1969–70, resulting in some large-scale sit-ins and highly publicized actions. At the urging of the national Anti-Apartheid Movement, local student groups investigated their own university finances to see if any university funds were supporting companies such as Barclays, which had heavy investments in South Africa and Rhodesia. Finding these investments at most universities, students pressured their respective university administrations to divest them to put further financial pressure on governments to end apartheid. British students were also encouraged in their campaign by reports of American SDS and Trinity College students forcing their colleges to sell their shares in South African companies.[74] These divestment campaigns, however, often brought up the issue of student power because of the fact that students had no way of influencing the financial decisions of their universities. As a consequence, many divestment campaigns evolved to include demands for student control over finances, and as a result, developed into significant protest actions in the late sixties.

At Edinburgh University, anti-apartheid activism spawned a much larger protest involving the issue of political files, similar to that of Warwick University. Edinburgh students had been particularly passive throughout most of the decade, but they finally rose up in protest over the issue of South African apartheid in January of 1970. One hundred students occupied the Appointments Board offices to prevent a Barclays Bank representative from recruiting on university premises. Students demanded a ban on the use of university facilities by firms with heavy investments in South Africa and Rhodesia, the publication of the full details of the university's investments in those firms, and an assurance that no individual who held investments in those firms be allowed to sit on the Appointments Committee. Like students at Warwick, Edinburgh students began reading through some files they discovered during the occupation and found a number of discriminatory comments about students' race, politics, and background, such as "possibly a Jew" and "undesirable political affiliations." They published this information in a seven-page document and called for an inquiry into the working of the appointments service. The University administration responded by sending in the police to remove the filing cabinets and suspending fifty-five students involved in the occupation. This led to further sit-ins against this disciplinary action involving hundreds more. Eventually, the university replaced the appointments office with a new organization which was explicitly non-discriminatory and allowed students to see their own files and withhold consent from any objectionable opinions in them.[75] In 1971, Edinburgh University sold all of its 500,000 pounds of South African shares.[76]

Similar anti-apartheid activism occurred at a number of other universities. At Liverpool University, for example, apartheid and racism were among five issues which precipitated an eleven-day sit-in.[77] While most anti-apartheid activists remained polite and cooperative in their negotiations with authorities, stronger disciplinary actions by university authorities and the angry rhetoric of the Conservative Party and press heightened tensions and polarized students against authorities at many universities. Such was the case at Essex University in the late sixties.

The Essex Socialist Society had investigated their University Court and found that many of them had connections with companies with investments in South Africa or Rhodesia.[78] When the Court ignored student demands that they sever these ties and ban recruiters from companies with ties to Rhodesia and South Africa, militant activists expressed their growing anger and frustration with the rhetoric of extreme American groups, such as the Black Panthers and Weatherman. Reflecting the language of Mark Rudd of Weatherman, one Essex student wrote

> Well, Senate baby, we know what you're into and we don't like it. Fuck you. We recognize that you are paid for by those who are manipulating the capitalist machine and supporting South Africa in their inhuman terrorisation [sic] of the black people. . . . Even if you did condescend to talk to us you wouldn't understand.[79]

The author went on to tell the Vice Chancellor and the Registrar to "watch their arses. . . . Guerrilla activity is never wantonly destructive but directed against strategic targets. Right on."[80] This language seemed out-of-place at English universities where faculty and administrators still commanded a respectful and deferential attitude from most students. The threatening and disrespectful language of militant students angered authorities and alienated many students. Borrowing language from the American movement may have given the militants a sense of solidarity with the global student movement and added meaning to their dissent, but the language itself became an obstacle to getting authorities, the public, and other students to take their struggle seriously. This also may have been one reason why this anti-apartheid campaign failed to arouse the Essex student population.

A second strategy that the student movement adopted to fight apartheid in 1969 was the harassment and disruption campaign against the all-white South African rugby team, the Springboks. This was a more symbolic protest against apartheid, designed to publicize British student opposition to apartheid and draw public attention to the fact that South African sports teams were segregated like the rest of its society. This strategy was actually first used by the Anti-Apartheid Movement earlier in the decade, but it was Peter Hain, a Young Liberal student at the Queen Mary College of London University, who popularized the issue among university students.

Exiled with his parents from South Africa for their anti-apartheid activism there, Hain was passionate about this issue and fearless in facing crowds of rugby supporters to force this mass audience to consider the immorality of apartheid. In 1969, he stood up at an anti-apartheid meeting and suggested that they use direct action to disrupt sporting events which included segregated South African teams. He later recalled:

> Direct action would disrupt the events and pose a challenge which could not be ignored by the sports elites, which had been impervious to moral appeals and symbolic protest. Because it was novel and had such a potential for impact, it also had the advantage of being highly

newsworthy, with strong visual images for the new television age. It was the product of the era of student sit-ins, Vietnam demos, the 1968 Paris revolt and the American antiwar movement.[81]

In 1969–70, Hain became the chairman of the Stop the Seventies Tour of the Springboks, which involved massive protests against the Springboks, including student groups invading the pitch and all sorts of disruptive behavior.[82]

He ran the campaign with the help of his parents and other students from his parent's flat in London, and was able to gain support from student unions, labor unions, churches, the RSSF, and other student groups across the nation. The protesters harassed the players everywhere they went—in their coaches and hotel rooms, as well as on the pitch. After two months of this, the players voted to go home and end the tour, but their government and management refused to let them. Even the vice-captain of the Springboks, Tommy Bedford, publicly supported Hain. As soon as the rugby tour ended in the spring of 1970, the cricket tour began and his supporters then threw their energies into similar tactics against the South African cricket team.[83] After this ground-swelling of disruptive actions, the NUS passed an emergency motion supporting organizations attempting to stop the rugby and cricket tours.[84] In 1969–70 alone, anti-Springboks demonstrations took place in Leicester, Swansea, Cardiff, Coventry, and Manchester, each involving thousands of protesters and hundreds of arrests.[85]

Hain and the Stop the Seventies Tour were very important in coordinating and encouraging protests against South African sports teams, but much of this action was also independently organized and carried out. Students from many universities would travel to the Springboks matches and join in the protests, often with no direct contact with Hain's group. Anna Davin and a group of Warwick students joined in several of these and thought that they were exciting. They were very organized, making sure they wore the right clothes to minimize getting caught or hurt, and they would "keep an eye on each other to make sure no one got left behind or lost." [86] They discussed tactics to work as a group to get through the police lines and did everything they could think of to ensure a successful demonstration. Davin's last demonstration, however, was the one at Manchester. The police were clearly better organized than the protesters. They would let the protesters through their line, then cut them off from the rest of the crowd, and arrest them. She felt completely frustrated and powerless because of this tactic. She later recalled:

> The confidence in your solidarity and strength was completely under-cut when you realized how organized they were and how they anticipated everything and how useless it was to try and break through a line because what did you do then even if you weren't arrested? It just seemed like playing games. I wanted something that would feel as

though you were getting somewhere, not just confrontation and the excitement that came out of it.[87]

Despite Davin's frustration, the movement did convince Harold Wilson and thirteen nations to oppose the 1970 Springboks cricket tour. Finally, the South African government, under pressure from the Labour government as well as other countries, cancelled the tour.[88]

WOMEN'S LIBERATION

The student movement not only developed new strategies in the aftermath of 1968, it also gave birth to a new social movement. The women's liberation movement emerged alongside and within the student movement in the late sixties, and would become one of the most widespread and important social movements of the seventies. Feminism was especially attractive to university students because of the blatant sexism in higher education. Throughout the 1960s, British universities remained a preserve of male privilege with female students comprising only twenty to forty per cent of the student population at most universities.[89] Society viewed college for women as a transition period toward marriage rather than a serious career choice. University officials acted paternalistically by imposing separate *in loco parentis* regulations for female students, punishing them more severely for sexual relationships and imposing earlier curfews than for male students. Female (and male) students had long resented the unequal and irritating *in loco parentis* regulations, and had successfully gotten their demands included in NUS and student union demands earlier in the era. By the late sixties, most of these regulations had disappeared, but student attitudes continued to reflect the wider sexism of British society in this period. Student and underground newspapers in the sixties featured photos of scantily-clad women in alluring poses and only mentioned women's issues when they discussed fashion or beauty contests.[90] Women were involved in all facets of political life at the university and in student union governance, but because of stereotypes that women were not interested in politics and that women lacked leadership ability, most political groups and student unions were led by male students, and male students published most articles on student politics. The student movement for much of the Long Sixties was thus male-dominated.

Although the student movement and the wider New Left had supported the end of discriminatory *in loco parentis* rules, they resisted other initiatives to eliminate wider sex discrimination in society. Juliet Mitchell, then an English lecturer at Reading University, was among the first to call upon the British New Left to begin to address the oppression of women in her 1966 article, "The Longest Revolution," published in the *New Left Review*.[91] Influenced by her readings of socialist theory and Simone de

Beauvoir's *The Second Sex*, Mitchell drew attention to "the problem of the subordination of women and the need for their liberation."[92] She argued that all of the great socialist thinkers of the nineteenth century, as well as many important thinkers in the twentieth century, had recognized the importance of addressing this problem, but that the British New Left had almost completely overlooked sexual equality as a fundamental element of the socialist ideal. Like similar pleas to the New Left in Germany and America, however, Mitchell's article failed to generate a significant response from the British New Left in the mid-sixties.

In the late sixties, this feminist awareness grew dramatically in response to a number of factors, including the women's rights movements in the United States and West Germany, and two women's industrial actions in Britain. These gave British women role models for their own movement and shaped their language and ideas about their own oppression. Sheila Rowbotham, an original participant in Britain's women's liberation movement, asserts that the American and German women's liberation movements were very influential in raising initial awareness of sex discrimination, but that women's campaigns within the British workers' movement actually touched off the British women's liberation movement. For her, the process of developing a feminist identity had begun when she encountered the radical psychology and Black Power movements at the Dialectics of Liberation Congress in 1967. These had helped her to perceive how women's experiences differed from those of men. The next year, press coverage of the fiftieth anniversary of female suffrage in Britain raised widespread interest in women's rights. Rowbotham, however, was more inspired by the Hull fish-house worker, Lil Bilocca, who was campaigning against unsafe trawlers and had inspired the formation of a women's group in support of the campaign. The highly publicized female machinists' strike at Ford that year and their claim that "It isn't about pay, it's about recognition," additionally helped her to "see how women workers were put down as women."[93] The machinists demanded pay equal to that of men for equal work. Although they did not achieve parity immediately, they did inspire the formation of a National Join Action Committee for Women's Equal Rights in 1969, which would go on to successfully win an Equal Pay Act in 1970.[94]

Around the same time, Rowbotham read some literature from women in the American New Left who were leaving it because of the discrimination they felt within that movement. She immediately identified with the American feminists and began thinking about how angry she was with some of her male comrades, who had always assigned her to secretarial duties or arranging dinners and socials, and rarely asked her to speak or otherwise lead the protests. In fact, the first time she spoke at a political meeting in 1969 at the LSE, she got catcalls and wolf-whistles. At the History Workshop at Ruskin College that year, she spoke with Anna Davin, Barbara Winslow, Hilary Wainwright, and others who felt the same anger and same concern for bringing women's issues into the wider student and worker struggle. When they discussed women at the workshop, however, they were jeered and laughed at. They decided to do something about it themselves. They began planning a women's conference for the next year and in the meantime would devote themselves to raising awareness of women's issues in other ways.[95] Rowbotham convinced Tariq Ali to have *Black Dwarf* designate 1969 as the "year of the Militant Woman." She wrote the main article for that edition, entitled "Women: The Struggle for Freedom." In it, she explained how personal relations, the family, and women's oppression lay at the heart of capitalism and must be addressed by all socialists as they struggled to overthrow the old system. Ali felt that it was probably the most important piece they ever published.[96]

Other female activists also recognized the sexism of the dissent movements in the late sixties. For example, after the October 1968 VSC protest, student activist Elisabeth Tailor believed that "These demos were organized as ego-trips by men who wanted to be at the front, get their pictures in the paper, and prove they were 'prolier' [more proletarian] than thou. The arrogance of a small elite, thinking they were leading the revolution and telling the working class what to do! They controlled the language— their Marxism was always better than yours–and made women feel like idiots."[97] Hilary Wainwright agreed that in the RSSF and at most demonstrations, women were excluded in all of the symbols and leadership, generating "the feeling that you were only partly there."[98] Sheila Rowbotham added that, "in the free-for-all combat of the student movement, men who could assert charisma or just sometimes aggression would tend to hold the floor. Although the Revolutionary Socialist Students' Federation had a rhetoric of participation, its anarchic style of meetings effectively excluded most women."[99] She also felt that some of the radical student literature portraying women was hostile and degrading to women.[100]

When female students brought their concerns to their male counterparts, they were initially rejected. This then forced feminist activists to form separate women's liberation groups. For example, in 1968 Anna Davin and some other women within the Warwick Socialist Society decided to meet separately from the male students, so that they could discuss issues unique to their situation. Some of the men in the group, however, objected that women's liberation was "diversionary" from the socialist revolution. The women decided to have occasional separate meetings anyway, because when the men were there, the women "could not get a word in edgewise."[101] In 1970, they extended membership of the women's group to students outside the Socialist Society and women outside the university. They discussed equal pay, birth control, and issues of physical appearance.

Likewise, at Essex University's Revolutionary Festival in 1969, women who attempted to discuss women's liberation were constantly interrupted by male activists who made disparaging remarks and who tried to dominate the meeting. The female activists decided to hold another meeting and exclude men. They decided to form their own women's liberation group, called the London Women's Liberation Workshop that year, and campaigned to improve nursery facilities.[102] This group would become an important part of the women's movement in the 1970s, when its *Women's Liberation Newsletter,* renamed *Shrew,* became the leading publication of the entire movement.[103]

Feminist students used these publications not only to communicate with each other, but also to reach out to and educate the rest of the student population. Essex students published a magazine in these early years containing a variety of articles, including topics such as women in advertising, equal pay, housework drudgery, and birth control. They explained:

> We have put together this magazine because we want more women to see that they have much more potential than society allows them to realize. Whether we have paid jobs or not, we all have to do housework, and are brought up to consider it our natural duty. We were also taught that women are *less important* than men, that we are weak, emotional and brainless. In relationships with men, it is all too often important that we smile invitingly without really meaning it, and give in in arguments, just for the sake of calming him down . . . Many of us know that to act like this is humiliating and dishonest, and we don't want any part of it.[104]

They urged interested students to contact their local women's liberation group and join them.

Rowbotham contributed extensively to the growing literature of the women's liberation movement. Her *Mayday Manifesto: Women's Liberation and the New Politics* was a particularly widely-read pamphlet, first published in 1969. This pamphlet attempted to work out a theory for women's liberation in relationship to Marxism and post-colonialism. Referencing Stokely Carmichael and Frantz Fanon, she revealed the influence of the American Black Power movement in one section:

> Similarly relevant is the understanding of the movement of Black America. For an oppressed group to successfully challenge those who control them they have to be able to construct a total alternative kind of being. Such an alternative does not drop neatly from the skies. It has to be hewn out through suffering, in struggle, over time, and with thought.[105]

Rowbotham would continue to study and participate in the women's liberation movement through the seventies, becoming one of its most famous activists.

The first Ruskin College Women's Conference in February of 1970 was a major turning point in the beginning of a women's liberation movement in Britain. Over 500 women attended the conference and set up an informal umbrella organization, the National Coordinating Committee, composed of two representatives from each local women's group. It promoted a simple agenda of four basic demands: free 24-hour nurseries, equal pay, equal education, and job opportunities.[106] Each group would continue to act independently, but the National Coordinating Committee would meet annually and organize support for campaigns on which they all agreed. They were determined to create democratic collectives, without leaders or hierarchies, so that women would be free to participate and develop in their own way. Rowbotham believes that this anti-authoritarianism and belief in participatory democracy came from the North American women there at the first meetings of British women's liberation groups as well as from C. Wright Mills via the New Left.[107]

While women's liberation gained considerable support from students at many British universities, it faced tremendous opposition and hostility from some students. Glasgow University was particularly resistant to women's liberation efforts. Female students there were greatly outnumbered by males, rarely journalists for student publications, almost never elected to the top positions in the student council and political groups, and excluded by the Men's Union. The only discrimination against which they voiced protest, however, was their exclusion from the Men's Union, and even then only a minority of women objected to this segregation.[108] Writing in 1966, a Glasgow student argued against the segregation of the sexes in the unions, asserting that

> there should be an examination and sweeping away of the unwarranted assumptions and suppositions which undeniably lie beneath this policy—that women are capable only of a dilettante approach to education, that for them university is a superior kind of finishing school; that they cannot be trusted not to distract earnest and industrious men students from their studies; that they have no right to be seriously career-minded, and that if they are allowed real and effective equality as students they will get "ideas above their station": their station being naturally in the vicinity of the kitchen sink.[109]

Glasgow's female students were aware of the prejudice of their male counterparts, but they did not organize themselves to fight this prejudice until the early 1970s, after publicity about the women's rights movement in America and elsewhere in Britain eventually inspired Glasgow's students. Despite the moderate tone of their arguments, a 1969 letter in the student newspaper referred to the Glasgow feminists as "five emasculated chickens" and concluded "No girls, when you grow up in a few years you will realize that marriage is not unfair drudgery, and if their marriages turn out that way they have only themselves to blame."[110] Even Glasgow's student Left ignored the women's rights issue until it was taken up by the major national Left organizations after 1970.

Traditionally male-dominated national student organizations also initially denigrated the idea of a women's rights movement. The RSSF and other socialist student groups criticized feminists for being bourgeois and counter-revolutionary. One early women's liberation newsletter, *Shrew*, responded to this criticism, stating, "I do not intend to neurotically consult Marxengleslenin before baring my teeth or my teats. I do not intend to give ladylike (read suck ass) reassurance to radical chauvinists during the course of this struggle, even if it means losing their friendship (i.e. patronage)."[111] Similar to the American and German SDS, many student organizations thus unwittingly pushed women into creating their own separate organizations by ignoring and ridiculing the initial demands for consideration of women's rights.

Women's rights activism is only one manifestation of the many ways in which the student movement was transformed at the end of the sixties. In the aftermath of 1968, students reflected on their movement, critically analyzing its limitations and possibilities. While feminist activists exposed the sexism within the student movement, others criticized it as too radical or too moderate, too violent or too weak, too bourgeois or too proletarian. Out of this dynamic critique emerged new perspectives, strategies, and protest issues, transforming the student movement in the process. At the same time that the student movement was evolving, social and political commentators constructed their own critique of the movement and formed a counterattack against it. Culminating in the Conservative victory in the 1970 election, the backlash against the student movement had a tremendous impact. The Conservative critique of the student movement, together with the repression of the student movements in the US, West Germany, and France, fed a sense of persecution amongst students in 1970. This sense of political persecution is what made the political files incident at Warwick such an important issue to students that year. The Warwick incident and the widespread protests they inspired were thus a result of and response to the national and global response to student protest in the late sixties.

Similar to protests at Essex University and the LSE in earlier years, the Warwick files protests were also a product of a unique combination of the local, national, and international circumstances of that particular place in that particular time. Created out of the postwar attempt to rebuild Coventry and reform the nation's higher education system, Warwick University reflected the highest hopes of the people of Warwickshire. Coming to Warwick with high expectations for a fully modernized and democratic university, progressive staff and students were greatly disappointed with the perceived conservatism of the administration of the university. After years of failed petitioning for a student and community building, the discovery of the political files was the last straw for Warwick's students. In the context of the growing conservative backlash against the student movement, students and many of the staff interpreted the files as a politically-motivated attack on progressive students and employees, and responded by joining together in defense of their rights.

While the changing national political climate in the aftermath of 1968 fed Warwick students' sense of persecution, it also contributed to many students' increased sense of power in the late sixties. The Wilson government and Vice Chancellors had given students significant victories in the lowering of the age of majority to eighteen, the elimination of lingering *in loco parentis* regulations, and an acceptance of student participation in university governance. Many on the Left publicly recognized the potential power of student activism and gave them further encouragement. This new recognition of the political power of the student movement, however, also made it a political target. Conservatives in particular used student protest as a symbol of the failure of Labour's "permissive" legislation and democratization of education. This critique became an important plank in their political platform in the spring of 1970 and contributed to their surprise victory in the June 1970 election. In the face of this new attack, students more clearly saw their place within national politics and their activism as more explicitly political. In this context, any attempt on the part of the government or university officials to limit the growing power of the student movement would be seen as a political attack.

Many university officials for their part were deeply alarmed by the strength and militancy of the British student movement in 1968. Student activists' increasing willingness and ability to shut down universities and shout down invited speakers in support of their demands especially angered university administrators and many staff. Even liberal and normally tolerant university authorities balked at students blatantly disregarding the freedom of speech and open access to university buildings. They were willing to allow students some representation on university committees, but were determined to prevent student protesters from disrupting the operation of their universities. Like the LSE, most universities created plans for minimizing the disruptive power of student protesters and protecting the rights of staff and other students. While personal files had been kept long before 1968, they became even more important in the years afterwards to help university authorities effectively eliminate disruptive student activists. Viewed in this context, the political files were indeed potential threats to the student movement.

Students responded to their new political status in a variety of ways. For some student activists, their victories had proved the essentially democratic and fair nature of the British political system, but for many socialist students, the victories had shown only a brief glimpse of the potential power of the student movement. They were encouraged to press even harder to reform the university system to reflect socialist values and to eliminate inequalities in wider society. Socialist societies dominated many student unions and used them to press for their goals. They advocated adopting new strategies in the changing political landscape of the late sixties, including attacking symbolic targets in the fight against apartheid and sit-ins in support of a wide variety of issues. They additionally attempted to refocus the student movement on bringing the revolution to Britain by building support for workers actions and struggling against university authorities and Conservative politicians. Socialist students would ultimately be victorious in these initiatives in the early seventies, but in 1970, Conservatives seemed to have the upper hand. As a result, students were especially concerned about political files and disciplinary actions as evidence of political persecution.

In their struggle to continually create sensational, news-worthy protests and combat the messages of Conservative politicians, however, student activists unwittingly played into the hands of their enemies. The student movement itself became a prominent component of national discourse in the aftermath of 1968, peaking in importance in the 1970 election. It contributed to a backlash against permissiveness and the welfare state, which began in that period and would continue to grow over the next several decades. The student movement thus played a significant role in the great shift in political tides, away from liberalism and socialism, and towards the conservatism which would dominate the nation in the next decade.

5 The Seventies and the Rise of the Unions

It was the Fifth of November 1973. On Oxford's High Street, just outside the elaborate façade of the nineteenth-century Examinations Schools building, several hundred students gathered together, bundled against the cold. They talked excitedly about their direct action strategy to win the creation of a Central Student Union (CSU), a central social facility for all of Oxford's students run by its own student government. Led by International Marxist Group and International Socialist students, the students entered the Examinations Schools and began the longest student sit-in at Oxford University in the Long Sixties.[1]

As soon as they entered the building, the students quickly organized committees to work on negotiations with the administration, publicity, internal communication, supplies, and entertainment. They immediately set to work on producing broadsheets to publicize their demands: a "legally binding agreement to provide a CSU in three years," "provision of sufficient interim facilities," and "no victimization of those involved in the occupation."[2] As they worked, the administration cut off the electricity and demanded that they leave the building. Anticipating this action, students brought in candles and a generator, and prepared to wait until the administration was willing to negotiate.

First-year Politics, Philosophy, and Economics undergraduate Peter Mandelson was there at the beginning and wrote about it for the Oxford University student newspaper, *The Cherwell*:

> Tension has ebbed away with the adrenalin here. The great yell of victory that accompanied the initial invasion at 2.30 this afternoon has developed into a general hubbub of voices, and laughter, bottles and crockery and guitars and mouth organs. The PA system informs people of sleeping and defense arrangements, requesting and instructing on behalf of the various committees that were set up shortly after the schools were taken. . . . Now with the electricity cut-off, candles only serve to enhance the communal atmosphere. Collected along the corridors are groups singing and playing chess and only vaguely thinking of what tomorrow will bring.[3]

Over the next seven days, these committees ran one of the largest sit-ins of the era, with up to 700 students in attendance at various times throughout the week. Over one thousand students participated in a demonstration march in the middle of the week in support of their demands as well as in support of a nation-wide campaign for increased student grants.

The administration, however, would not tolerate the occupation for long. At the end of the week, the university Registrar Geoffrey Caston sent a letter to the occupiers threatening to use a High Court injunction against them and bring in the police to evict them. He did, however, offer that the university would discuss their demands with the Student Representative Council at their next meeting. Although the IMG students wanted to continue the protest until their demands were met, the majority of the students were satisfied with the offer of compromise and the new feeling of solidarity and revolution generated by the occupation. They were also worried that if they stayed longer, the administration would carry through with their threat to bring in the police and arrest them. At a final meeting, over one thousand students voted to end the occupation on a successful note, clean up the building, and march out en masse. Just as the campus police came in with the court summonses, the students marched out in an impressive candlelight procession.[4]

In the weeks that followed, the university magazine *Isis* reported that the occupation was a great success:

> This week's occupation was bigger, better and more organized than any in Britain for five years . . . The idea of student power has finally found a home in that last cloistered refuge of academic feudalism. For some that is something to regret, but for the great majority of students it is an exciting feeling. . . . Never has such cooperation or goodwill been felt among students, never had sectarianism been so routed in favor of the common cause. That students could take over a shell of a building and provide those inside with electricity, food, music, fireworks, theatre, films and run an extensive publicity and defense network outside gives new confidence to all student radicals. If nothing else is achieved, the occupation has given self-respect back to the armchair socialists of the University.[5]

IS students added that the occupation gave hundreds of students the "novel experience of being able to take complete control of at least a part of their lives, acting as they want to and not as a remote and alien university, college authority or union bureaucracy decide for them."[6] Both the IS and the IMG would effectively use this occupation as a launching pad for a campaign which would escalate in the coming months and last throughout the academic year.

As the administration dragged its feet in the weeks following the occupation, one hundred students demonstrated at the end of November, demanding that administrators meet with student negotiators. In its defense, administrators were reeling not only from the protesters' actions, which the bursar claimed caused over £9,000 worth of damage, but from a growing backlash from irate students, staff, and townspeople who demanded an end to these kinds of disruptions. In a letter to the Proctors (the top administrators) that November, student Timothy Lemmer complained that the occupiers were violating his rights as a student member of the university:

> their conduct is opposed to the spirit of free speech and the orderly persuit [sic] of knowledge and toleration of others that is the heritage and policy of this great institution. They are victimizing those students who want to get on with the education they are here to get. They debase the ideals and the good name of the university which they claim to represent. . . . Most of the students are fed up with this kind of behavior which could be considered infantile and laughed off if it didn't constitute a threat to the rights of others and to the order of our university.[7]

In a local newspaper, *Oxford Mail*, resident F. S. Flood wrote a letter to the editor opposing the "noxious behavior" of the Oxford protesters, arguing that "those who opt for tumult and vandalism" were a moronic, uncivilized minority who should be thrown out.[8] To satisfy these critics and prevent further disruptions, the administration created new disciplinary rules, explicitly prohibiting occupations and creating contingency plans for calling in the police to evict students, new penalties for occupiers, and a new disciplinary court to hear cases against student protesters. Finally in January of 1974, the University recognized an Oxford University Student Union (OUSU) as the representative of all of the university's students, but rejected student requests for a Central Student Union (CSU) to house the new union and social facilities for the general student population, arguing that this would take away funding from the Junior Commons Rooms.[9]

The new OUSU held its first meetings that January. Its agenda for a meeting on 4 February 1974 reveals the wide range of issues inspiring the student movement at Oxford and elsewhere that year. In addition to demanding a CSU building, they reaffirmed their commitment to ending investments in South Africa as part of their opposition to apartheid, pledged support for the working class struggle against the Tory government, demanded increased student grants to keep pace with the rate of inflation, demanded that women be admitted to all Oxford colleges on an equal basis, supported the NUS campaign for crèche facilities, nurseries, and equal pay for women, and condemned the British government's brutality in Northern Ireland.[10] At that meeting, 337 students voted in support of a demonstration march demanding a CSU, and in support of "the miner's fight for a fair wage, a struggle in alliance with the working class . . . against the Tory Government."[11] Although the motion for another occupation in support of the CSU failed, seventy of the 200 marching students attempted to occupy the Indian Institute on 13 February. Led by the Proctors and staff, the campus police forcefully ejected the occupiers. Outside, the civil police then arrested eight of the students.[12]

The next day, the left-wing student newspaper *Oxford Strumpet* described the scene and its impact:

> The shock of standing outside the Indian Institute and watching ones comrades and friends being beaten, kicked and thrown downstairs, whilst the Proctors exhort further violence from the keepers of the peace, has by no means worn off as this is written, the bruises, the arrests, the bloke in hospital, the shocked comments of dons who witnessed the violence all testify to the fact that there seem to be no lengths to which the University authorities will not go in order to deny Oxford students their political rights . . . Our wishes for an effective Union, for men and women to be taught and to live side by side, for the updating of ancient academic courses, all have been frustrated by University intransigence and now, when registering our protest in a non-violent manner, we can be beaten up and sent down by courtesy of the disciplinary section of the same University. We must now register our anger and disgust not only about the things that were done to our friends, but also about the authorities' reaction to our reasonable wishes. We *are* right to demand certain things from the University and to express these wishes forcibly if necessary. If Wednesday shows anything it shows the real nature of what we are up against—not conciliatory liberalism, but ruthless reaction.[13]

Reflecting the polarized political climate of the era, Oxford students thus interpreted this as a politically-motivated assault and called upon all students to attend a general meeting to decide upon what response they should make.

On 21 February, the Proctors provoked further outrage when they charged nineteen students with major university offenses stemming from the Indian Institute scuffle. Students retaliated with a demonstration march of 900 through the streets protesting the Proctors' actions. They planned a national demonstration against the victimization of student protesters, supported by student unions from all over the country, to coincide with the trial in March. Hundreds of students from several universities demonstrated outside administrative offices on Little Clarendon Street on 4 March, pushing the police lines backwards and breaking the glass. At the hearings in the second week of March, 400 students stormed the gates where the disciplinary hearings were being held, and stood outside the doors protesting the trials. The nineteen accused students protested the hearings every step of the way, refusing to sit down, and shouting out their objections. One of the students, Sue Lukes, asked Tariq Ali to be her adviser for the trial. He refused to sit down at the trial, shouting that the trial was a farce that brought discredit to Oxford University. At the end of his diatribe, he "walked out, clenched fist aloft, to the cheers of students in the court, as University police came in."[14] Finally on 29 March, the disciplinary court convicted eighteen of the students and ordered that the students be "sent down." Ten students appealed the verdict, but their appeals were dismissed.[15] At the end of the trial, the Senior Proctor warned that a core of radicals were determined to disrupt the university again and that it was essential that the university not "make any concessions which will in the slightest impair its power to defend itself. We found its present powers barely sufficient."[16] Both students and administration were frustrated, angry, and exhausted by this drawn-out power struggle.

The Oxford protests of 1973–74 represented not only the culmination of years of activism to create a Student Union at Oxford, but also a new belief in the power of student unions and in workers' unions in general. In the midst of the largest industrial crisis of the post-war period, Oxford's students were emboldened to fight for a student union as never before. As such, the Oxford protests of 1973–74 illustrate some important changes in the student movement in the seventies. As is clearly indicated by the student movement at Oxford University, the British student movement did not die in the early seventies. In fact, it escalated and took on a new focus in response to the economic and political crises of that period.

OXFORD'S ANCIENT INSTITUTIONS

To truly understand the meaning of Oxford's protests, however, one must begin with its local context. More than any other university in the country, Oxford represented the highest ideal for universities and it was the role model for universities not only elsewhere in the country, but in the world. Begun in the twelfth century, it had been the elite training ground for most of the nation's political leaders and for many of its leading writers and scientists for centuries. Indeed, Prime Ministers Macmillan, Wilson, and Heath were all Oxford men. Most of its staff and students were proud of its ancient traditions and spired stone buildings. The robes and the coldness and quirks of the buildings, while uncomfortable at times, still held a certain mystique, connecting staff and students to the centuries of history embodied in this institution of higher learning. Oxford University, however, also epitomized the contradiction between Britain's former model of the university tradition and the modern, youthful zeitgeist of the sixties. Caught between the ancient and the modern, Oxford's student movement would reflect the unique context of its local setting as well as national and international trends.

Oxford University was a confederation of colleges, which were residential communities, "to which all members owed their first allegiance." As the Master of Balliol college explained in 1960,

> Every true Oxford man would agree that the essence of Oxford is college life. To have one's own rooms, on one's own staircase, making one's

friendships with undergraduates and dons, to have meals together, to drop into one's own JCR, read in one's College Library, worship in one's own College chapel, to play on one's own field or row from one's own boathouse-all these, taken together, make up the experience men come to Oxford to get and always treasure. It is on this intimacy of daily life that an Oxford education is based. From this it derives its unique value . . . There is nothing quite like it . . . in the whole world.[17]

This collegiate system set Oxford apart from most other universities in Britain. Oxford undergraduates were admitted into one of its colleges, and spent nearly all of their time and classes in that college. Each college elected a student president and other officers, and these officers had some say over the rules within their own college, but little real power.[18]

The tradition of calling students "undergraduates" or "junior members," and staff "senior members" also promoted the sense that all were life-time members of this community, with inherent rights and responsibilities. This unique sense of privilege, however, waned over the course of the Long Sixties. For example, at the beginning of the era, all members of the community wore distinctive gowns denoting their membership in the community, but by the end of the sixties, students gradually ceased to wear them at tutorials and eventually even at dinner.[19] Oxford students began identifying themselves with university students elsewhere, dressing like other youth their age, and behaving like the rest of their generation instead of elitist "junior members" of an ancient institution. The wider discourse of democratization had spread to Oxford and this would have far-reaching consequences.

These surface changes reflected wider transformations taking place within the university. Similar to universities elsewhere, Oxford's student population grew rapidly throughout the era, from roughly 7,000 in the 1940s to 11,000 in 1970.[20] This put tremendous strain on facilities, especially accommodation. Students were first packed into the old college housing, then forced to live off-campus. By 1968, 45 per cent of students lived in off-campus lodgings, shifting student orientation away from the colleges to the university in general and weakening the bond between faculty fellows and students.[21] Because of the growth of the university and especially the growth in science and technology, which was funded directly by the central university administration, the central administration increased in bureaucracy and power. The university administration was led by two Proctors, senior members elected by other senior members. Meetings of all senior members, called Congregation, made the most important decisions, but the Proctors handled day-to-day decisions. Power, consequently, grew ever more distant from students, who had little say in the rules imposed upon them or even in the governing of their individual colleges.

In response to these changes, students began demanding to have a student union or committee to represent students' interests to the university as a whole in the early sixties. The university consequently established a Student Representative Council (SRC) in the spring of 1961. Each college sent one representative to this council, and the council discussed issues which affected all students, such as housing and facilities. Unlike student unions at most other British universities, however, Oxford's SRC had no formal power, no offices, and no social facilities. Whereas student unions elsewhere received funds from the government to support bars, dance-halls, sports facilities, and other large-scale amenities, Oxford University divided its union funding between the Junior Commons Rooms of each college, so that none of the commons rooms could provide more than a bar and some small amenities. While some of Oxford's students enjoyed their unique commons rooms, left-wing students wanted a real central students union which they believed would help to make the university more democratic and would be a more powerful tool to use in negotiating with university authorities. As early as 1963, students in *The Cherwell*, argued that, "What Oxford students need is a hard hitting trade union organization which is willing not only to protest but to employ sanctions where necessary."[22] Throughout the sixties, Oxford activists repeatedly demanded a Central Students Union and were repeatedly denied.

By the early seventies, the International Marxist Group and International Socialists had replaced the New Left as the most powerful student activist groups at Oxford, and were attempting to gain support from Oxford's students for their organizations' more traditional "Old Left" goals of workers' power and a worker-led socialist revolution. A key part of this strategy was to recruit more students to their organizations, and get them to support workers' strikes and to think more like the working class. Creating a student union which could act like a workers union in the fight against capitalism was thus an important goal for both of these organizations, and they believed that direct action in support of this goal would serve as an important radicalizing event which would bring more students into their organizations.[23] In the October 1973 edition of their newspaper *Oxford Strumpet*, they outlined this strategy. They argued that while students would not "rally round petitions," SocSoc meetings, or agit-prop, "an occupation is a positive and an obvious blow—it clearly represents what many people feel. . . . effective direct action, coupled with coherent strategic demands, presents the only way forward for the CSU campaign at this stage."[24] The protests of 1973–74, therefore, were only one part of a long-term left-wing campaign that had actually begun in the early 1960s.

THE NATIONAL AND GLOBAL CRISES OF THE SEVENTIES

The Oxford student movement, however, also reflected national and international political, social, cultural, and economic trends in the early seventies. Underlying the Oxford protest and the rest of the British student movement in the early seventies was the shortage of funding for higher education, which was a direct result of the growing crisis of global capitalism. As the global economy slowed, profits declined, and unemployment rose, but at the same time, the cost of energy, food, and rents skyrocketed. This economic trend, labeled "stagflation," was a transnational phenomenon, with many different causes and effects. In Britain, stagflation caused a political, economic, and social crisis nearly equal to that of the Great Depression. In the soaring inflation, many British citizens on government pensions or aid, including students with grants, faced serious poverty. They found that they could not afford to pay their rent and some used rent strikes to protest the rising rents. Workers demanded higher wages to keep pace with inflation, but employers feared falling profits and tried to cut wages. Both Labour and Conservative politicians struggled to find a solution to the escalating crisis. The newly-elected Conservative government led by Edward Heath attempted to deal with this crisis by aiding British corporations, limiting the power of trade unions, cutting government programs including educational funding, and instituting a national wage freeze. These moves were extremely unpopular with workers and students who joined forces to bring about the downfall of the Heath government.

The sense of economic crisis in the industrialized countries was compounded by a sense of political and social crisis precipitated by left-wing terrorist activities in many countries, including Britain. The most famous of these terrorist groups are probably America's Weatherman Underground, West Germany's Red Army Faction (the Baader-Meinhof gang), and Japan's Red Army. Each of these groups justified their use of violence by arguing that government authorities routinely used violence against protesters and workers to defend capitalism and imperialism. The Japanese Red Army hijacked airplanes, bombed embassies, and assassinated and kidnapped people in the struggle to end imperialism. The German Red Army Faction hoped to spark a revolution through bombing US military buildings, assassinations, and attacks on the Springer press. In 1971, polls showed that up to a fourth of young West Germans sympathized with them. By the 1980s over 100 Red Army Faction bombing and arson attempts had claimed more than fifty lives.[25] The American Weatherman group likewise set off hundreds of bombs in draft offices, government facilities, and military research establishments across the country in an attempt to terrorize the government and society into ending its imperialistic practices.[26] Although these groups had sympathy amongst some student activists and attracted some former students, these organizations operated outside of universities were self-consciously separate from the student movement. Their importance, however, lay in how they added to the sense of crisis growing across the post-industrial world.

The British Isles additionally had their own crisis with bombings in the 1970s. In response to Irish Republican Army violence, the British government resorted to interning suspects without charge or trial in 1971. Anti-internment organizations emerged across the British Isles and 30,000 turned out to protest the new internment law in a series of demonstrations in London. When a January 1972 civil rights march turned into a riot, British paratroopers swooped in and shot fourteen unarmed civilians dead. Known as Bloody Sunday, this event spurred protests across the British Isles. Thirty thousand demonstrators burned the British embassy to the ground in Dublin.[27] Parliament dissolved the Stormont government and began direct rule of Northern Ireland, and a more intensive campaign against the IRA. Soon afterwards, the IRA began its retaliatory bombing campaign in England. Bloody Sunday thus set off an escalating cycle of terror and repression which would go on for decades. Amidst the spiraling violence, a fearful public turned to the Conservative government to uphold "law and order" at home.

Even before Bloody Sunday, however, there had been 120 bombings in England and Wales since 1968. Although most of these caused little damage and were unattributed, the police blamed many of them on an infamous group of home-grown revolutionaries called the Angry Brigade.[28] Their bombing campaign and highly publicized trial in 1971 increased the nation's sense of crisis and forever tarnished the student movement with an image of anarchic violence.

Four of the eight people charged in the trial, John Barker from Cambridge, Christopher Bott from Strathclyde, and Anna Mendelson and Hilary Creek from Essex, had been radical student activists in the late sixties. Their frustrations with the student movement, the examples of the American Weather Underground and the Red Army Faction in Germany, and the heightened sense of class warfare in the early seventies, convinced them to drop out of university to become full-time revolutionaries.[29] John Barker had ripped up his final examination at Cambridge in 1968 as part of his protest against the elitism which he believed was "the twin of exploitation."[30] Barker later described the Angry Brigade as "libertarian communists," who were serious about contributing to the working class struggle against the Heath government and leading capitalists, whom they believed were destroying the nation. Barker had participated in numerous Vietnam demonstrations in the sixties, but felt that they had become routine and useless. After leaving university, the Angry Brigade had no connection to student or leftist organizations because of their perceived ineffectiveness. Instead, they turned to using small bombs against government and corporate targets because "it felt like it was hurting them without hurting ourselves. . . . and that there was a need for action not constrained by capitalistically defined legality."[31] The Heath government's Selsdon policy and internment law especially shocked them and motivated them to escalate their actions.

Barker distinguished the Angry Brigade from other groups such as the Red Army Faction in Germany, claiming that the Angry Brigade had none of their "vanguardist assumptions" and were more interested in having a good time, "smoked a lot of dope," and were "not that serious."[32] Indeed, journalist Martin Bright recently called them "a quaint Pythonesque version of their more murderous continental counterparts."[33] Influenced by the Situationist manual, *The Society of the Spectacle,* they wrote confusing communiqués to underground newspapers, discussing their theories and announcing their intentions to attack symbols of repression and the Establishment. While it is still difficult to ascertain which bombings they actually committed, the police charged them with twenty-five bombings, including the January 1971 bombing of Conservative minister Robert Carr's home.[34] No one was killed in any of these small bombings and only one person was slightly injured, but they were a serious embarrassment to the Heath government, which created a Bomb Squad in January 1971 specifically to hunt them down. The squad launched an all-out attack on the London counterculture, its communes, newspapers, and bookshops, and quickly flushed out the amateur revolutionaries.[35]

The mainstream press had a field day with the trial, evoking the specter of "sinister forces massing behind the scenes." [36] In an article entitled "The Red Badge of Revolution," the *Evening Standard* linked the Angry Brigade to the student movement and other protest movements: "These guerrillas are the violent activists of a revolution comprising workers, students, trade unionists, homosexuals, unemployed and women striving for liberation. They are all angry."[37] The judge at their trial undoubtedly perceived them as a product of the student movement, stating that "I am sorry to see such educated people in your situation. Undoubtedly a warped understanding of sociology has brought you to the state in which you are."[38] Commenting on the Angry Brigade, J. C. Gunn of the Institute of Psychology at London University more directly linked the two, arguing that "One of the factors which must be taken into account is the way they were affected by their exposure to university life. The broader spectrum of society now attending and mixing in universities is creating an entirely new sociological picture."[39] Indeed, even many students and workers believed that the Angry Brigade were expressing their anger at the Heath government, and thousands of "I'm in the Angry Brigade" badges were worn during and after the trial.[40] Although the Angry Brigade members had left the student movement because of its lack of radicalism, in the public mind, the Angry Brigade was a direct result of the student movement if not secretly still part of it.[41] As such, the Angry Brigade and other left-wing terrorist organizations could be used by the enemies of the student movement to discredit and attack it.

The sense of economic and social crisis in the early seventies led many Britons to support tougher laws to target the student movement and left-wing organizations for prosecution so as to limit their ability to disrupt society. In 1978, Stuart Hall pointed to the Angry Brigade as the key to the conservative turn against the forces of liberalism in the early seventies. He argued that the Angry Brigade:

> gave the forces of law and order precisely the pretext they needed to come down on the libertarian network like a ton of bricks. It strengthened the will of ordinary people, for whom explosions in the night were

a vivid self-fulfilling prophecy, to support the law-and-order forces to "do what they had to do," come what may. The "Angry Brigade" thus unwittingly provided a critical turning-point in the drift into a 'law-and-order' society. It provided such proof as seemed to be needed that a violent conspiracy against the state *did* exist, and was located in or near the mass disaffiliation of youth.[42]

With a new Conservative government in power on the basis of a "law and order" campaign, the legal system began attacking all organizations suspected of supporting disruptive behavior. Although the forces of conservatism would ultimately succeed in riding this moral panic to a resounding victory over the student movement and the entire Left in the 1980s, it would first have to face a formidable enemy in a powerful student movement and workers' revolt in the early seventies, and the students and the workers would win this first round.

TOWARDS A WORKER-STUDENT ALLIANCE

The Conservative attacks on students and workers in the early seventies reveal the strength of these movements as well as their importance in the history of the nation in that era. As workers' unions resisted the Conservative government's attacks on union privileges and wages, student unions supported the workers by joining in strikes, holding sympathy actions, raising money for striking workers, and helping to advertise the demands of the workers. In the climate of an impending working class revolution, the Communist Party, IMG and IS thrived within the student movement, encouraging students to view themselves as workers and their student unions as workers' unions. Within this context, student unions felt obligated to show solidarity with workers' struggles, and workers' unions conversely felt obligated to support student union struggles. Although this discourse failed to convince all workers and students, these groups did join together on many occasions in the early seventies and through their unity, were able to play a role in toppling the Heath government in 1974.

The main cause of the conflict between the Heath government and the workers was the Industrial Relations Act of 1971. This Act carried through with many of the ideas first proposed by Labour in the late sixties, requiring unions to officially register with the government, establishing an Industrial Relations Court to negotiate between employers and unions and impose prison sentences on those who broke its agreements, and outlining a number of other requirements designed to undermine workers' ability to strike. [43] At the same time the Conservative government was passing this Industrial Relations Act, it passed a new Criminal Damages Act, which imposed stronger penalties for damage to property and had the potential to be used against strikers, squatters, and protesters.[44] Workers' unions unsurprisingly responded with massive protests from the time these were proposed in 1970 through when it took effect in 1972. One of the largest of these was the December 1970 national day of action against the Industrial Relations Bill in which 600,000 students and workers participated with strikes, marches, and other protests.[45]

In addition to protest against the Industrial Relations Act, workers held a number of successful strikes for higher wages and against management schemes to declare workers redundant. In 1972 the Upper Clyde Stewards in Glasgow's shipbuilding industry held a mass work-in until the government and employers agreed to cancel redundancies there. This fight involved the support of students and workers from throughout Britain, and brought confidence to other workers and students through their ability to fight and win against capitalism.[46] In January 1972 the National Union of Miners held a six-week strike demanding higher wages to keep up with inflation. This strike crippled the nation, forced the government to call a three-day work-week to conserve energy, and ended with major concessions to the miners. With its flying pickets and massive demonstrations, this struggle reinforced hope in the tactic of mass united action. When the miners went on strike again in November 1973 demanding another wage increase to keep pace with inflation, Prime Minister Heath again called a three-day work week and admitted that his government faced a tremendous amount of opposition. Both miners' strikes received the support of a number of other unions, as well as students and much of the general public.[47] The second miners' strike and its widespread support was the last straw for the embattled Heath government, which called a national election in 1974. Harold Wilson of the Labour Party defeated Heath by promising to make major concessions to the trade unions and repeal the Industrial Relations Act.

This national political struggle had a tremendous impact on the student movement. One major result was the increased popularity of "Old Left" political organizations within the student movement. While New Left theorists of the sixties had argued that the British working class was incapable of leading a revolution and emphasized a student vanguard, Old Left groups such as the CP and IS had maintained that the working class would lead the revolution in Britain and urged students to support workers' strikes. The industrial struggles of the seventies and the increased militancy of many trade unions and workers' organizations appeared to prove the validity of the latter interpretations and made New Left theories seem irrelevant.

As the New Left declined in influence in the early seventies, groups such as the IS, IMG, and the CP dominated campus Socialist Societies, the NUS, and other student organizations by stressing worker-student unity and trying to transform student unions true trade into unions. Writing in 1975, IS students Alex Callinicos and Simon Turner explained the importance of the worker-student alliance both for the student movement and for achieving a working class revolution. They argued that most students were no longer part of the ruling class, but would become workers upon graduation.

Until then, they were a transitional social group, neither working class nor ruling class, but they were also an oppressed group because of their lack of control over their lives. The goal of revolutionary groups was to harness the rebellious energy and anger of the student movement, and direct it towards supporting revolutionary politics and the workers' movement. At that time, Callinicos and Turner believed that IS Societies could play a crucial role in uniting the student movement and the revolutionary workers movement, and thus contribute to the overthrow of the capitalist system. There were already ninety IS groups at universities and colleges across the nation, poised to take advantage of the economic and political crisis and recruit large numbers of students to the revolutionary struggle.[48]

Indeed the case of Oxford University in the early seventies appeared to support their theories. The IS and IMG were powerful forces in the Oxford protests of 1973–74 and echoed the rhetoric of the Old Left in their own analysis of their movement. For example, in the aftermath of the Indian Institute trial, two students in the Oxford IS group, Paul Taylor and Nick Illesly, published a pamphlet expressing their perspective on the events of that year. Placing the Oxford student movement within a framework of global economic and political changes, they argued that students were no longer members of the ruling class and that they were instead being trained to serve the ruling class in government or industry, and as such had come to challenge bourgeois ideology. They had succeeded in creating an OUSU that year, but the "victimization" of the students on trial was part of a nation-wide campaign "to frighten them away from direct action."[49] They believed that the protests that year had succeeded in increasing their own numbers on campus and had given them hope that the student movement could indeed help the workers to overthrow capitalism.

Informed by the CP, IMG, and IS, socialist societies at most universities supported workers in industrial struggles throughout the period by manning picket lines, raising money for strike funds, and providing public hearings for the workers' demands. Jimmy Reid, the leader of the Upper Clyde Shipbuilders' struggle, became a hero to student activists across the country.[50] He not only led the workers' struggle, but also championed student rights within universities and supported the student-worker alliance, even becoming the rector of Glasgow University in 1972.[51] The 1972 Miners' strike likewise attracted considerable support from student activists. Oxford University students offered their rooms to miners picketing the Didcot power station and helped to man the picket line.[52] At Essex, students belonging to the IMG, the Claimants Union, the IS, and other activist organizations created a "United Front" to support the miners and fight against the government and ruling class.[53] That spring hundreds of students at Essex supported actions by the United Front, donating money and working for the Miners, even taking over the student newspaper office to use as headquarters for their "Defense of the Miners' Strike."[54]

While socialist students whole-heartedly supported a student-worker alliance, other students remained less convinced. Many continued to see students as separate from but sympathetic to workers. One Essex student asked rhetorically: "Us, working class? How many of us have ever even *spoken* to a real worker? What the hell would we say?"[55] Students came from all classes in society, and it would be ridiculous to assume that all would support workers' struggles. By the early seventies, however, activists in the student movement would increasingly identify themselves with the workers, creating the perception of one united front against the Conservative government.

STUDENT UNION AUTONOMY

In addition to taking part in this larger industrial struggle, student activists defended their own earnings and unions from the Conservative government. A struggle over union autonomy began in 1971 with a consultative document issued by the Department of Education and Science and promoted by Minister of Education Margaret Thatcher. This White Paper asserted that student unions at many universities had been irresponsible with the money given to them by the University Grants Committee and broke their constitutions by using the money to support political groups. It proposed to make union membership voluntary and to have a general registrar to monitor student union finances. Clubs and societies would receive no funds from the unions and would have to rely entirely on student dues for support. Student unions and many university officials objected to the White Paper. Officials saw this as an attack on their budgets, while students saw it as a Conservative attempt to prevent student unions from supporting left-wing groups and give authorities more direct control over union finances.

The NUS of course opposed the Thatcher proposals, but was divided over the goals of their opposition. The CP-dominated executive wanted the government to simply drop the proposals, while the IS, IMG, and independent socialist delegates wanted the entire system revised so that student unions would be totally autonomous from the control of both government and university authorities. The latter groups formed the Liaison Committee for the Defense of Student Unions and sought an alliance with workers in a general strike against the Tory government.[56] In 1971–72, the NUS and the Liaison Committee sponsored several massive demonstrations against the Thatcher proposals. The NUS estimated that over 350,000 students participated in their December 1971 national day of action.[57] Fifty thousand attended the London demonstrations and some of the largest demonstration marches of the Long Sixties took place at universities across the nation.[58] Even the Federation of Conservative Students opposed the proposal.[59] By April 1972 the Department of Education had bowed to the pressure and shelved the proposals. The NUS executive declared victory and ended its campaign, but the Liaison Committee continued to fight for increased union autonomy for through the next year.

In addition to these national actions against the Thatcher proposals, hundreds of local protests took place across the nation. Glaswegian students attended a rally of 4,000 at Strathclyde University, but their boycott of classes was a miserable failure.[60] An article in the student newspaper explained that Glasgow students "ignored the call for a student strike, realizing that in this fight the authorities . . . were on our side, and that orderly demos were more likely to win public support than wild-cat action . . ."[61] At Essex, over ten per cent of students participated in a demonstration against the Thatcher plans in December 1971.[62] Essex, however, had disaffiliated from the NUS in 1968 and its protests were in support of the Liaison Committee demands.[63] Most Essex socialists believed that the Communist-dominated NUS was too conciliatory to the government and not radical enough in its demands. The fight for union autonomy, therefore, carried on long after the NUS had declared victory. Influenced by the Liaison Committee's arguments, Essex students fought for a completely autonomous union until 1973, when the University Council finally relinquished financial control over the union and allowed student dues to go directly to the Student Council.

These protests reveal some important dimensions of the student movement in this period. Union autonomy, unlike the issues of student representation, was interpreted as a defensive action against the government attacks on the rights of students to control their own organizations. Those students, such as the supporters of the Liaison Committee, who sought to take the offensive in the fight and gain progressive reform were in the minority in this huge campaign. The thousands of students who became active on this issue did so out of a desire to preserve what they thought were their traditional rights, rather than to gain new rights and privileges.

THE STUDENT GRANTS CAMPAIGN

Another defensive campaign within the student movement of the early 1970s was the grants campaign. By the early sixties, all full-time students over eighteen who had been accepted to a full-time higher education program, and passed two Advanced Level exams, were provided with government grants to cover fees, living expenses, books, equipment, clothes, and travel for the entire year. Students who were married women or dependent on parents would receive less according to how much their spouses or parents earned. At first students saw this grant as a privilege, allowing those with less money to attend college, but by the late sixties, most students saw grants as a form of payment for their studies and the right of every British citizen. With the influence of revolutionary socialists in the late

1960s, many student activists came to see their education as part of a job in which the government paid for their training. In this view, students were essentially the workers, while the administration and government were the employers. Grants, therefore, were effectively their wages while they were at university, and student unions were effectively industrial unions to negotiate wages (grants) and working conditions.[64]

By 1973 most leaders of the NUS saw themselves as a trade union and identified student interests with those of the working class. The NUS President Charles Clarke asserted that since the vast majority of students would find themselves as trade union members later in life, the workers unions "are the natural allies of the student body."[65] In this light, it was important for students to gain the support of workers for their grants campaign and for students to support workers in their industrial struggles. Many trade unions and socialist groups concurred with this idea of the university and the situation of students, but many conservative and liberal British workers disagreed and continued to see students as a privileged minority who consumed their taxes and should be thankful for whatever donations they received in grants. One "disgusted rate-payer" near Essex University responded to Essex' students demands for adequate grants by stating:

> Why should taxpayers provide grants for you and your long-haired, dirty, sex-ridden so-called students. I am an OAP [old-age pensioner] and have never asked for, or been given charity. . . . For God's sake stop being parasites and branch out and work for your own education, this . . . is being done by a few who do not deprive the poor to help keep them in drink, cigarettes, sex, drugs, etc. The majority of people are sick to death of students, who do the students think they are? A special privileged community? . . . Students are now considered the lowest of the low, it would help this country if most of the Universities were closed down.[66]

Many conservative citizens and government officials agreed with this rate-payer and resisted any increases in student grants, but trade unions, socialist groups, and educators agreed with student demands for grants to keep pace with inflation. This nation-wide debate over the role of students and educational funding lay at the heart of disagreements over union autonomy, grants, and student participation in university governance, putting universities at the center of the political battles of the early seventies.

Although the grants issue had been debated since the introduction of full government educational grants, the struggle between students and the government over this issue peaked in the 1972–73 academic year. By that time, students and others with fixed government incomes were suffering financial hardship because of inflation. The NUS, long a pressure group for increased student grants, began a massive campaign to force the government to increase grants and, at the local level, to pressure university authorities into lowering rents and food prices. In March 1973, an estimated 400,000 students from across Britain participated in the NUS campaign for higher grants.[67] Demonstration marches, canteen boycotts, and pickets were also held at universities across the nation that year.[68]

At Essex, for example, the grants issue attracted considerable support and eventually led to another large-scale student strike. In November 1973, a core of 100 Essex activists, with the official backing of their student union, participated in the NUS day of action for higher grants by boycotting classes and forming picket lines outside of lecture halls. A few days later a smaller group of student radicals broke into the administrative offices, read private files to uncover evidence of political spying, and occupied the building for three weeks, demanding that no disciplinary action be taken against the occupiers and that the university support the students' grants campaign. They specifically demanded a fifteen per cent reduction in catering prices and a 55 per cent reduction in rent for university housing.[69] Over the course of the protest, more than 400 students out of a student body of 2,000 participated in some part of the occupation.[70]

Many Essex students participated in the protest because of accumulated frustrations with poor facilities, poor food standards, and a general lack of social provisions for the 50 per cent of students who lived on the bleak and isolated campus at Wivenhoe.[71] The student body felt that the university was not sufficiently dedicated to giving its students a decent standard of living and felt that they needed to use their collective power of protest to pressure university officials into solving the grants problem. University officials contended that they were powerless to solve these problems because the government and the University Grants Committee allocated the university's budget, which dictated grants as well as university services. They consequently viewed student protests as a fruitless and unwarranted disruption of university functions, and accordingly brought disciplinary charges against thirty-four students involved in the occupation.

Once again, disciplinary action provoked an escalation in the protests as more students joined in to oppose "victimization." Student radicals compared their action as parallel to industrial union actions, in which individual strikers could not be disciplined because of participation in collective actions, and argued that this was therefore a clear case of victimization. Aware of the mounting conservative backlash against the student movement, activists additionally accused university officials of "using the events to purge any politically conscious student from the community to protect their own image in the eyes of the public."[72] Within the context of the conservative attack against the unions and the student movement, these arguments seemed plausible and convincing to a large number of students at Essex and elsewhere.

After the disciplinary committee expelled one student activist, students picketed the university and closed its main entrance with barricades. This action attracted widespread coverage in the press, and in the climate of industrial strife, sixteen labour unions and a large number of student unions pledged support for the Essex student struggle. The NUS officially supported the strike and sent more than 200 students to man the barricades. Police dispersed and arrested the demonstrators, but students retaliated by occupying the Vice Chancellor's office and holding him hostage for a few hours. Up to 1,000 students attended the mass meetings and about sixty members of the staff opposed the disciplinary procedures of the administration. When police arrested over 100 students for obstruction and trespassing, and the public demanded an official inquiry, the Vice Chancellor appointed a friend, Lord Annan, to make a full report of the events. The Annan report predictably laid the blame for the entire affair on the shoulders of revolutionary student activists, roughly seven IMG, twenty IS, and to a lesser extent twenty CP members, asserting that these students duped the student body into joining the criminal disruption of the university.[73]

Unlike Oxford's CSU protest, Essex students continued to protest through the 1974–75 academic year. One of the prominent demands of the previous year had been that the university reduce rents by 50 per cent, but in November of 1974, the university proposed increasing rents by 40 per cent. The Student Union responded by calling a rent strike. All student tenants of university accommodations were asked to put their rent payments in a special rent strike fund administered by the union instead of paying it to the university. Since the demonstrations and massive protests of the previous year had little effect on relieving their financial difficulties, they concluded that this new tactic might be more successful and unite them more closely with the workers' movement. A member of the Essex IMG asserted that the Essex rent strike was part of a larger working class effort to prevent the ruling class from forcing them to bear the brunt of suffering from high inflation and unemployment. By the spring of 1975, over 200 students had participated in the rent strike by paying into the strike fund. The university responded by threatening to withhold exam results from students who refused to pay their rent, but the strike continued into June 1975. The strike involved fewer Essex students and was less sensational than earlier occupations and marches, but it is nevertheless evidence of continuing activism around the issue of student financial rights.[74]

Many other students used the rent strike as another way to fight for higher grants. One reason that higher grants were necessary was that rents continued to increase at an alarming rate throughout the period. The rent strike was actually an old working class tactic to protest against greedy landlords, but it became more popular in the seventies as rent inflation became a widespread problem.[75] Workers and students formed renters' unions to coordinate withholding rents and negotiate with landlords. Since most universities managed student housing, they were the landlords on the other side of student rent strikes. By 1973 the NUS had adopted rent strikes as part of their campaign for increased grants and more than forty universities and colleges, including Oxford University, held rent strikes.

The rent strikes and grants campaigns continued through the mid-1970s, as the recession continued and the new Wilson government failed to dramatically increase student grants or increase funding to the universities. At Warwick University, the student rent strike campaign escalated into a four-week long occupation in April and May of 1975. After a strong rent strike throughout the fall term, the university administration continued to refuse their demands to lower rents. Faced with the choice of either giving up the rent strike and paying the rents and fines, or escalating the campaign to potentially win their demands, the student union executive voted to occupy the central administration offices until the administration lowered their rents. Having learned from previous sit-ins, the executive carefully planned the occupation, with each member taking the responsibility of forming committees to organize cleaning, security, entertainment, and negotiations. They brought in generators when the power was cut off and set up study areas so that students could continue to study for exams. When the administration rejected their demands and threatened to withhold exams and grant money to the occupiers, as well as send in the police to enforce a court injunction to evict them, over 1,000 students at a general meeting voted to continue the occupation. Support poured in from the NUS, trade unions, teaching unions and even the local MP, Audrey Wise.[76] Eventually, however, Warwick students succumbed to the pressure of exams and summer holiday without an agreement on rents.

The grants and the union autonomy campaigns garnered tremendous student participation, but they also attracted the support of many trade unions and other workers' organizations. Although the popular news media consistently reported that the working class disliked students and that the students ignored workers' interests, the reality was that many workers' unions supported the student grants campaign and the vast majority of students supported the working class struggle against the Conservative government. Indeed, the expansion of higher education and student grants allowed many of the working class to send their children to university for the first time. In an October 1973 Glasgow student grants demonstration, the Glasgow Trades Council, and fifty local shop stewards committees expressed their solidarity with the student protesters.[77] Trade unions also supported Essex students' struggles for adequate grants. While many British citizens may have disapproved of student protesters who demanded more of their taxes, many workers' organizations saw the student attack on the government as part of a wider left-wing attempt to gain power over their lives and working conditions, and as such, deserving of their support.

With the help of working-class organizations, student rights activists achieved some important victories in the early seventies. They successfully blocked Thatcher's proposals to control student unions and after the Wilson government came to power, students eventually won a 25 per cent increase in the standard grant, an annual review of grants to keep up with inflation, and a 40 per cent increase for married women students, who had typically received much less than male students.[78]

STUDENT POWER

While the student grants and union autonomy issues rose to the forefront of the British student movement in the early seventies, the related issue of student rights remained an important part of the movement as well. Students had made significant progress on this issue in the late sixties so that by 1974, most universities allowed student representation on at least some university committees, and 25 out of 67 universities and colleges had at least one student as a full member of the University Council or Court.[79] Even these student representatives, however, were greatly outnumbered in university governance and consequently had little real power over decision-making. Most universities had no student representation on the governing board or allowed students to attend Council, Senate, or Committee meetings only as consultants or observers. University governing structures across the country also remained virtually unchanged. Because of this continued inequality, the NUS continued to pressure the Vice Chancellors for increased student participation in university governance and many student unions also acted independently for increased student decision-making power. Reflecting the growing influence of the Old Left within the NUS and student unions, however, this issue was often framed as an issue of workers' control of their workplace.

The most prominent illustration of this tendency is the case of the LSE. Students there had successfully fought for and won significant increases in student representation within their university. Six of the LSE's ninety-eight full members of Court were students, and LSE students were allowed to be observers upon invitation by the Senate.[80] Student activists, however, recognized their lack of real power in these arrangements and continued to struggle to restructure their university in order to gain more real representation in decision-making. In the seventies, however, they began to pair this goal with gaining "workers' control" of the university. In 1971, LSE student union Vice President John Fisk argued that all those who worked in the university— staff, porters, cleaners, and students— should be allowed to participate in a decentralized democratic university government.[81] This argument reflects the overall tenor of the LSE Union Council in the early seventies. Influenced by labor unions' demands for worker's control and their IS and IMG controlled Socialist Society, LSE student leaders refused to accept the moderate reforms which had allowed them minority participation in most levels of university government. While the leadership remained militant, the vast majority of LSE students rarely supported strikes and disruptions on this issue. LSE radicals were reduced to militant speeches and articles in the newspaper, and participating in off-campus struggles for worker's control and against the government. Without the support of masses of students, they could not achieve their goal of restructuring the university.

One of the most infamous student rights protests of the 1970s occurred in 1972 during Queen Elizabeth's visit to the recently built University of Stirling in Scotland. University officials there diverted a considerable amount of money to prepare for the festivities surrounding this visit. The Student Union opposed this expenditure and held a protest demonstration during the Queen's visit. The press claimed that students shouted obscenities at the Queen, raised a clenched fist salute to the crowd, and committed other outrageous and disrespectful acts. Under tremendous pressure to take some action against the students, the university administration singled out twenty-four students to charge with failing to maintain order and drinking from a bottle in the Queen's presence, "which act was abusive and discourteous to the Queen and her accompanying party." [82] NUS Scotland soon set up a Stirling Appeal Fund and organized a mass rally on the first day of the disciplinary hearings, which was attended by 4,000 students from all over Britain. Protests continued in the spring when Linda Quinn, the Stirling Student Union president, was suspended for participating in a meeting at which the protest against the Queen was planned, failing to maintain order at the meeting, and playing a leading role in other occupations. Pickets of the disciplinary proceedings and rallies demanding an official inquiry into the matter and the resignation of University Vice Chancellor Tom Cottrell continued through the spring. In the midst of the protests and enquiry, Cottrell died of a heart attack. Many British faculty and administrators, as well as many students, were stunned by his death and attributed it to continual student harassment. The press then used this negative reaction to fuel its attack on the student movement. [83] By the mid-seventies, incidents like the Stirling protest and the consequent negative press coverage would reify the narrative of the student movement as irrational, un-British, and illegitimate.

WOMEN'S LIBERATION

While student rights and the student-worker alliance dominated the student movement in the early seventies, feminist ideology continued to spread throughout the movement. Women's liberationists convinced the majority of student activists to back the goals set by feminists in 1970: free 24-hour nurseries, equal pay, equal education, and job opportunities. Student unions across the country voiced support for these goals, as well as other more university-specific goals. In some cases, feminist students carried out their own direct actions in support of these goals, but this activism met with mixed success. The university system and even the bulk of the student population were slow to change.

Probably the most famous women's liberation action of the early seventies was the November 1970 Miss World protest at Albert Hall in London. Inspired by the 1968 protest against the Miss America competition, London feminists disrupted the Miss World pageant to raise consciousness of the sexism at the heart of this commercial commodification of women's bodies. In front of a large British and American audience, "radical feminists began to shout from the stalls—perhaps as many as a hundred—and caught [emcee Bob] Hope off guard."[84] Hope was clearly annoyed with the repeated rattles, whistles and shouts interrupting the program. After sacks of flour, bags of ink, and stink bombs were thrown at Hope and the contestants, a group of protesters rushed the stage and were physically ejected from the event. Five were arrested and their trial inspired further protests.[85] The protesters definitely succeeded in attracting the attention of the world, but the symbolism and message were not always communicated effectively. Many Britons were appalled at the disrespectful and disruptive behavior, but many students were made aware of feminist issues for the first time, adding to the feminist movement which was growing on universities across the nation.

Inspired by the Miss World protest and the first women's liberationists, university students continued to form their own consciousness-raising groups and attempted to alleviate sexism amongst students and within the educational system. For example, LSE's Women's Liberation Group joined with women's organizations from other London University schools in November 1970 to protest a sexist article in its newspaper, *Sennet*, and the Miss Fresher competition, which they called "an outrageous violation and degradation of women and human relationships. . . . of men viewing the girls entering colleges simply as pieces of meat to be graded, consumed, and discarded."[86] After picketing the *Sennet* offices, the women's group attended the Miss Fresher competition to challenge the students "to explain why they were participating in such blatant exploitation and oppression of women. The only responses were booing and mockery."[87] The situation for women at LSE changed little in the early 1970s. A letter to the editor in 1974 showed that the Careers Advisory service refused to give women information on jobs which specified "men only," that only one-third of LSE undergraduates and only one-tenth of the graduate students were women, and that male students still dominated the Student Union Executive and gave little consideration to women's issues.[88] Regardless of this lack of change, LSE's feminist students continued to press for reforms to create a university nursery and a women's studies course at LSE. They succeeded in getting the sociology department to create a women's studies course in the 1975–76 academic year, but the nursery was not forthcoming.[89]

A more successful women's rights group formed at Hull University in the spring of 1971. Demonstrating the influence of Marxist theories of sexual oppression in an article in the student newspaper *Torchlight*, they urged women to "unite with the working class to achieve a society which eliminates all prejudice—racist, chauvinist, sexist, for only through this struggle can any group achieve true liberation."[90] This article immediately received sharp criticism from other students. One stated, "If you ask me, the rise of the Women's Liberation Organization is the end of femininity. The organization is made for Tom Boys who want to act just like men—except when they are in bed."[91] Despite this negative reaction, feminists gained the support of the Student Union and successfully pressured the Vice Chancellor into providing students and faculty with a campus crèche.[92]

The more radical Essex women's liberation group, which was founded in 1969, moved from reform initiatives, such as providing child care, to the more revolutionary goal of transforming sex roles altogether. Writing in 1971, four members of the Essex Women's Liberation group stated that "we want to change the existing division of sex roles and the framework within which they operate. . . . both the family and the economic system are closely interconnected agents for the constraint and restriction of people into pre-determined roles."[93] Writing in 1972, Essex feminist Eve Hostettler revealed the extent of sexual inequalities at Essex: the ratio of male to female undergraduates was about four to one, there were far less women than men on the academic staff, and five times as many men as women were awarded higher degrees at Essex.[94] She pointed out that these inequalities began in the socialization of women at home, which led them to adopt service and support roles rather than developing their own abilities. Hostettler also revealed the success of women's liberation on campus, claiming that it had given women a new direction, an opportunity to assert themselves as individuals, and strength and solidarity by organizing them around their own oppression. As a consequence, men and women were questioning gender stereotypes and more women were playing a prominent role in campus political activities.[95]

By the 1974–75 academic year, Essex women were heavily involved in student politics and the student body had come out strongly in favor of the women's rights movement. They elected a female president of the Student Union and passed a motion stating:

> the removal of all barriers to equality for women in education, training and job opportunity is an essential part of the students' demands for a fairer education system. . . . students alone will not win these demands, and need to develop strong links with all groups in the local communities working for the same ends.[96]

The Union further resolved to support the Working Women's Charter Group, work for the NUS women's campaign, and send a coach to London to support the International Women's Day celebration in March. Women's liberation gained considerable support among Essex students, but never involved as many students as did activism for union autonomy and student grants. This was largely because feminists used different strategies to promote their cause, placing more emphasis on liberating individual women through consciousness-raising groups, successfully exposing and challenging gender stereotypes, and increasing student and administrative sensitivity to women's issues, rather than large public demonstrations.

The NUS was slow to respond to women's liberation, but followed the lead of the Communist Party when it took a strong stand in support of women's rights in 1972. At its national conference that year, the NUS passed a long motion on women's equality, but made it secondary to the class struggle:

> Conference recognizes that the oppression faced by women in British Society cannot be seen in isolation from the capitalist system class structure and realizes that there can be no *meaningful* Women's Liberation until the Class System is destroyed since the subjugation of women is directly related to the economic and social roles cast for them regardless of class.[97]

It did, however, become a leading supporter of women's rights in the universities for decades afterwards, holding annual conferences on women's rights, and campaigning to achieve equal grants for married women students, university nurseries, the availability of contraception and abortion on demand, and increased educational opportunities for women.[98]

Women's rights involved small numbers of highly dedicated students throughout the 1970s. Although their actions were generally unspectacular, student women's liberation groups provided crucial support groups for women who struggled against sexism. They achieved better childcare facilities and health care for women, and built new women's centers and safe houses for victims of sexual abuse.[99] They also eventually won the support of many trade unions, students, and socialist organizations for equal pay for equal work, and greater access to higher education and contraception. Despite its widespread growth and strength in the early seventies, however, the women's liberation movement failed to convince many Britons to make deeper changes in their personal approach to gender stereotypes and sexual relations. Women's rights organizations made some gains in ending sex discrimination in the work place and higher education, but in this era they fell far short of their larger goal of ending sex inequalities and discrimination in Britain.

GAY LIBERATION

The women's liberation movement, together with the counterculture, civil rights movements, and the American gay liberation movement, also gave rise to gay liberation groups on many British campuses in the seventies. At many universities, women's liberation groups worked very closely with gay liberation groups, holding mutual conferences and sharing ideas on sexual oppression and tactics. Although homosexual students in Britain had no incident like the Stonewall riots, which had sparked gay rights activism in America in 1969, nor a prominent off-campus gay liberation movement to draw from, they were inspired by the American gay liberation movement and their experiences within the British counterculture and student movement. The *Sexual Offences Act of 1967* had legalized homosexuality in England and Wales for consenting males over 21, but it was still socially unacceptable and illegal in Scotland, Northern Ireland, and the British armed forces. Gay students, like women, faced the prejudice of their fellow students in addition to social discrimination in the wider society. Heterosexuals ridiculed gay students, and they had few places where they could meet socially or be themselves. Similar to feminists and other activists of the sixties, gay students organized a mass movement to fight for their civil and social rights. They fought for the lowering of the age of consent for homosexuals to eighteen, the same as for heterosexuals, and for increased public understanding and acceptance of homosexuality. Like the women's liberation movement, student gay rights activism in Britain involved far fewer participants than did other issues, but provided crucial support to gay students and gained the support of many students.

The inaugural meeting for the British Gay Liberation Front (GLF) was held at the LSE in October 1970. This was the brain-child of LSE student Bob Mellors and Aubrey Walter, who had visited America earlier that year, become immersed in the American Gay Liberation Front, and met each other at a Revolutionary People's Constitutional convention in Philadelphia. Inspired by both experiences, they determined to begin a GLF movement in Britain.[100] Twenty LSE men and women attended their first meeting. This group showed the influence of the American movement at their first meeting when Mellors and Walter spoke of their experiences in the Gay Liberation Front in the United States. They asserted that they were fighting to end the oppression of gay people and to liberate themselves. Their first target was *Sennet*, which had published an article offensive to women in its male chauvinism and to gays who were called "queers." The GLF joined Women's Liberation and Agit-Prop in protesting at the *Sennet* offices. Later that year, the GLF also held a candlelight march to protest the arrest of a gay student charged with gross indecency. The LSE GLF remained active in defending gay rights and providing an important forum for sharing mutual concerns for the next several decades.[101]

David Fernbach, who was a former LSE student, an editor of the *New Left Review,* and Walter's partner, soon afterwards became a full-fledged gay rights activist. Fernbach had "a fairly easy time of it as a gay person" in that he felt accepted by the CND group he had joined as a youth and that even at the LSE, it was okay to be gay as long as he kept quiet about it. He had never seen it as a part of his political activism, however, until he began reading about the gay liberation movement in America. When

Walter came back with his plans to redirect his activism towards gay rights, Fernbach was forced to rethink his own politics. He then participated in the mass gay liberation actions of 1971–72, seeing the Festival of Light counter-demonstration as the highlight of these.[102] Hundreds turned up at their weekly London GLF meetings and hundreds more were involved in various workshops and other groups. Fernbach recalls his time in the gay liberation movement as his happiest time in the Long Sixties, and believes that the London gay rights movement provided social facilities and critical support to gay people which they had never had before.[103]

Essex students also founded a Gay Liberation Front in 1971, which was outspoken in its defense of the gay community and homosexual rights. In 1973 Essex students held a GLF conference which attracted 120 delegates from universities across the country. Delegates discussed the main issues confronting Gay people: repression, aggression, discrimination and alienation. The conference also held Gay Marxist and feminist workshops. To eliminate any sex intimidation, women at the feminist workshop excluded men from participating. Later the conference discussed the dual oppression faced by gays and women, and agreed that unification and solidarity was necessary for their mutual success. Reporting on the conference for the wider student body, Essex student Simon Pringle explained the wider meaning of Gay Liberation in relationship to Marxist discourse, arguing that the GLF was subversive to capitalism because it undermined the family-unit-as-consumer-producer on which capitalism is based.[104] These interconnections between the students', women's, socialist, and gay rights movements were discussed in many GLF publications across the country in this period, as gay rights activists worked out their place within the wider social movements of the era.

Gay rights groups formed at several other universities in the seventies, but not all students accepted homosexuality as a right. Gay rights activists found especially strong resistance at Glasgow University. Reflecting their contempt for homosexuals, student journalists derogatorily referred to gays as "poofs," "perverts," and "queers," and used the NUS's backing of the gay liberation movement as a reason for not affiliating with the union.[105] In this atmosphere, it was extremely difficult for Glasgow's gay students to come "out of the closet" and join the gay liberation movement. It was not until 1975 that a gay society was created at Glasgow, and even then it was at the initiative of the student council rather than gay students themselves.[106]

Despite the continued homophobia of many students, gay rights activists made considerable progress in providing meeting places and support groups for homosexual students. The number of gay student societies rose from nineteen in 1973 to eighty in 1974.[107] The NUS became a strong advocate for gay rights after 1973, working with trade unions to protect people from dismissal on the grounds of sexual orientation, reporting on gay rights and the problems of homosexual men and women, holding teach-ins and campaigns to educate tutors and students about gay rights, helping to form Gay

Societies, and fighting to lower the age of consent for homosexual behavior.[108] While student gay rights activists succeeded in creating gay societies at universities across the nation and increasing student awareness of gay rights, like feminists, they failed to seriously undermine public stereotypes and prejudice or eliminate discrimination against them.

APARTHEID

At the same time the British student movement was branching out into new issues in response to the changed social, economic, and political context of the 1970s, the issue of apartheid in South Africa, which had emerged at the very beginning of the Long Sixties era, remained prominent in the student movement throughout the seventies. In 1975, there were still seventy student groups affiliated with the Anti-Apartheid Movement.[109] Students continued to use the strategies they had developed in the late sixties, including divestment of university shares in corporations engaged in trade in South Africa as well as demonstrating against segregated South African sports teams. The politicized NUS attempted to lead this movement, launching its own Anti-Apartheid Movement Campaign in 1972, but most activism against apartheid continued to be organized at the local university level.[110] While union autonomy, grants, rents, and workers strikes preoccupied most student activists in the early seventies, anti-apartheid protests could still attract widespread support and even spark large-scale actions at some universities in this period.

At Hull University, for example, this issue led to a massive strike and campaign led by the Hull Anti-Apartheid Society to force the university to divest its shares in Reckitt and Colman Ltd.[111] This campaign dragged on for several years, leading to a sit-in of hundreds of students in 1972 and continued pressure on university authorities from the student council. In 1975 the university still refused to take moral consideration into account in its investments and continued to hold the shares. Students, therefore, employed a new tactic: they purchased a share of stock in Barclays Bank to allow their union to participate in the bank's general meetings and press for withdrawal of investments in South Africa.[112] After years of tactics such as these, and many other students joining in the Barclays protests, the bank finally sold their South African subsidies in the 1980s.

Students also continued to boycott and protest against South African sports teams playing on British soil. The NUS participated in this campaign against South African sports teams by coordinating local actions and advertising the issue. The campaign against the Springboks achieved some success in 1974, when several Labour MPs signed a letter calling for the cancellation of the Springboks' tour.[113] Activism against apartheid, however, was not without its costs. The South African government had a long history of assassination and harassment of anti-apartheid activists both inside and outside of its borders. Peter Hain, who had continued to lead actions against South African sports teams in the early seventies, believes that they were behind an attempt on his life and a legal prosecution mounted against him in 1972. In June of 1972, he received a letter bomb, which was defused by Scotland Yard. Later that year, he was brought up on criminal conspiracy charges for all of the disruptions against the South African sports teams. After a four-week trial, in which he defended himself, he was freed when the jury was split in its decision.[114] In this case and in many others where students were expelled and lost their careers, student activists paid a high price for their idealism.

The fight against apartheid was one important thread within the student movement, weaving its way through all periods of the Long Sixties, from the late fifties through the mid-seventies. Indeed, it was one issue that distinguished the British student movement from its counterparts in other countries—no other student movement outside of Africa protested against apartheid as consistently or as passionately. Because of their nation's imperial past and continued economic ties with South Africa and Rhodesia, British students probably felt a greater obligation to help solve this problem. As one strategy after another failed to end apartheid, students adapted by using new tactics such as confrontational pickets at sports matches and becoming shareholders in companies with ties to apartheid. Through years of devoted activism, however, students saw some success on this issue. Eighteen English universities withdrew their financial investments in South Africa in the early seventies.[115] The NUS additionally campaigned to raise money for African liberation movements, and together with Southampton and Sussex universities, raised £3,000 in 1973.[116] That year it began one of its longest and ultimately successful campaigns: the campaign for the release of Nelson Mandela. While all of this activity failed to immediately end apartheid in South Africa, it did succeed in turning most of the British public against South African trade, putting considerable pressure on the South African government, and contributing to the ultimate release of Mandela and the downfall of apartheid.

The campaign against apartheid illustrates how some issues remained at the core of the student movement throughout the Long Sixties. Like apartheid, the issues of imperialism and university reform were central to the student movement at the end of the fifties and remained prominent through the mid-seventies. Student activists used many of the same strategies as they had in the first Suez, CND, and anti-apartheid protests: sit-ins, demonstration marches, and pickets. Yet the movement continued to evolve in the seventies as it was confronted with the political and economic crises of the time. Confronted with the feminist and homosexual critique of the sexism and homophobia of the university system, the student movement embraced the issues of women's and gay rights in the seventies, significantly contributing to both of these social movements long afterwards. Faced with an increasingly hostile press and Conservative government which attacked its unions and student grants, the student movement was also forced to go on the defensive. As a consequence, it mobilized some of the largest national student protests of the era in defense of union autonomy and adequate grant funding. The student movement of the seventies had thus finally reached the zenith of its power to mobilize the masses of students and influence national politics.

The most important cause of this escalation in the student movement was the climate of economic and political crisis in the early seventies. Swept into office on the heels of economic woes, rising industrial conflict, and a conservative backlash against the student protests of the late sixties, the Conservative government went on the offensive in the early seventies. It attacked both student and industrial union power as it attempted to solve the problems of stagflation and perceived permissiveness. Students and labor unions responded with massive protests and strikes, crippling the nation in the early seventies and eventually forcing the Heath government out. In this unprecedented wave of dissent, students joined workers on the picket line and workers supported student struggles for union autonomy and grants. Orchestrated by the CP, the IS, the RSSF and the newly politicized NUS, this student-worker alliance was tentative and short-lived, but powerful in helping both groups to win their demands.

The militancy of the workers' movement in this period hastened the downfall of New Left theories of a student-led revolution, and appeared to confirm the arguments of the IS and CP in favor of student support for a worker-led revolution. As a result, the influence of these Old Left groups increased dramatically within socialist societies and student unions across the nation. While a New Left emphasis on extra-parliamentary direct action, participatory democracy, and humanist socialism remained firmly embedded within the student movement, Old Left rhetoric and styles proliferated. Socialist students repeatedly interpreted issues such as student representation, student union autonomy, and student grants within the context of the wider struggle of students and workers against capitalism. While this rhetoric did not convince all students or workers, it did help to reorient the student movement away from viewing itself as a part of a global youth movement towards identifying itself as part of a national socialist workers' movement.

The prolonged protests at Oxford University in 1973–74 were thus only one manifestation of a much larger trend within the student movement emphasizing the power and importance of student and workers unions as important agents of change. Oxford's student activists had been demanding a Central Student Union since the early sixties, but in the midst of massive industrial strikes and the enormous NUS campaigns in defense of student union autonomy and student grants, it became even more vital for them to have their own student union to help them to join this fight and fully mobilize the power of their own students in support of student rights and a socialist revolution. This was the reason why the IMG and IS led the fifth of November occupation and pushed the campaign for a CSU forward so passionately. Of course, students also supported the CSU to gain better social and sports facilities, but the main initiative of the campaign was far more political. Socialist students wanted to use this CSU to support the student-worker movement to topple the Heath government. What at first glance may have seemed like a parochial protest was actually a response to the social, economic, and political forces shaping the nation in the seventies. The Oxford protests and the massive wave of other student protests in the seventies clearly demonstrates how the student movement remained vibrant through at least the middle of the decade and continued to shape the national political and social debates of that critical era in British history.

Epilogue and Conclusions

Student activism did not suddenly come to an end at the end of the sixties, nor did it end in 1975. Student activism continued throughout the end of the twentieth century, but received far less media coverage than in the sixties and attracted less attention from social commentators who had grown accustomed to youth involvement in social movements. Students continued to sponsor a variety of small actions around many different issues in the later seventies, but except for a few extraordinary examples, this activism was no longer widespread enough or sustained enough to be truly considered a "movement."

The NUS continued to lead most student activism after the Long Sixties, but with dwindling support. For example, the NUS held another demonstration against cuts in education funding in February 1975, but drew much smaller numbers than in previous years. Another NUS demonstration for fair grants attracted 20,000 in February 1976, but activism on the issue at the local level dwindled.[1] Rent strikes began to fail as students realized that their university administrations could not afford to reduce rent rates and penalized them for non-payment. The NUS and individual student unions continued to support international causes, such as solidarity with leftists in Chile and civil rights protesters in Northern Ireland, but few held occupations or sit-ins over these issues and they did not escalate as was the case with the Vietnam War issue. Women's rights continued to gather support from student groups, but student activists noticed that their actions were attracting little support amongst the student population and felt that extensive militant activity could no longer be sustained. Despite sporadic protests after the mid-seventies, the media and the majority of students no longer framed it as a movement or as a decisive political, social, or moral challenge for the nation.

There are several possible reasons for this move away from defining student protest as a social movement and indeed the overall decline of activism (at least until the new upsurge in 2010). By the mid-seventies, protest activism was becoming passé as a new generation of students entered universities. Shaped by the economic, social, and political shocks of the early seventies, this new generation was perhaps bored with the activism that had dominated more than a decade of university history, and was more concerned with their careers and finding a job in the more competitive job market of the late seventies. In May 1975, for example, the Oxford student newspaper reported that "many women as well as men have dismissed International Women's Year as one overwhelming bore."[2] Similar comments and criticisms of student protests that year in other newspapers indicate considerably less enthusiasm for activism, and considerably more attention to films, fashions, and female nudity than to political or social issues. Perhaps protest, which continued to be widespread outside the universities in the late seventies and eighties, moved from being associated with youth and students to being a middle-aged activity. After all, the original student protesters from the beginning of the Long Sixties were in their thirties by the late seventies. Many of them had become leaders of other social movements, labor unions, and political parties. This demographic trend would make it more difficult for students to see protest as truly youthful or their own.

The cultural climate of the nation too changed in the eighties and nineties, inevitably affecting the prospects of student activism. Higher education continued to expand, so that by 2000, forty per cent of young people went on to university or college, but the nation could not sustain the increased cost associated with this expansion. As a result, student grants diminished and universities began to charge tuition. Students reacted to these financial measures with sporadic outbursts of protests, but no sustained student movement emerged prior to 2010. The political culture of those decades no longer framed university students as essential to the national economy or saw student grants as a sort of wage for their university work. The liberal welfare state and reputation of mass movements had eroded so much so that most students no longer believed that mass direct action was appropriate in defense of their grants. In the changed cultural and economic climate of the eighties and nineties, student protest thus attracted smaller numbers of devoted activists, while the majority of students turned their attention to their personal and career development.

To some extent, the decline of the student movement was also the result of the victory conservatives had achieved in defining student protest as mindlessly destructive "hooliganism." The mainstream media had contributed to this narrative as early as the 1967 Troubles at the LSE, but by the early seventies, the press was already announcing the death of the student movement as an unimportant fashion relic of the swinging sixties. Writing in 1975, former NUS president and student activist Digby Jacks explained that in the late sixties "the press sought to stigmatize students, alienate the general public from them and weaken the effect of their actions. More recently the press has come to regard what students do as irrelevant or not 'newsworth,' presumably because it has happened before and there is not enough violence, etc. Some journalists have been taken in by their own clichés and from time to time pronounce the student movement "dead."[3] He argued that, to the contrary, the student movement was stronger and more successful in the mid-seventies than ever. Perhaps student activism did not die in the mid-seventies, but the student movement of the Long Sixties, as it was defined by the press and many of the students themselves, was over.

CONCLUSIONS

The student movement of the Long Sixties thus extended well beyond one decade, stretching from the late fifties to the mid-seventies. The movement had coalesced out of hundreds of actions on the local level and dozens of national protest demonstrations around similar issues, including imperialism, nuclear weapons, racism, and university reform, using similar protest forms, including demonstration rallies and marches, sit-ins, and pickets, and similar ideology and rhetoric, including the participatory democracy and humanist socialism of the New Left. Despite continuities in many issues and strategies, the era witnessed three distinct generations of activism, including liberal activism focused on nuclear weapons and racism from 1958 to 1963, New Left protests focused on student rights and imperialism from 1964 to 1968, and Old Left actions focused on building a worker-student alliance against the Conservative Party from 1969 to 1975. Each of these generations had its own distinct identity, responding to specific local, national, and transnational developments, as well as building upon previous generations of activism. The movement transformed as students critiqued their own movement, reacted to criticism leveled by social commentators, politicians, and the mainstream media, and responded to national and international issues, such as the Suez crisis, the development of apartheid in South Africa and Rhodesia, the Vietnam War, the Industrial Relations Act, and national higher education reforms.

   Each individual protest also had a local flavor, however, as it responded to developments within each individual university, as well as national and international issues. In the Troubles at the LSE in 1967, long-term student concern over racism and representation in decision-making evolved into protest when administrators ignored student wishes and appointed the Principal of University College in Rhodesia to be the new Director of the LSE. Dissent at Essex had likewise simmered around local problems for years until university officials unjustly disciplined student activists and protests escalated into a mass movement in 1968. Disciplinary actions against activists sparked mass movements in many places throughout the Long Sixties, raising deeper questions about the nature of authority, the structure of the university, and student rights. Warwick's protests originated in students' desires for the kind of university community they had been promised, but spiraled into a much larger movement when students discovered administrative files which made it seem as though their own administrators were conspiring with conservative industrialists against the student movement and left-wing staff. Lastly, the protests at Oxford University emerged out of a decade-long student movement demanding their own student union, and were brought to a head by administrative reaction and the powerful example of workers' union actions. Each of these protests arose out of the national and global climate in which they emerged, but were uniquely shaped by the each university's students, staff, administrators, physical structures, and traditions.

The unique local and national contexts of the British student movement distinguished it from all other student movements. The influence of Britain's own New Left and Campaign for Nuclear Disarmament helped British students to form their activist movement years earlier than many other countries and shaped their rhetoric, symbols, ideology, and protest strategies through the sixties. Because of Britain's unique imperial past, the British student movement focused more attention on apartheid in South Africa and Rhodesia than any other student movement outside of Africa. The loss of Britain's empire also shaped the student movement's desire for a revival of national prestige by becoming a moral leader in a new world order. This desire led it to demand British intervention against apartheid, unilateral nuclear disarmament, and condemnation of US actions in Vietnam. The strength of Britain's Marxist Left also uniquely shaped its student movement. While the Old Left was obliterated by anti-communism in West Germany and the United States, in Britain, the Communist Party and various Marxist-Leninist groups survived to take part in the emerging student movement. By the end of the sixties, their arguments and ideologies had infused the student movement, and by the early seventies, they had taken over the major organizations of the student movement to lead it towards a worker-student alliance. These groups gave the British student movement an ideological vigor lacking in many other student movements, and helped it to join with workers in achieving remarkable successes in the early seventies, including the ultimate downfall of the Heath government. As student movements elsewhere declined, the British student movement reached the zenith of its national power.

While the British movement was unique in all of these ways, it was also similar to other global student movements in a number of important ways. Each of the national student movements emerged out of the social, cultural, and political climate which dominated the industrialized West in the fifties. Similar to their counterparts in Western Europe, Japan, and North America, British students were born in the baby boom following the Second World War, raised in the Cold War rhetoric of freedom and democracy, and its contradictory emphasis on nuclear weapons, racism, and polarizing politics. Coming of age when their economies were thriving, this student generation did not fear unemployment and had high expectations for their educations and their societies. Hoping to train this large generation for highly-skilled positions in their modernized economies, governments in all of these nations expanded their systems of higher education. When students found crowded conditions and their universities and societies revealed that students were not as free, equal, and democratic as they had expected to be, they were disillusioned and became more critical of their universities and societies. These structural factors, together with the contradictions between the ideology and reality of the Cold War, and the consequent rise of a dissenting global New Left, contributed to the development of student movements in all of these regions in the Long Sixties. The British movement, therefore, was indeed similar to these other movements, but not because it was imitating them. Rather, it emerged out of the same forces and interacted with the global student movement through conferences, the mass media, and student exchanges, resulting in similar perspectives, rhetoric, and forms of protest.

In comparison with its counterparts elsewhere, the British student movement was just as significant, involving comparable numbers of students, and having a similar impact on the nation's media, politicians, and public. Like countries such as France and the United States, British students participated in several spectacular national protests in 1968, most notably the October VSC demonstration, as well as a number of other large-scale protests with the CND in the early sixties, and in support of student union autonomy, grants, and workers' movements in the early seventies. These were indeed massive protests, causing quite a stir amongst the media and Parliament. Violent confrontations between police and protesters occurred, but they were not as dramatic as at the barricades in the French May or the Chicago Democratic National Convention. This relative lack of violence was a result of effective crowd management on the part of the police and the British culture of respectable behavior, rather than a lack of passion on the part of the protesters. Similar to other nations, most student activism took place in independent, local actions around similar issues, using similar tactics. The British student movement did not have a powerful left-wing organization, like the German and American SDS, but it did have the smaller RSA and RSSF, the NUS which became a strong activist organization in the late sixties, strong local socialist societies and student unions, and strong adult activist organizations in the CND, VSC, and CP. The British movement may have had less of a cohesive national organizational identity, but that did not prevent student activists from identifying themselves with their counterparts in struggle, expressing solidarity for each other's actions, joining in specific protests together, and frequently coordinating their local actions with actions elsewhere.

Similar to student movements everywhere, the British student movement always struggled against the apathy of the majority of students. Even at the height of worldwide student protests in the sixties, the majority of students in almost every country were interested primarily in careers and related professional issues. Only a minority of students in all places and at all times chose to act upon their discontent. A number of opinion polls taken during the sixties confirm that politically radical student activists in most of the world only consisted of one or two per cent of the student population.[4] The transitory state of studentship and the lack of involvement of the majority of students have made student movements very difficult to sustain beyond a few weeks, and extremely difficult to maintain from the end of the academic term in the spring to the beginning of the new academic term in the autumn. Given all of these factors, sustained student activist movements are indeed historical anomalies. Despite the difficulties in maintaining the support of large numbers of students, disciplined and dedicated socialist societies succeeded in involving larger numbers of British students for their protests when they gained student union support or were persecuted by university administrators. Even when they could not rally large numbers to their protests, socialist societies played an important role in translating New Left and Old Left ideologies to the student movement and the student population as a whole, convincing the majority of students to support participatory democracy and racial equality by the end of the sixties.

Despite the small numbers of highly involved student activists, the British student movement had a significant influence not only on universities, but also on national politics. They won student representation in university decision-making, reforms in curriculum and assessment, increased autonomy for student unions, and increased student grants. They were able to gain the support of workers' groups for a number of student actions and helped workers to win their demands in the seventies. They shaped national debates over racism, apartheid, Vietnam, educational reform, the limits of social democracy, the welfare state, youth rebellion, and permissiveness. Parliament discussed student protests in several debates in the late sixties and early seventies, and the Conservative Party used the student movement as a political target in their 1970 election campaign. Student activists even helped to topple the Heath government in the 1970s. The British student movement was obviously not just some bit player in a cultural revolution— it was a key player in national politics.

While much of this activism resulted in significant victories for the student movement, it also played an unintentional role in strengthening conservative forces after the late sixties and contributing to their victories in the 1970 election and their dominance at the polls in the eighties. A key to this development was the conservative media, which consistently depicted student protests as illegitimate, infantile, naïve, destructive, and criminal. Beginning with the LSE Troubles of 1967, the media, aided by conservative staff and administrators, constructed a narrative of the student movement as being overtly influenced by Americanism, implying that British students really had no reason to complain and were merely playing at politics, or somehow inventing issues or problems around which they could organize. Although a handful of American students did participate in British protests, as has clearly been shown, most activists were born in Britain and responded to the political, social, and economic context in which they lived. British students did in fact have legitimate grievances at the heart of their protests. While the civil rights and anti-apartheid movements may have begun in America and South Africa, and racism may have been stronger in those countries, there is no denying that racism was a serious problem in Britain as well. The race riots in Notting Hill, as well as the everyday racial discrimination witnessed by many minorities, were clearly a social problem which needed to be addressed. Similarly, universities clearly needed reforms, women and homosexuals clearly needed equal rights, and the Vietnam War and nuclear escalation clearly needed to be stopped. This is not to deny the presence of American influence on the British student movement, but cultural influences ran both ways. American students read British authors, attended British universities, listened to British music, and watched British films, just as British students interacted in the same ways with American culture. Regardless of where ideas, rhetoric, or strategies originated, they resonated with students in specific local and national contexts, and students adopted, altered, or dismissed these influences based upon their own specific identities, experiences, contexts, and goals. British students, not Americans or any other foreigners, were thus the primary active agents in their own movement.

Although students were the primary actors in the student movement, they were inspired and encouraged by a number of important older intellectual activists and the dominant political discourses of the era. Bertrand Russell, E. P. Thompson, C. Wright Mills, and Herbert Marcuse were especially important role models for students, sharing their vision for a new world order based upon participatory democracy and socialist humanism. They influenced students both directly at demonstrations and gatherings, and indirectly through their publications and actions. They helped to link radical students to older generations of activist intellectuals and grounded the student movement within a wider national and international discourse of dissent. Academic staff, mostly associated with the New Left, too had a strong influence on student activists. Not only did they convey New Left perspectives to their students through their teaching and writing, they actively met with student groups, encouraging them to take action in defense of their principles, sometimes joined in student protests, and were occasionally dismissed or otherwise punished for their part in the student movement.

While older dissenters provided a model for activists, the dominant political discourses of the era raised student expectations for a more democratic and modernized society, government, and system of higher education. Using the liberal rhetoric of reform, democracy, freedom, human rights, morality, and respectful political participation, the student movement contributed to the national debate over liberalism, social democracy, and youth, pushing the Labour government to further reforms and defending itself against a Conservative reaction. In all of these ways, the student movement showed itself to be a substantial social and political movement, and not just a generational or cultural youth revolt.

While much of the conservative media-generated narrative has been clearly disproven by the evidence, it must be admitted that not all protesters had high ideals or obeyed the law. One problem with large social movements with open memberships is that anyone can join in a protest and it is difficult for organizers to control their behavior. Any large-scale protest will therefore attract a variety of participants, some of whom may act in ways that discredit the movement. Journalists who wished to accurately report on the purpose of the protest and its overall impact could do so by interviewing its organizers and putting all of the events of the protest in perspective. Some journalists did this in the Long Sixties, but many other journalists focused on the actions of the naïve, foolish, extremist, and criminal elements in the crowds of protesters to support the dominant conservative narrative.

This initial narrative played a critical role in the Conservative Party's "law and order" campaign in the 1970 election. Conservatives effectively used this narrative to criminalize the student movement and use it in its attack on Labour's "permissiveness." Building on a public backlash against the student movement, the Conservative Party used this anti-student feeling to help it to win the election and afterwards attack funding for student unions and grants, and take legal action against protesters. This political attack, however, caused the student movement to gain sympathetic support from the majority of the student population, resulting in a strong upsurge in student protests in the early seventies against the Tory government. With the support of labor unions and many staff, students defeated the Thatcher proposals to control student unions and eventually won increases to student grants. While students and workers fought off this first Conservative attack in the seventies, Thatcher would effectively use the specter of student and worker strikes, and the perceived legacy of permissiveness to win elections in the 1980s. In these ways, the student movement was an important element in national politics not only in the Long Sixties, but also in the decades that followed.

MEMORY AND LEGACY

The student movement not only affected national politics, the media, and public opinion, but it also had a tremendous impact on the lives of the activists themselves. Some activists paid a high price for their idealism. Some were expelled, imprisoned, excluded from jobs, and threatened physically for their participation in protests to improve their universities, society, and world. Other activists, however, used their experiences within the student movement as a springboard into related careers. Many activists went on to pursue radical studies in various disciplines in the universities. Stuart Hall and Colin Crouch, for example, went on to extremely successful academic careers. For others, such as Sheila Rowbotham, Tariq Ali, and Anna Davin, their student experiences were merely the beginning of long careers as activists outside the universities. Rowbotham and Davin remained active in the women's liberation movement and taught women's history classes at universities, and Ali continues to speak out against capitalism, imperialism and racism around the world to this day. Others, such as Tom Fawthrop, David Fernbach, and Christopher Hitchens, began their careers as student activists writing manifestos for the student movement and went on to professional journalism and writing careers afterwards, often continuing to write and speak about social and economic injustice. Still others carried their political activism over into professional political careers within the Labour party. David Triesman, Jack Straw, and Peter Hain, for example, all achieved high-level positions in Labour governments in the 1990s and 2000s. Perhaps some former activists are embarrassed by their youthful protests and have moved towards the right politically, but most of the activists in this study have never renounced the high ideals they had as students.

The student movement had a direct impact on the students themselves, but it also left an important legacy of activism that has shaped the nation since the Long Sixties. The student movement of the sixties opened the doors to the massive social and political movements that shook the foundations of Britain in the seventies. They directly led to the feminist and gay and lesbian liberation movements, and helped to shift the Labour party to the Left in the seventies and eighties. Students and former students also helped to resurrect the Campaign for Nuclear Disarmament at the end of the seventies, mobilizing a record 400,000 demonstrators for a protest in London against the deployment of Pershing missiles in Britain in 1980. Campaigns against apartheid and racism continued through the 1990s, eventually freeing Mandela and contributing to the downfall of apartheid in South Africa.[5] The student movement may not have achieved all of its highest aspirations in the Long Sixties, but it did have a significant long-term impact on countless lives afterwards.

Most importantly, the student movement of the Long Sixties showed how powerful mass protests can be. This is one reason why student activism has continued to the present day. As the protests of 2010–11 illustrate, students still believe that if they unite together in one voice, in massive demonstrations that cannot be ignored by the media or politicians, they can indeed influence decision-making and "make history." Students continue to protest because the reality of our world still does not live up to our highest ideals and expectations. We still face a world and society dominated by global capitalism, consumerism, and inequality. Indeed, our societies are arguably more alienated and unequal than ever before. Many individuals feel powerless amidst overwhelming global forces. For all those who wish to eliminate these problems, the student movements of the Long Sixties offer strategies, theoretical frameworks, and lessons from which to learn. One important lesson is the simple fact that individuals alone stand little chance of effecting real change, whereas joined together with hundreds or thousands of other like-minded individuals, student movements can affect the course of history.

Engaged, earnest, and passionate, student activists in the Long Sixties used their liberal arts educations and critical thinking skills, as well as the discourse of modernization and democracy, to expose the hypocrisy of their society and push university and government authorities to live up to their nation's highest ideals. Perhaps this effort was naïve and misguided, but it was a valuable corrective force in the political, social, and cultural debates of the era. Student activists ultimately forced their universities to become more democratic and forced their government to modify its policies. These victories had long-lasting consequences which should never be forgotten.

Notes

NOTES TO THE INTRODUCTION

1. John Rose, interview with Ronald Fraser (1984), quoted in Ronald Fraser, *1968: A Student Generation in Revolt* (New York: Pantheon, 1988), 133.
2. David Widgery, "NUS – The Student's Muffler," in Robin Blackburn and Alexander Cockburn, eds. *Student Power: Problems, Diagnosis, Action* (Harmondsworth: Penguin, 1970), 140.
3. Edward Short, House of Commons Orders of the Day, *Hansard Online Collection*, HC Deb 29 January 1969 vol. 776 cc1341–464 <http://hansard.millbanksystems.com/commons/1969/jan/29/universities#S5CV0776P0_19 690129_HOC_292> accessed 3 May 2010.
4. Nick Thomas, "Will the real 1950s please stand up? Views of a contradictory decade," *Cultural and Social History* 5: 2 (April 2009), 228.
5. Christopher Connery and Hortense J. Spillers, "The Still Vacillating Equilibrium of the World," *boundary 2* 36: 1 (Spring 2009), 2–3.
6. For a good recent analysis of press coverage of student protests against the Vietnam War, see Nick Thomas, "Protests Against the Vietnam War in 1960s Britain: The Relationship between Protesters and the Press," *Contemporary British History* 22: 3 (2008): 335–354.
7. A. H. Halsey and Stephen Marks, "British Student Politics," in *Students in Revolt*, ed. Seymour Martin Lipset and Philip G. Altbach (Boston: Houghton Mifflin Company, 1969).
8. Jack Straw, Albert Sloman, and Paul Doty, *Universities: Boundaries of Change* (London: Panther, 1970), 29–46.
9. Arthur Marwick, "How We Taught the World to Swing," *The Times (UK)*, May 30, 2004, <http://www.timesonline.co.uk/tol/life_and_style/article428608.ece> accessed 10 May 2010.
10. Arthur Marwick, "The 1960s: Was There a 'Cultural Revolution?'," *Contemporary Record* 2 (October 28, 1968): 18–20; Arthur Marwick, *The Sixties: Cultural Revolution in Britain, France, Italy, and the United States, c.1958–c.1974* (New York: Oxford University Press, 1998); Arthur Marwick, *British Society Since 1945* (Harmondsworth: Penguin, 1982); Marwick, "How We Taught."
11. Richard Cockett, "The New Right and the 1960s: The Dialectics of Liberation," in Geoff Andrews et al., *New Left, New Right and Beyond: Taking the Sixties Seriously* (New York: Palgrave Macmillan, 1999), 91.
12. Ibid., 92–97.
13. Dominic Sandbrook, *White Heat: A History of Britain in the Swinging Sixties* (London: Little, Brown, 2006), 511–512.

14. See also Dominic Sandbrook, "The swingers who never were," *New Statesman*, 21 March 2005, <http://www.newstatesman.com/200503210015> accessed 29 January 2012.

15. Thomas Nicholas Thomas, "The British Student Movement 1965–1972" Ph. D. diss. (University of Warwick, 1996).

16. Nick Thomas, "Challenging Myths of the 1960s: The Case of Student Protest in Britain," *Twentieth Century British History* 13: 3 (2002): 277–297.

17. Ibid., 293.

18. Ibid., 296.

19. Ibid., 293.

20. Thomas, "Will the real 1950s please stand up? Views of a contradictory decade."

21. Fredric Jameson, "Periodizing the 60s," in *The 60s without Apology*, ed. Sohnya Sayres, Anders Stephanson, Stanley Aronowitz, and Fredric Jameson (Minneapolis: University of Minnesota Press, 1984), 178–209.

22. Ibid., 181.

23. See for example: Joseph Califano, *The Student Revolution: A Global Confrontation* (New York: Norton, 1969); David Caute, *Sixty-Eight: The Year of the Barricades* (London: Hamish Hamilton, 1988); Martin A. Klimke and Joachim Scharloth, *1968 in Europe: A History of Protest and Activism, 1956–1977* (New York: Palgrave Macmillan, 2008); Fraser, *1968*; Gerd-Rainer Horn, *The Spirit of '68: Rebellion in Western Europe and North America, 1956–1976* (New York: Oxford University Press, 2007); George Katsiaficas, *The Imagination of the New Left: A Global Analysis of 1968* (Boston: South End Press, 1987).

24. Klimke and Scharloth, *1968 in Europe*.

25. A number of good histories of the global sixties have been published in recent years, including Gerard J. DeGroot, *The Sixties Unplugged: A Kaleidoscopic History of a Disorderly Decade* (Cambridge: Harvard University Press, 2009); Carole Fink et al., *1968: The World Transformed*, First Edition. (New York: Cambridge University Press, 1998); Jonathon Green, *All Dressed Up: The Sixties and the Counterculture*, New Ed. (London: Pimlico, 1999); Martin Klimke, et al, *Between Prague Spring and French May: Opposition and Revolt in Europe, 1960–1980* (New York: Berghahn Books, 2011).

26. This manuscript uses the broad definition of a social movement as "a conscious, collective, organized attempt to bring about or resist large-scale change in the social order by non-institutionalized means" used by John Wilson, *Introduction to Social Movements* (New York: Basic Books, 1973), 8.

27. Mark Edelman Boren, *Student Resistance: A History of the Unruly Subject* (New York: Routledge, 2001); Eric Ashby and Mary Anderson, *The Rise of the Student Estate in Britain* (London: Macmillan, 1970).

NOTES TO CHAPTER 1

1. "Aneurin Bevan, 1956" *New Statesman* online (4 February 2010), http://www.newstatesman.com/uk-politics/2010/02/aneurin-bevan-1956-speech(accessed 7 June 2011.

2. Stan Newens, "Memories of a Seminal Year," *International Socialism* 112 (12 October 2006), http://www.isj.org.uk/index.php4?id=252&issue=112 (accessed 24 January 2012).

3. Ibid.

4. Stuart Hall, "The 'First' New Left: Life and Times," in *Out of Apathy: Voices of the New Left 30 Years On*, ed. Oxford University Socialist Discussion Group (London: Verso, 1989), 11–38.
5. Alain Badiou quoted in Christopher Connery, "The End of the Sixties," in *boundary 2*, 36: 1 (March 2009), 206–207.
6. Walter L. Arnstein, *Britain Yesterday and Today: 1830 to the Present*, 6th ed. (Lexington, MA: DC Heath, 1988), 370.
7. David M. Goldberg, "The Union Today: Generation Gone Wrong," *Glasgow University Magazine*, December 1955, 117–119
8. See Thomas, "Will the Real 1950s Please Stand Up? Views of a Contradictory Decade."
9. Rodney Lowe, *The Welfare State in Britain since 1945* (New York: St. Martin's, 1993), 196–206.
10. Brian Simon, *Education and the Social Order, 1940–1990* (Palgrave Macmillan, 1991), 597.
11. Lowe, *Welfare State*, 193.
12. Mark Donnelly, *Sixties Britain: Culture, Society and Politics* (New York: Pearson Longman, 2005), 17.
13. Harold Macmillan, *Riding the Storm 1956–1959* (London: Macmillan, 1971), 350, quoted in Peter Hennessy, *Having It So Good* (London: Allen Lane, 2006), 533.
14. Marwick, *The Sixties*, 248–258.
15. Bill Osgerby, "Youth Culture," in *A Companion to Contemporary Britain, 1939–2000*, ed. Paul Addison and Harriet Jones (Oxford: Blackwell, 2005), 128.
16. Marwick, *The Sixties*, 383.
17. Thomas, "Will the Real 1950s Please Stand Up?"
18. Ibid.
19. Hennessy, *Having It So Good*, 491.
20. Ibid.
21. Osgerby, "Youth Culture," 130.
22. Ibid.
23. Bill Osgerby, *Youth in Britain Since 1945* (Blackwell Publishers, 1998), 42.
24. Osgerby, "Youth Culture," 131.
25. Osgerby, *Youth in Britain Since 1945*.
26. Peter Lewis, "Mummy, Matron and the Maids: Feminine Presence and Absence in Male Institutions, 1934–63," in *Manful Assertions: Masculinities in Britain Since 1800*, ed. Michael Roper and John Tosh (London: Routledge, 1991) 179–80.
27. Marwick, *The Sixties*, 55.
28. For an interesting survey of students at Oxford and Manchester in the early sixties, see Ferdynand Zweig, *The Student in the Age of Anxiety; A Survey of Oxford and Manchester Students* (New York: The Free Press of Glencoe, 1963).
29. Rowbotham recalls these experiences in an interview with Ronald Fraser, May 1984, *British Library Sound Archive*, transcript 896/17 and in her own book, *Promise of a Dream: Remembering the Sixties* (London: Allen Lane, 2000).
30. Richard Ivan Jobs, "Youth Movements: Travel, Protest, and Europe in 1968," *American Historical Review* 114: 2 (April 2009): 376–404.
31. Rowbotham, *Promise of a Dream*, 7.
32. Harold Macmillan quoted in Harriet Jones, "The Impact of the Cold War," in *Companion to Contemporary Britain*, 37.

33. Jones, Ibid., 35; and Addison, "The Impact of the Second World War" in *Companion to Contemporary Britain*, 3–22.
34. Wendy Webster, "Immigration and Racism," in *A Companion to Contemporary Britain, 1939–2000*, 96.
35. Michael F. Hopkins and John W. Young, "The 'Special Relationship,'" in *Companion to Contemporary Britain*, 500.
36. Jones, "The Impact of the Cold War," 28
37. Lawrence Wittner, *Confronting the Bomb: A Short History of the World Nuclear Disarmament Movement* (Stanford, CA: Stanford University Press, 2009), 59.
38. Richard Taylor, *Against the Bomb: The British Peace Movement, 1958–1965* (Oxford: Clarendon, 1988), 118.
39. Ibid.
40. Hall, "The 'First' New Left," 13–38.
41. Peter Sedgwick, "America Over Britain," *Oxford Left* (1954), 4–9 reprinted in *Marxist Internet Archive*, http//: www.marxists.org/archive/sedgwick/1954/xx/america.htm (accessed 17 May 2010).
42. Addison, "The Impact of the Second World War," 16.
43. Hennessy, *Having It So Good*, 463–466.
44. Interview with Stan Newens, "Protesting against Both Imperial Powers in 1956," *Socialist Worker* 1987 (11 February 2006),http://www.socialistworker.co.uk/art/php?id=8250 (accessed 20 May 2010).
45. David Widgery, *The Left in Britain 1956–68: Volume 1* (Harmondsworth: Penguin, 1976), 59; Addison and Jones, *Companion to Contemporary Britain*, 25.
46. Addison, *A Companion to Contemporary Britain*, 126.
47. "Students in Hungary Protest March to Whitehall," *Times*, 12 November 1956, 4.
48. Widgery, *The Left in Britain 1956–68*, 51.
49. Madeleine Davis, "The Origins of the British New Left," in Klimke and Scharloth, *1968 in Europe*.
50. Ibid.
51. Hall, "The 'First' New Left: Life and Times," 13.
52. Editorial, *Universities & Left Review* 1:1 (Spring 1957), ii.
53. Madeleine Davis, "The Marxism of the British New Left," *Journal of Political Ideologies* 11, no. 3 (2006): 344–345.
54. Lin Chun, *The British New Left* (Edinburgh: Edinburgh University Press, 1993), 10–15.
55. Hall, "The First New Left," 36.
56. Chun, *The British New Left*, xvii.
57. Hall, "The First New Left," 24.
58. Ibid., 26–27.
59. Ibid., 28–29.
60. Chun, *The British New Left*, 55.
61. Seth Moglen, "Introduction," in *Out of Apathy*, ed. E. P. Thompson (London: New Left Books, 1960), 5.
62. Holger Nehring, "'Out of Apathy': Genealogies of the British 'New Left' in a Transnational Context, 1956–1962," in *Between Prague Spring and French May*, 19.
63. Davis, "The Marxism of the British New Left," 342.
64. C. Wright Mills, *C. Wright Mills*, ed. Pamela Mills and Kathryn Mills (Berkeley: University of California Press, 2000), 241, 243, and 316.
65. Daniel Geary, "'Becoming International Again': C. Wright Mills and the Emergence of a Global New Left, 1956–1962," *Journal of American History* 95: 3 (December 2008): 715.

66. C. Wright Mills, "Letter to the New Left," *New Left Review* 5 (September–October 1960), 18–23.
67. Ibid.
68. See Martin Klimke, *The Other Alliance: Student Protest in West Germany and the United States in the Global Sixties* (Princeton University Press, 2009).
69. Bret Eynon, "Community, Democracy, and the Reconstruction of Political Life: The Civil Rights Influence on New Left Political Culture in Ann Arbor, Michigan, 1958–1966." Ph.D. diss. (New York University, 1993), 238, 259, 306; and Tom Hayden, *Reunion: A Memoir* (New York: Random House, 1988), 76, 74, 102, 96, 99.
70. Barbara Ehrenreich, "Legacies of the 1960s: New Rights and New Lefts," in *Sights on the Sixties*, ed. Barbara Tischler (New Brunswick, NJ: Rutgers University Press, 1992), 234.
71. Rowbotham, *Promise of a Dream*, 53–63.
72. Willie Thompson, Interview by Caroline Hoefferle, 21 April 1997, Glasgow.
73. British students had been struggling to increase their power within the university almost since the beginning of the university system in the middle ages. See Mark Edelman Boren *Student Resistance: A History of the Unruly Subject* (New York: Routledge, 2001).
74. Graham Machin, "Attack on Proctors," *The Cherwell* 28 January 1961, 1.
75. "Politics in Union," *Torchlight* 18 October 1960, 4.
76. *Minutes of the Union Council* 9 November 1959, 4 in the *Hull University Archives*, Brynmore Jones Library, Hull.
77. *Minutes of the Union Council* 14 January 1963, 3 and *Hull* 15 January 1963, 1.
78. *Hull* 11 June 1963, 1 and 15 October 1963.
79. D. J. Grennan, president of NUS, "NUS Council Meeting at King's College on April 1960," 2.
80. Smith, "True Lies," 62.
81. J. B. Priestly, "Britain and the Nuclear Bomb," *New Statesman*,1 November 1957, quoted in Hennessy, *Having It So Good*, 523–524.
82. Nigel Young, *An Infantile Disorder: The Crisis and Decline of the New Left* (London: Routledge & Kegan Paul, 1977), 72.
83. Ibid.
84. Excerpted in Widgery, *The Left in Britain 1956–68*, 116.
85. Excerpt from Edward Thompson and John Saville, *The New Reasoner*, Spring 1968 in Ibid., 124.
86. Editorial, *Peace News*, 6 March 1959, 4 quoted in Holger Nehring, "Searching for Security: The British and West German Protests Against Nuclear Weapons and 'Respectability', 1958–1963," in *Peace Movements in Western Europe, Japan and the USA during the Cold War*, ed. Benjamin Ziemann (Essen: Klartext, 2008), 176.
87. Richard Taylor, *Against the Bomb: The British Peace Movement 1958–1965* (Oxford: Clarendon, 1988), 33.
88. Wittner, *Confronting the Bomb*, 60 and 82.
89. Ibid., 72.
90. Taylor, *Against the Bomb*, 209.
91. Ibid., 211.
92. Ibid., 64.
93. Jones, "The Impact of the Cold War," in *Companion to Contemporary Britain*, 24.
94. Taylor, *Against the Bomb*, 198–199.
95. Widgery, *The Left in Britain 1956–68*, 459.

96. Taylor, *Against the Bomb*, 222.
97. Russell quoted in Ibid., 223.
98. Ibid., 224–226.
99. Martin Smith, "True Lies," *History Today* (July 1999), 62.
100. Adam Lent, *British Social Movements Since 1945: Sex, Colour, Peace, and Power* (New York: Palgrave, 2001), 42.
101. Taylor, *Against the Bomb*, 228.
102. Green, *All Dressed Up*, 22.
103. Fraser, *1968*, 35.
104. Frank Parkin, *Middle Class Radicalism: The Social Bases of the British Campaign for Nuclear Disarmament* (Manchester: Manchester University Press, 1968), 158.
105. Ibid., 157.
106. Donnelly, *Sixties Britain*, 40.
107. Parkin, *Middle Class Radicalism*, 163.
108. David Triesman, quoted in Fraser, *1968*, 35.
109. *Peace, Protest and the Nuclear Threat: Archives of the Campaign for Nuclear Disarmament, 1958–1972*, Edinburgh: Edinburgh University Library, Microfilm, 14: 8/2 and 2: 1/33.
110. Wittner, *Confronting the Bomb*, 84.
111. "CND and Cuba . . . an Appeal," *Torchlight*, 8 November 1962, 5.
112. "Labour Club Plan Proctorial Survey," *The Cherwell* 4 November 1959, 1.
113. "Militants on the March," *The Cherwell* 2 December 1959, 1.
114. Catherine Fiske, "Why I Am Marching," *The Cherwell* 8 March 1961, 3.
115. Simon Maguire and David Miller, "Nuclear Disarmament Society," *Glasgow University Students Handbook, 1960–61*, Glasgow University Library, 166.
116. Widgery, *The Left in Britain*, 459.
117. "Nuclear Disarmament Club," *Glasgow University Students Handbook 1961–62*, 151.
118. "The NUS Council Meeting held at Margate on the 25th, 26th, and 27th of November 1960," NUS Archives, Modern Records Centre, Warwick University62 and 67.
119. "The NUS Council Meeting held at King's College, Newcastle upon Tyne on the 7th, 8th, 9th, and 10th of April, 1960," NUS Archives, 58.
120. Wendy Webster, "Immigration and Racism," in *A Companion to Contemporary Britain*, 97.
121. Roger Fieldhouse, *Anti-apartheid: A History of the Movement in Britain: A Study in Pressure Group Politics* (London: Merlin, 2005), 20.
122. "The NUS Council Meeting held at the University of Hull on the 3rd, 4th, 5th, and 6th of April, 1959: Minutes and Summary of Proceedings," NUS Archives, 5 and 57.
123. Fieldhouse, *Anti-apartheid*, 61.
124. *Beaver* 14 March 1957.
125. John L. Fryer, "What is this Thing called Law? London Students Beaten Up," and Dave Lindley, "Politics and the Student: An Inquiry," *Beaver,* 10 March 1960, 1 and 3.
126. "Oxford Clubs Ban Apartheid Goods," *The Cherwell* 31 October 1959, 1.
127. *The Cherwell* 7–14 May 1960.
128. *Glasgow Guardian*, 27 October 1962, 1 and "1965–66: A Review," *Glasgow University Students Handbook 1966–67*, Glasgow University Library, 65.
129. Alan Travis, "After 44 Years Secret Papers Reveal Truth about Five Nights of Violence in Notting Hill," *The Guardian* 24 August 2002, http://guardian.co.uk (accessed 20 May 2010).

130. Hennessy, *Having It So Good*, 501.
131. "NUS Council Meeting at Margate in November 1960," NUS Archives, 21.
132. "The NUS Council Meeting held at King's College, Newcastle upon Tyne on the 7th, 8th, 9th, and 10th of April, 1960," NUS Archives, 2.
133. Ibid.
134. Don Esslemont, editorial, *Beaver*, 16 June 1960, 2.
135. "LSE Boycott Snowballs," *Beaver*, 24 October 1963, 1.
136. "NUS Council Meeting at Margate in November 1960," 123.
137. "SRC and Pettigrew in Colour-Bar Battle," *Glasgow Guardian*, 13 October 1961, 1.
138. "SRC Verbatim Minutes 1961–62," University of Glasgow Archives, 7 December 1961.
139. Hugh Macpherson, "Colour Prejudice in Glasgow," *Glasgow Guardian*, 9 February 1962, 3.

NOTES TO CHAPTER 2

1. Lord Ralf Dahrendorf, *L.S.E.: A History of the London School of Economics and Political Science, 1895–1995* (New York: Oxford University Press, 1995), 452–453.
2. Colin Crouch, *The Student Revolt* (London: Bodley Head, 1970), 49.
3. Ibid., 50.
4. Harry Kidd, *The Trouble at L.S.E. 1966–67* (London: Oxford University Press, 1969).
5. Tessa Blackstone et al., *Students in Conflict, L.S.E. in 1967* (London: Weidenfeld and Nicolson, 1970), 163.
6. Crouch, *Student Revolt*, 54–55.
7.   8.   Ronald Faux, "Hunger Strike by Students: Girls among Volunteers for LSE Protest," *Times*, 15 March 1967, 1.
9. Blackstone et al., *Students in Conflict*, 168.
10. Jonathon Green, *All Dressed Up: The Sixties and the Counterculture* (London: Pimlico, 1998), 250.
11. Kidd, *Trouble at LSE*, 113.
12. Peter Watherston, "LSE's New president Peter Watherston Asks: When Will They Ever Learn?" *Beaver*, 11 May 1967, 2.
13. *Manchester Guardian*, 15 March 1967, 1 and 16 March 1967, 5.
14. "New-style Protests May Spread to other Universities," *Times*, 15 March 1967, 1.
15. *Daily Telegraph*, 21 November 1966, quoted in Alan Shelston, "Students and the Press," in *Anarchy and Culture: The Problem of the Contemporary Culture* ed. David Martin (London: Routledge and Kegan Paul, 1969), 94.
16. Robert Pitman, *Daily Express*, 15 March 1967, 12 in Thomas, "The British Student Movement 1965-1972," " (Ph.D. diss., University of Warwick, 1996), 182.
17. Alan Shelston, "Students and the Press," in *Anarchy and Culture: The Problem of the Contemporary Culture* ed. David Martin (London: Routledge and Kegan Paul, 1969), 95.
18. Blackstone et al., *Students in Conflict*, 135, 175, 181, 193, and 302.
19. Hennessy, *Having It So Good*, 540.
20. "Great Britain: You Can Walk Across it on the Grass," *Time*, 15 April 1966.
21. Green, *All Dressed Up*, 86.
22. Roy Jenkins, "Is Britain civilised?" (1959) quoted in Green, *All Dressed Up*, 57.

23. *Higher Education, Report of the Committee Appointed by the Prime Minister under the Chairmanship of Lord Robbins, 1961–1963,* presented October 1963, Cmnd. 2154, Parliamentary Papers xi-xiv, 1962–63.

24. *The Years of Crisis, Report of the Labour Party's Study Group on Higher Education,* Labour Party (1963), quoted in Brian Simon, *Education and the Social Order 1940–1990* (New York: St. Martin's, 1991), 229.

25. Simon, *Education,* 597 and 261.

26. Kenneth S. Davies, Paul Walker, David Tupman, "Universities, Numbers, Money, Policies, 1945–85," in W.A.C. Stewart, *Higher Education in Postwar Britain* (London, 1989) footnote in Simon, *Education and the Social Order,* 401.

27. John Carswell, *Government and the Universities in Britain, Program and Performance, 1960–1980* (Cambridge: Cambridge University Press, 1985), 172.

28. Dahrendorf, *LSE,* 427.

29. Ibid., 429.

30. Ibid., 439.

31. Brewster, "Revolt," 19.

32. Blackstone, *Students in Conflict,* 33.

33. Ibid., 19, 23, and 27.

34. Ibid., 14.

35. Reminiscences of David Fernbach (3 May 1984), on pages 1, 2, and 13 in the Columbia University Center for Oral History Collection (hereafter CUCOHC).

36. Colin Crouch in Joan Abse, *My L.S.E.* (London: Robson Books, 1977), 192–193.

37. Edward Thompson in *Peace News,* 29 November 1963, quoted in David Widgery, *The Left in Britain, 1956–68* (Harmondsworth: Penguin, 1976), 131.

38. Geoff Andrews, "The Three New Lefts and Their Legacies," in *New Left, New Right and Beyond: Taking the Sixties Seriously* (Palgrave Macmillan, 1999), 73–75 and Davis, "The Marxism of the British New Left," 347–350..

39. Avishai Zvi Ehrlich, "The Leninist Organizations in Britain and the Student Movement 1966–1972" (Ph.D. diss., University of London, 1981), 87.

40. *Agitator,* 9 November 1965, 1.

41. Mark Tishman, "Introduction to a Critique of the New Left," *Agitator,* 26 November 1965, 6–7.

42. Fernbach reminiscences, page 10. The Fourth International was formed by Leon Trotsky of the Russian Communist Party in 1938 as a new revolutionary organization to replace Stalin's Comintern. After Trotsky's assassination it split into the Paris-based International Secretariat and the International Committee, affiliated with the British Socialist Workers Party. (Widgery, *The left in Britain,* 484).

43. *Agitator,* 9 November 1965, 1–12.

44. Boren, *Student Resistance,* 130–131.

45. Ray Steding, "Sorbonne Revolt," *The Cherwell,* 26 February 1964, 1.

46. W. J. Rorabaugh, *Berkeley At War* (New York: Oxford University Press, 1989) and Wini Brienes, *Community and Organization in the New Left, 1962–1968: The Great Refusal* (New Brunswick: Rutgers University Press, 1989), 22–24.

47. Chris Piening, editorial, *Wyvern,* 5 February 1965, 3.

48. Boren, *Student Resistance,* 144.

49. Louis Menashe and Ronald Radosh, eds. *Teach-Ins USA: Reports, Opinions, Documents* (New York: Praeger, 1967), 152.
50. Bret Eynon, "Community, Democracy, and the Reconstruction of Political Life: The Civil Rights Influence on New Left Political Culture in Ann Arbor, Michigan, 1958–1966" (Ph.D. diss., New York University, 1993), 424.
51. University Committee on Vietnam, "Vietnam Teach-In," 12 November 1965, Student Activism Files, UCLA University Archives; and Student-Faculty Committee on Vietnam, Minnesota Student Association, Union Board of Governors, and the Department of Concert and Lectures, "Vietnam Teach-In," 24 May 1965, Minnesota University Commission on Campus Demonstrations File, University of Minnesota Archives.
52. James Tracy, *Direct Action: Radical Pacifism from the Union Eight to the Chicago Seven* (Chicago: University of Chicago Press, 1996), 128 and 141.
53. Laurence Mayer, editorial, *Wyvern*, 13 June 1966, 2.
54. Tariq Ali, *Street Fighting Years: An Autobiography of the Sixties* (London: Collins, 1987), 1.
55. Tariq Ali interview with Ronald Fraser, 3 April 1984, British Library Sound Archive, C896/02.
56. Chris May, "Vietnam Row Enters its Second Phase," *The Cherwell*, 24 February 1965, 3.
57. "Oxford Left Wing Join Protest Over Vietnam," *The Cherwell*, 17 February 1965, 12.
58. Ashok Advani, "Ali Cleared by Magistrate," *The Cherwell*, 28 April 1965, 3.
59. Ali, *Street Fighting Years*, 50.
60. Ibid., 51.
61. Ali interview.
62. Ehrlich, "The Leninist Organizations," 114.
63. *Declaration of the British Campaign for Peace in Vietnam*, quoted in Thomas, "The British Student Movement 1965–1972", 53.
64. Ibid., 88.
65. *Torchlight* photo caption, 9 March 1965, 1.
66. Michael Dackson, Lynda Townsend, Patricia Townsend, Maggie Smith, Philip Heselton, Letter to the Editor, *Torchlight*, 5 May 1966, 4.
67. Thomas, "The British Student Movement 1965–1972," 56.
68. Ibid., 61.
69. Ibid., 60.
70. "Banner Call," *Beaver*, 10 December 1964, 8.
71. "Sharpeville March Plans Change," *Beaver*, 4 March 1965, 1.
72. Ibid.
73. Tariq Ali interview and "The Proctors Run into Trouble," 7 October 1964, 1.
74. Oxford University joined thousands in Trafalgar square for an April 1963 anti-apartheid protest ("Jeffrey Meets Barbara in the Square," *The Cherwell*, 27 April 1963, 12); Hull students held anti-apartheid protests in 1964 (*Torchlight*, 3 December 1964, 1); and Nick Thomas notes that student protests against apartheid occurred at Leicester University (1964 and 1965) in his thesis, *The British Student Movement 1965–1972*, 288–290.
75. Fraser, *1968*, 109.
76. "Council Meeting held at Queen's University, Belfast on the 7th, 8th, 9th, 10th and 11th of April 1961: Minutes and Summary of Proceedings," MSS 280: Box 101C and "The National Union of Students Executive Report, 1966," MSS 280: Box 96, Modern Records Centre, Warwick University.

77. Thomas, "The British Student Movement," 290–291.
78. "Rhodesia," *Agitator,* 26 November 1965, 3; "Rhodesia: Runge Walks Out," *Beaver,* 28 October 1965, 4; and "Immigration: the Background," *Beaver,* 28 October 1965, 4.
79. *Agitator,* 26 November 1965, 3.
80. Avishai Zvi Ehrlich, "The Leninist Organizations," 98.
81. Willie Thompson, "Notes on Communist Work Among Students" (Communist Party Great Britain, October 1965), Personal collection of Willie Thompson, Glasgow.
82. Reminiscences of David Triesman (17 April 1984), on pages 40–41 in the CUCOHC.
83. *A Radical Student Alliance* (London: R.S.A., 1966) in Digby Jacks, *Student Politics and Higher Education* (London: Lawrence and Wishart, 1975), Appendix 2.
84. Triesman reminiscences, page 26.
85. Ibid., page 42.
86. Ehrlich, "The Leninist Organizations," 104–105.
87. *Darts* 2 March 1967, 5 quoted in Thomas, "The British Student Movement 1965–1972." 67.
88. Although many students felt that the increase in overseas student fees revealed racism on the part of British politicians, the Labour government made a major effort to combat racial discrimination with its Race Relations Act of 1966. This act created a Race Relations Board to deal with cases of proven racial discrimination and was the first of its kind in Britain.
89. Fraser et al., *1968,* 130; and Thomas, "The British Student Movement 1965–72," 68.
90. Thomas, "The British Student Movement 1965–1972," 68.
91. "Minutes of the Union Council," 6 February 1967, Hull University Archives, Brynmore Jones Library Special Collections, 2200.
92. "Rebel 300 March as president Stops Strike," *Torchlight,* 24 February 1967, 1; and "R.S.A. Hits at NUS," *Torchlight,* 2 November 1967, 1.
93. "How well connected is your college?" Broadsheet by the Anti-Apartheid Movement, undated and unsigned, John Johnson-Bulkeley Collection, Oxford University New Bodleian Library.
94. "The National Union of Students of the Universities and Colleges of England, Wales and Northern Ireland: April Council Meeting held at Goldsmith's College, London on the 11th, 12th, 13th, 14th, and 15th of April 1965, Minutes and Summary of Proceedings" NUS Collection, Modern Records Centre, University of Warwick, 44.
95. Savage, "The National Union of Students Executive Report," NUS Collection, 17–18.
96. Geoff Martin, president of NUS, "National Union of Students Executive Report 1967" NUS Collection, 9.
97. Stay Gray, "A Student Trade Union for Oxford," *Oxford Left* 5 (1966) in the John Johnson-Bulkeley Collection, Oxford University New Bodleian Library.
98. Ibid.
99. *Glasgow Guardian,* 7 February 1966, 1.
100. "Banned Students: Scrap the Whole Proceedings Say SRC," *Glasgow Guardian,* 2 March 1966, 1.
101. Dahrendorf, *LSE,* 442.
102. "1963–64 Annual Report of the Student Union of the London School of Economics" (London: British Library of Political and Economic Science Archives), 2.

103. "Union Council Meeting Minutes," 17 June 1964, British Library of Political and Economic Science Archives,.
104. Tim Gopsill, editorial, *Beaver,* 18 February 1965, 2.
105. "LSE Union Minutes," 17 March 1965, British Library of Political and Economic Science Archives,.
106. Crouch, *The Student Revolt,* 35.
107. "LSE Union Minutes," 31 January 1966, 21 February 1966, and 10 March 1966.
108. Kidd, *Trouble at LSE,* 12.
109. "Elect your Director," *Agitator,* 16 March 1966, back cover.
110. LSE Socialist Society, *LSE's New Director: A Report on Walter Adams,* 1966, British Library of Political and Economic Science Archives.
111. Crouch, *Student Revolt,* 42.
112. "Strike—Emergency Meeting," *Beaver,* 17 November 1966, 1.
113. Blackstone et al., *Students in Conflict,* 154–157.
114. Ibid., 157–158; Crouch, *Student Revolt,* 45.
115. "New-style Protests May Spread to other Universities," *Times,* 15 March 1967, 12.
116. Crouch, *Student Revolt,* 47.
117. Blackstone et al., *Students in Conflict,* 160.
118. Sociologist Tom Burns introduced this term. Tom Burns, "The Revolt of the Privileged," *SSRC Newsletter* 4 (November 1968): 5–11.
119. Thomas, "Protests Against the Vietnam War in 1960s Britain," 296.

NOTES TO CHAPTER 3

1. David Triesman, written evidence, Tribunal of Enquiry, May 1968, no. 42, 3, Essex University Special Collections.
2. David Triesman, "Essex," *New Left Review* 50 (July–August, 1968), 70 and Reminiscences of David Triesman(17 April 1984), on pages 58–60in the Columbia University Center for Oral History Collection (hereafter CUCOHC).
3. "Students in Porton Protest," *Wyvern,* 10 May 1968, 1 and 8; and Lord Gifford (Chair), "University of Essex Report of the Tribunal of Enquiry on the events of May 7ᵗʰ 1968 and the events leading up to them," June 1968, 12, Essex University Special Collections.
4. Triesman reminiscences, 60, 61, and 65. Triesman does not mention Archard by name in the reminiscences.
5. "Surprise University Death: Hundreds Feared Living in Disaster," *Wyvern,*21 June 1968, 1.
6. Colin Crouch, *The Student Revolt* (London: Bodley Head, 1970), 103–105.
7. Ibid.
8. Adrian Sinfield quoted in Paul Thompson and Joanna Bornat, "Myths and Memories of an English Rising: 1968 at Essex," *Oral History* 22: 2 (Autumn 1994): 50.
9. "Surprise University Death," 2.
10. Triesman reminiscences, 62.
11. "Free University of Essex—An Announcement," *Wyvern,* 21 June 1968, 8.
12. Jean-Luc Godard was there filming for his *British Sounds AKA: See You at Mao* (1969).
13. Triesman, reminiscences 69–70 and "Surprise University Death", 2.
14. "Essex Catalyst in CBW Control" and "London March," *Wyvern* 21 June 1968, 8.

15. Triesman reminiscences, pages 72, 73, 78, and 79. .
16. Tony Scase, transcript from *Look East*, BBC program, 20 May 1968, Essex University Special Collections.
17. Memo from Senate Group on Decision-Making in the University, May 1969, Essex University Special Collections.
18. "Progress Report on Developments in Student Participation in University Government," *In Brief*, 3 October 1968, Essex University Special Collections.
19. Brian MacArthur, "Students' Right to Private Life," *The Times*, 14 October 1969, 8.
20. R.A. Butler, "Rab: From Our Chancellor," *Wyvern*, 1 December 1964, 1.
21. Mike Gibson, "Essex v. Warwick and Kent," *Wyvern*, 5 February 1965, 6.
22. "Avoiding the Draft," *Wyvern*, 13 January 1967, 4.
23. "Essex Receives Its Charter," *Wyvern*, 5 February 1965, 10.
24. "Where the Power Lies," *Wyvern*, 9 October 1970, 8.
25. By the mid-1970s, the student population had only risen to 2,500.
26. Albert Sloman, transcript of "A University in the Making," *Reith Lecture 1* (9 November 1963), 2 *BBC Website*,http://downloads.bbc.co.uk/rmhttp/radio4/transcripts/1963_reith1.pdf (accessed 19 July 2011).
27. Ibid., 7.
28. Thompson and Bornat, "Myths and Memories of an English Rising: 1968 at Essex," 44.
29. Stephen Hatch, "Easier to Get in to Essex," *Wyvern*, 2 February 1966, 10.
30. Triesman reminiscences, pages 1, 2, 3, 4, 7, 9, 12–15, 16, 17, 23, 24, and 32–37.
31. "Frankly Speaking: Student Views Surveyed," *Wyvern* 5 February 1965, 4–5.
32. Chris Piening, editorial, *Wyvern*, 2 November 1965, No. 5.
33. "Men have Campus Majority," *Wyvern*, 2 November 1965, 10.
34. Thompson and Bornat, "Myths and Memories," 44.
35. David Triesman reminiscences, pages 35–36.
36. Ronald Fraser et al., *1968: A Student Generation in Revolt*, American ed. (New York: Pantheon Books, 1988), 35.
37. Dave Kendall, comment, *Wyvern*, 2 February 1966, 2.
38. Rick Coates, "Coates' Concept," *Wyvern*, 28 February 1966, 3.
39. Andrew Renshaw, "Anti-Crosland Demonstration for Tomorrow," *Wyvern*, 10 February 1967, 1.
40. Andrew Renshaw, "Strike a Great Success," *Wyvern*, 24 February 1967, 1.
41. Brian Hanrahan, "Essex Leaves NUS," *Wyvern*, 10 February 1967, 1.
42. See Suri, *Power and Protest: Global Revolution and the Rise of Detente* for an excellent overview of the Cold War and dissent movements of the sixties.
43. Fraser, *1968*, 178.
44. Klimke and Scharloth, *1968 in Europe*.
45. Ali, *Street Fighting Years*, 172.
46. Klimke and Scharloth, *1968 in Europe*.
47. Klimke and Scharloth, "West Germany, in *1968 in Europe*, 103–104.
48. Ingrid Gilcher-Holtey, "France," in Klimke and Scharloth, *1968 in Europe*, 112–113.
49. Fraser, *1968*, 203–230.
50. Thomas Hecken and Agata Grzenia, "Situationism," in Klimke and Scharloth, *1968 in Europe*, 23–24 and Gordon Carr, *The Angry Brigade: The Cause and the Case* (London: Victor Gollancz, 1975), 18.
51. Jerry Avorn, *Up Against the Ivy Wall: A History of the Columbia Crisis* (New York: Atheneum Press, 1968), 243.

52. Columbia Strike Coordinating Committee, "Columbia Liberated," (Fall 1968), in *The Sixties Papers: Documents of a Rebellious Decade*, ed. Judith Clavir Albert and Stewart Edward Albert (New York: Praeger, 1984), 237.
53. Terry Anderson, *The Movement and the Sixties: Protest in America from Greensboro to Wounded Knee* (New York: Oxford University Press, 1995), 203.
54. Daniel Walker, Director of the Chicago Study Team, *Rights in Conflict: The Violent Confrontation of Demonstrators and Police in the Parks and Streets of Chicago During the Week of the Democratic National Convention of 1968* (New York: Bantam, 1968), vii.
55. James Kirkpatrick Davis, *Assault on the Left: The FBI and the Sixties Anti-war Movement* (Westport, CT–: Praeger, 1997), 131; and Kirkpatrick Sale, *SDS* (New York: Random House, 1973), 460462.
56. Boren, *Student Resistance*, 166–171.
57. Mike Farell and Eamonn McCann interview quoted in Anthony Barnett, "People's Democracy: a Discussion on Strategy," *New Left Review* 55 (June 1969): 4.
58. Eamonn McCann, quoted in Dochartaigh, "Northern Ireland," in *1968 in Europe*, ed. Klimke and Scharloth, 141.
59. Simon Prince, "The Global Revolt of 1968 and Northern Ireland," *The Historical Journal* 49: 3 (2006): 852–853, and 863.
60. Fraser, *1968*, 232–236.
61. Ibid., 236.
62. Maryvonne Fear, Essex Soc Soc, "Message and an Appeal to all Students," June 1968, M. J. Sommerlad Collection, Essex University Special Collections, Albert Sloman Library, University of Essex, Wivenhoe; "Uproar at Meeting," *Torchlight,* 7 June 1968, 3; and Green, *All Dressed Up*, 251.
63. Trevor Pateman, "1968: Student Revolt and the Making of a Course-Critic," in *Counter Course: A Handbook for Course Criticism* (Harmondsworth: Penguin, 1972) reproduced in *Trevor Pateman Selected Works*, http://www.selectedworks.co.uk/ (accessed 30 January 2012).
64. Reminiscences of Hilary Wainwright(17 June 1984), on pages 1 and 2/15 in the CUCHC.
65. Pateman, "1968: Student Revolt."
66. Gareth Stedman Jones, Anthony Barnett, and Tom Wengraf, "Student Power: What is to Be Done?" *New Left Review* 1: 43 (May–June 1967), 4.
67. Ibid., 5.
68. Ibid., 6–7.
69. Martin Shaw, "On Students," *New Left Review* 1: 44 (July-August, 1967), 88.
70. Ernest Mandel, "The New Vanguard," in *New Revolutionaries: Left Opposition*, ed. Tariq Ali (London: Peter Owen, 1969), 50.
71. Ibid.
72. Ali, *Street Fighting Years*, 184.
73. *The Black Dwarf* 13: 6 (15 October 1968).
74. Ali, *Street Fighting Years*, 133–137.
75. Tariq Ali, *Street Fighting Years: An Autobiography of the Sixties* (London: Collins, 1987), 2 and 184; and Tariq Ali, "The Extra-Parliamentary Opposition," in *New Left Revolutionaries*, 70 and 73.
76. "The People Rule," *Challenge* 9 (Fall 1968), 12. Issues of *Challenge, the Journal of Britain's Young Communists* published between 1968 and 1972 are filled with similar references to democracy and attempts to attract student activists.

77. The estimates of student CP members were provided by Fergus Nicholson, the National Student Organizer for the CPBG in "NSC Notes," 22 May 1969, in Willie Thompson personal collection.
78. James Craighead and Secretary Leslie Jardine, "The Marxist Society," *Glasgow University Students Handbook 1968–69*, Glasgow University Library.
79. "Young Socialist (Marxist)," *Glasgow University Students Handbook, 1969–70*, Glasgow University Library, 104.
80. Thompson interview.
81. Triesman reminiscences, 53–55.
82. Ehrlich, "The Leninist Organizations," 12.
83. Green, *All Dressed Up*, 164.
84. David Cooper, ed., *The Dialectics of Liberation* (Harmondsworth: Penguin, 1968), 7 and back cover.
85. Ibid., back cover.
86. Herbert Marcuse, "Liberation from the Affluent Society," (1967) in *The Dialectics of Liberation*, 175.
87. Ibid., 189.
88. Fraser, *1968*, 169.
89. Green, *All Dressed Up*, 164.
90. Ibid., 166–167.
91. *IT* 51 (28 February–13 March, 1969) in Ibid., 244.
92. Triesman reminiscences, pages 43–44.
93. Ibid.,45–46.
94. Avishai Zvi Ehrlich, "The Leninist Organizations in Britain and the Student Movement 1966–1972" (Ph.D. thesis, University of London, 1981), 123.
95. Ibid., 122, 117, 124, 137.
96. David Fernbach, "Revolution and the Student Movement," undated article in RSSF file of Trevor Pateman Correspondence, Box 1 in the Pateman Collection of the John Johnson Collection, Special Collections of the Oxford University Bodleian Library.
97. "Manifesto," pamphlet, n.d., Essex University Special Collection.
98. "RSSF—Manifesto for a Political Program, 1968," Adopted by the 2nd RSSF conference—London: November 10, 1968, in Digby Jacks, *Student Politics and Higher Education* (London: Lawrence and Wishart, 1975), appendix 3.
99. Ibid.
100. Ehrlich, "The Leninist Organizations," 138.
101. Ibid., 134.
102. *Oxford Left* 2: 10 (September 1968), inside cover, in the John Johnson-Bulkeley Collection, Oxford University New Bodleian Library.
103. Ibid., back cover.
104. Jenny Bingham, "Ives is Dead: Long Live Ives," *Wyvern*, 8 November 1968, 2. Ives refers to Keith Ives, a member of the Student Council, who consistently opted for moderate means and reforms as alternatives to the more extreme actions advocated by the extreme left.
105. "LSE Union Council Meeting Minutes," 4 November 1968, British Library of Political and Economic Science Archives.
106. "LSE Union Council Meeting Minutes," 4 November 1968. The minutes over the next several years reveal the high turnover of presidents and their negative opinion of the tactics of the far left.
107. Ehrlich, "Leninist Organizations," 126–140.
108. David Gilles, "NUS Conference, Liverpool, April 8–12, 1969," 19 April 1969, NUS Collection, , 1.
109. Ehrlich, "Leninist Organizations," 107; David Triesman, "The CIA and Student Politics," in Alexander Cockburn and Robin Blackburn, eds., *Student*

Power: Problems, Diagnosis, Actions (Harmondsworth: Penguin, 1969), 141–159.

110. Ali, *Street Fighting Years*, 123–125.
111. Tariq Ali, quoted in Fraser, *1968*, 133.
112. Ali, *Street Fighting Years*, 115–119.
113. Ibid., 115.
114. "Appeal Nets 150 Pounds," *Wyvern*, 27 October 1967, 1.
115. "Staff and Students Allege Manhandling by Police: Socialist Chairman Arrested in Rally," *Wyvern*, 27 October 1967, 1.
116. Ibid.
117. Horace Ove quoted in Jonathon Green, *Days in the Life: Voices from the English Underground, 1961–1971* (London: Heinemann, 1990), 244–245.
118. David Widgery quoted in Fraser, *1968*, 186.
119. Tariq Ali quoted in Ibid., 185.
120. Rachel Dyne quoted in Ibid., 185–186.
121. This type of media reaction to mass protests had a long history in Britain. For a more complete discussion of the media reaction to the Vietnam protests, see Nick Thomas, "Protests Against the Vietnam War in 1960s Britain: The Relationship between Protesters and the Press," *Contemporary British History* 22: 3 (2008): 335–354.
122. Quoted in Stuart Hall et al., *Policing the Crisis* (London: Palgrave, 1978), 243.
123. Green, *All Dressed Up*, 268.
124. Thomas, "Protests Against the Vietnam War in 1960s Britain," 348.
125. Ali, *Street Fighting Years*, 216.
126. Tom Iremonger, q *Daily Telegraph*, 24 October 1968, quoted in Green, *All Dressed Up*, 267.
127. Ibid., 269.
128. Ali, *Street Fighting Years*, 216.
129. Tariq Ali, *Street Fighting Years*, 219 and 216; and Carr, *The Angry Brigade*, 42.
130. *How We Marched for Peace: a personal account of the London Peace March Sunday, 27 October, 1968,* (Institute of Current World Affairs, n.d.), Ross Collection, University of Minnesota Archives, Walter Library, University of Minnesota-Twin Cities, Minneapolis, 12.
131. Ibid., 11; and Al McConagha, "Serious Trouble Averted in London Anti-US March," *Minneapolis Tribune*, 28 October 1968, 2.
132. Robin Jenkins, "This Could be the Last Time," *Wyvern*, 8 November 1968, 5.
133. Ibid.
134. "Vietnam Fast," *Glasgow Guardian*, 2 November 1967, 3.
135. *Times* 22 February 1968, 2 and 8 March 1968; and *Guardian* 19 March 1968, 3.
136. *Daily Telegraph* 9 March 1968.
137. Paul Rock and Frances Heidensohn, "New Reflections on Violence," in David Martin ed. *Anarchy and Culture: The Problem of the Contemporary Culture* (London: Routledge and Kegan Paul, 1969), 110.
138. Ibid., 111.
139. Ibid., 104.
140. David Barrow, Letter to the Editor, *Torchlight*, 2 November 1967, 10.
141. George Bridges, "Join the Green Berets and Get Away with Murder," *Challenge* 15 (1969), 5 and Barney Davis, "America on Trial," *Challenge* 17 (1969), 2.

142. Thomas Nicholas Thomas, "The British Student Movement 1965–72" (Ph.D. diss., University of Warwick, 1996), 62.
143. Fred Lindop, "Racism and the Working Class: Strikes in Support of Enoch Powell in 1968," *Labour History Review* 66: 1 (Spring 2001): 80.
144. Philip Whitfield, "University mob kick and trample MP's wife," *Daily Mail* 4 May 1968.
145. "Up Against the Wall," *Torchlight*, 9 May 1969, 5.
146. Enoch Powell quoted in Dominic Sandbrook, *White Heat: A History of Britain in the Swinging Sixties* (London: Little, Brown, 2006), 641.
147. Ibid., 643.
148. "LSE Student Union Council Meeting Minutes," 24 April 1968.
149. Ibid., 2 May 1968.
150. *Manchester Guardian*, 2 May 1968, 1.
151. Editorial, *Agitator*, 7 May 1968, 1–2.
152. "Backlash to Press Attack," *The Cherwell*, 6 March 1968, 1.
153. "Oxford Revolutionary Socialist Students" [broadsheet, undated, unsigned (October 1968)] John Johnson Collection-K. Jones Archive, Box 1, Oxford University Bodleian Library Special Collections.
154. "How They Foiled Guerilla's Plot" and "Don't Stop Enoch's Speech," *The Cherwell*, 22 January 1969, 1 and 7.
155. "A Right-Wing Club for Debates?" *Glasgow Guardian*, 22 April 1968, 7.
156. Alexander Shaw, "Smithy for Rector?" *Glasgow Guardian*, 22 April 1968, 1.
157. Ross McKay, editorial, *Glasgow Guardian*, 14 March 1968, 3.
158. "Enoch Powell: Is Apathy Disappearing from G.U. at Last?" *Glasgow Guardian*, 13 May 1968, 1.
159. "Mr. Peter Archard's Actions Last Friday," *Wyvern*, 1 March 1968, 1 and Tony Scott, "Powell Has a Rough Night of It," *Wyvern*, 1 March 1968, 5.
160. Bill Rodger, "No Capitulation on Powell Charges," *Wyvern*, 15 March 1968, 1.
161. Ibid.
162. Editorial, *Wyvern*, 15 March 1968, 2.
163. Shaun Leslie, editorial, *Wyvern*, 1 March 1968, 2; and 15 March 1968, 2.
164. David Triesman, "Violence as a Tactic," *Wyvern*, 26 April 1968, 4.
165. Ibid.
166. Ibid., 5.
167. Ibid.
168. "NUS Statement," 13 June 1968, reprinted in Brian MacArthur, "The Course of Student Protest," *Higher Education Review*, Autumn 1968, 72–73.
169. "The Vice Chancellor's Reply," June 1968, reprint in MacArthur, "The Course of Student Protest," 73.
170. "The National Union of Students Executive Report, 1968," NUS Archives, 17.
171. Ibid. 102 and 99; *Manchester Guardian*, 24 May 1968, 1; and *Times*, 7 June 1968, 3.
172. "Hull University Union Council Minutes," 16 October 1967, Special Collections, Brynmore Jones Library, Hull University,, 2415.
173. Tom Fawthrop, "Hull," *New Left Review* 50 (July–August, 1968), 59 and 64.
174. "Student Challenge," *Torchlight*, 21 June 1968, 12.
175. Lisa Tickner, *Hornsey 1968: The Art School Revolution* (London: Frances Lincoln, 2008), 21–29.
176. Ibid., 29.

177. Tom Nairn and Jim Singh-Sanhu, "Chaos in the Art Colleges," in *Student Power: Problems, Diagnosis, Actions*, Alexander Cockburn and Robin Blackburn, eds. (Harmondsworth, Middlesex: Penguin, 1969), 104; and Crouch, *Student Revolt*, 111.
178. Tickner, *Hornsey 1968*, 38.
179. Ibid., 41.
180. Ibid., 100.
181. Nairn and Singh-Sanhu, "Chaos in the Art Colleges," 113; Tom Nairn, "Hornsey," *New Left Review* 50 (July-August, 1968), 65; and *Times* (4 June 1968), 3.
182. Tickner, *Hornsey 1968*, 79–80.
183. "LSE Union Minutes," 8 November 1968.
184. "LSE Union Minutes," 24 January 1969.
185. Fraser, *1968*, 282.
186. *LSE Union Minutes*, 12 February 1969 and 19 February 1969.
187. Paul Hoch, quoted in Green, *All Dressed Up*, 255.
188. "Strike Newsletter No. 3," in "LSE Union Minutes," 24 April 1969; "LSE Union Minutes," 21 April 1969 and 21 July 1969; and LSE Strike Committee, "Why We Are Demonstrating," appendix, "LSE Union Minutes," 21 May 1969; "Strike News Letter No. 8," 2 May 1969, "LSE Union Minutes", appendix.
189. Ehrlich, "The Leninist Organizations," 59 provides statistics for IMG membership in 1969 and a wealth of information on revolutionary socialist student theories and politics. Peter Shipley, *Revolutionaries in Modern Britain* (London: Bodley Head, 1976), 219 estimates the membership of the Young Communist League (of the Communist Party) to be 3,850 in 1969, but this organization included many non-student communists as well.

NOTES TO CHAPTER 4

1. Bryan D. Palmer, "Homage to Edward Thompson, Part II," *Labour/Le Travail* 33 (Spring 1994), 13–68 and E. P. (Edward Palmer) Thompson, *Warwick University Ltd.: Industry, Management and the Universities*, (Harmondsworth: Penguin, 1970), 50–51.
2. Ibid.
3. Ibid., 47.
4. Ibid., 48–51.
5. Ibid., 52.
6. Reminiscences of Anna Davin (20 April 1984), on page 84 in the Columbia University Center for Oral History Collection (hereafter CUCOHC).
7. Ibid., 78–79.
8. Thompson, *Warwick University Ltd.*, 52.
9. Ibid., 54.
10. Ibid., 54–56. The Chancellor was a figure-head position only. The Vice Chancellor was the head of the administration.
11. Davin, reminiscences, 79.
12. Ibid., 91.
13. Thompson, *Warwick University Ltd.*, 57–58.
14. Ibid., 58.
15. Ibid., 18–28.
16. Ibid., 42–43.
17. Davin, reminiscences, 39.

18. Ibid., 30–31.
19. Ibid., 41 and 62–64.
20. Ibid., 76–77.
21. "Documents on the SDS and the Split," 1969, State Historical Society of Wisconsin Library Pamphlet Collection, Madison and Todd Gitlin, *The Sixties: Years of Hope, Days of Rage*, rev. ed. (New York: Bantam, 1993), 382–388.
22. *Student Left Caucus*, August 1969, broadside, Ross Collection, University of Minnesota Archives, Walter Library, University of Minnesota.
23. Kenneth J. Heineman, "'Look Out Kid, You're Gonna Get Hit!': Kent State and the Vietnam Antiwar Movement," in *Give Peace a Chance: Exploring the Vietnam Antiwar Movement*, ed. Melvin Small and Willian D. Hoover (Syracuse: Syracuse University Press, 1992), 201 and Alexander Astin, et. al, *The Power of Protest: A National Study of Student and Faculty Disruptions with Implications for the Future* (San Francisco: Jossey-Bass Publishers, 1975), 36.
24. Seymour Martin Lipset, *Rebellion in the University* (Chicago: University of Chicago Press, 1971), 46.
25. Gerd-Rainer Horn, "The Working-Class Dimension of 1968" in Gerd-Rainer Horn and Padraic Kenney, *Transnational moments of change: Europe 1945, 1968, 1989* (Rowman & Littlefield, 2004), 95–118.
26. Boren, *Student Resistance*; Klimke and Scharloth, *1968 in Europe*.
27. Green, *All Dressed Up*, 243.
28. Tony Aldgate, "The Newsreels, Public Order and the Projection of Britain," in *Impacts and Influences: Essays on Media Power in the Twentieth Century*, edited by J. Curran, A. Smith, and P. Wingate (London: Methuen, 1987).
29. Hall et al., *Policing the Crisis*, 224.
30. Ibid., 240–242.
31. *Sunday Telegraph* 10 March 1968.
32. Sandbrook, *White Heat*, 509.
33. Quoted in *The Hornsey Affair*, 207.
34. Louise Lemkov, "Student Detonators," *Wyvern*, 25 October 1968, 3.
35. "The Press is Free. Liberate the Press," *Wyvern*, 28 February 1969, 1.
36. For a more complete explanation of the rise of conservatism in the sixties, see Sandbrook, *White Heat*.
37. Fraser, *1968*, 242–243.
38. Tom Vague, *Anarchy in the UK: Angry Brigade* (London: AK Press, 1997), 26–30.
39. Max Beloff, "Can the Universities Survive?" In C. B. Cox and Boyson, eds., *Black Paper 1975: The Fight for Education* (London: J. M. Dent, 1975), 45–50; Max Beloff, "The Myth of Student Power," *British Universities Annual* (1968): 89.
40. Edward Boyle, "Student revolt, a lecture given in Canterbury Cathedral" (Lecture, Canterbury, November 5, 1969), 2–8 held in the National Library of Scotland.
41. Geoffrey Martin, "Organizational Forms and Styles of Protest," in David A. Martin, ed., *Anarchy and Culture; The Problem of the Contemporary University* (London: Routledge & Kegan Paul, 1969), 85–93.
42. Tariq Ali, ed., *New Revolutionaries: Left Opposition* (London: Peter Owen, 1969), 47–75.
43. Tom Fawthrop, "Towards an Extra-Parliamentary Opposition," in *New Left Revolutionaries*, 57.
44. Ibid., 56.

45. Alexander Cockburn, "Introduction," in *Student Power: Problems, Diagnosis, Actions*, ed. Alexander Cockburn and Robin Blackburn (Harmondsworth: Penguin, 1969), 7–21.
46. David Adelstein, "Roots of the British Crisis," in Ibid., 59–81.
47. David Widgery, "NUS—The Student's Muffler," in Cockburn and Blackburn, *Student Power*, 119–140.
48. Simon, *Education and the Social Order, 1940–1990*, 258 and 261.
49. Committee on the Age of Majority and John Latey, *Report of the Committee on the Age of Majority* (London: H.M.S.O., 1967).
50. Geoff Martin (president), "National Union of Students Executive Report 1967," 9, MSS 280: Box 99: File 12, Modern Records Centre, Warwick University.
51. Colin Crouch, *Student Revolt* (London: Bodley Head, 1970), 122.
52. Ibid., 123.
53. *Manchester Guardian*, 30 January 1969, 1.
54. U.K. House of Commons, *Report from the Select Committee on Education and Science, Session 1968–69: Student Relations*, Vol. I–VII (London: HMSO, 25 July 1969).
55. Simon, *Education and the Social Order, 1940–1990*, 396–398.
56. Hall et al., *Policing the Crisis*, 274–276.
57. See further discussion in previous chapter. "NUS Statement," 13 June 1968, reprinted in Brian MacArthur, "The Course of Student Protest," *Higher Education Review*, Autumn 1968, 72–73.
58. Gilles, "NUS Conference," 18.
59. "Comment," *Wyvern* 9 October 1970, 3.
60. Jack Straw, Speech to the NUS Universities Conference, Bradford, 6 January 1970; and Jack Straw, Paper Presented to the Delegates at Turku International Student Week 1970, April 1970, Glasgow University Archives, 3.
61. Simon, *Education and the Social Order, 1940–1990*.
62. Fraser, *1968*, 13.
63. "Mayday Commitment," *Beaver*, 24 April 1969, 8 and "LSE Union Council Meeting Minutes," British Library of Political and Economic Science Archives, 2 May 1969; "No Response to May Day March," *Torchlight*, 9 May 1969, 2; and "Soc. Soc. Show Solidarity with B.S.R. Strikers," *Glasgow Guardian*, 23 October, 1969, 3.
64. David Crook, "The Cambridge Garden House Hotel Riot of 1970 and its Place in the History of British Student Protests," *Journal of Educational Administration and History* 38: 1 (April 2006): 19–28.
65. Ibid.
66. Christopher Hitchens, *Hitch-22: A Memoir* (New York: Twelve, 2010), 124.
67. Ibid., 125.
68. Mike Prior, "Warwick Files," *Wyvern*, 27 February 1970, 2.
69. See for example, "Hull and the Files Row," *Torchlight*, 6 March 1970, 3; "No Occupation: But Full Support for Other Unions," *Beaver*, 5 March 1970, 1; and "The Sit-In Comes to Glasgow," *Glasgow Guardian*, 5 March 1970, 1.
70. Editorial, *Wyvern*, 13 March 1970, 1.
71. Keith Thomas, "College Life, 1945–1970," in Brian Harrison, *The History of the University of Oxford: Volume VIII: The Twentieth Century* (Oxford: Clarendon, 1994), 706.
72. *The Fight Begins*, broadsheet by the Campaign for a Democratic Society (ca. March 1970), John Johnson Collection/K. Jones Archive, Box 1, New Bodleian Library, Oxford University.

73. See Chapter 5.
74. "World in Revolution," *Wyvern*, 30 January 1970, 9.
75. Stewart J.A. Copland, "Century of Activity: The History of Edinburgh University Students' Representative Council" (Edinburgh University, 1982), 1–7, Edinburgh University Student Representative Council Offices.
76. "The National Union of Students of the United Kingdom Executive Report: Presented to November Conference 1973," October 1973, NUS Collection, 62.
77. For an in-depth account of this Liverpool protest, see Gerry Gordon, "An Emotional Involvement," (2009) *Chronicles of the Student Occupation of Liverpool University Senate House, March 1970*. http://senatehouseoccupation.wordpress.com. Accessed 9 May 2012.
78. "The Nine 'Just So' Men," *Wyvern*, 25 April 1969, 4; "How to Stop It," *Wyvern*, 25 April 1969, 4; and "Senate No Action on South Africa," *Wyvern*, 13 February 1970, 2.
79. "Guerrilla Action on the Essex Campus," *Wyvern*, 16 January 1970, 1.
80. Ibid.
81. Peter Hain, "Away Defeat for the Springboks," *New Statesman* 125: 4307 (25 October 1996), 28.
82. Ibid.
83. Ibid.
84. "LSE Union Minutes," 19 November 1969; and David Gilles, "NUS Conference, Margate, November 21–24, 1969," 3 December 1969, NUS Collection, 2.
85. Thomas, "The British Student Movement 1965–1972," 300–301.
86. Davin reminiscences, 103–104.
87. Ibid.
88. Lent, *British Social Movements Since 1945*, 113.
89. Tessa Blackstone, et al, *Students in Conflict, L.S.E. in 1967* (London: Weidenfeld and Nicolson, 1970), 15; "Men Have Campus Majority," *Wyvern*, 28 November 1965, 10; and A. L. Brown and Michael Moss, *The University of Glasgow 1451–1996* (Edinburgh: Edinburgh University Press, 1996), 118.
90. Lent, *British Social Movements*, 59.
91. Juliet Mitchell, "Women: The Longest Revolution," *New Left Review* 40 (December 1966): 11–37.
92. Ibid., 11.
93. Rowbotham, *Promise of a Dream*, 203.
94. Ibid.
95. Sheila Rowbotham, "Ronald Fraser Oral History Collection," interview by Ronald Fraser, Sound Recording, May 1984, Transcript C896/17, British Library Sound Archive.
96. Ali, *Street Fighting Years*, 232.
97. Fraser, *1968*, 281.
98. Reminiscences of Hilary Wainwright (17 June 1984), pages 3–11 in the CUCOHC.
99. Rowbotham, *Promise of a Dream*, 221–222.
100. Rowbotham, "Ronald Fraser Oral History Collection," 12.
101. Davin reminiscences, 65–68.
102. "Women's Liberation," *Wyvern*, 13 March 1970, 8.
103. Lent, *British Social Movements Since 1945*, 66.
104. *Anvil no. 2 women's liberation* [undated, Wivenhoe] in the Pateman Collection, Box 2 of the Oxford University John Johnson Collection, Special Collections of the Bodleian Library.

105. Sheila Rowbotham, *Mayday Manifesto: Women's Liberation and the New Politics* (1969), 5–6 in Ibid.

106. Green, *All Dressed Up*, 406; Juliet Mitchell, *Woman's estate*, First edition. (Pantheon Books, 1971), 44.

107. Rowbotham, *Promise of a Dream*, 221–222.

108. "Apartheid," *Glasgow Guardian*, 29 November 1966, 3.

109. Ibid.

110. Malcolm Le May, Letter to the Editor, *Glasgow Guardian*, 30 April 1969, 4.

111. *Shrew* 3 (July 1969), quoted in Sheila Rowbotham, "The Beginnings of Women's Liberation," in *The Body Politic*, 95.

NOTES TO CHAPTER 5

1. *Oxford Strumpet* [International Marxist Group student newspaper], 31 October 1973 and Letter from the Negotiating Committee for the Open Occupation to the Vice Chancellor, Regents, Proctor and Junior Proctor, 10 November 1973, Proctor's Office Collection in the Oxford University Bodleian Library Special Collections, PR 1/23/30/1.

2. "From the CSU Occupation in Schools to All Members of the University," [broadsheet], 14 November 1973 in Proctor's Office Collection in the Oxford University Bodleian Library Special Collections, PR 1/23/30/1.

3. Peter Mandelson, "Letter from the 'Inside'–Monday Midnight," *The Cherwell*, 8 November 1973.

4. Letter from Geoffrey Caston to Those Occupying the Examination Schools," 12 November 1973; "Its All Yours, Proctors," *The Cherwell*, 15 November 1973; and "CSU Sit-in," *Isis*, 16 November 1973 in Proctor's Office Collection in the Oxford University Bodleian Library Special Collections, PR 1/23/30/1.

5. *Isis* 16 November 1973, 5 in Oxford University Bodleian Library University Archives, PR 1/23/30/2.

6. Ibid., 6.

7. Timothy Lemmer to the Proctors, 7 November 1973 in Oxford University Bodleian Library University Archives, PR 1/23/30/1.

8. F. S. Flood, Letter to the Editor, *Oxford Mail* 9 November 1973, 12.

9. "Oration by the Senior Proctor for 1973–4," *Oxford University Gazette*, 1 August 1974, 1179 in Proctor's Office Collection PR 1/23/32/2.

10. "Proposed Agenda for General Meeting on 4 February 1974," in Proctor's Office Collection in the Oxford University Bodleian Library Special Collections, PR 1/23/31/1.

11. James Baldwin and John Cantrell, "OCC Flop," *The Cherwell*, 13 February 1974, 1.

12. "NUS Week of Action Starts Here," [undated broadsheet] in Proctor's Office Collection in the Oxford University Bodleian Library Special Collections, PR 1/23/26/5

13. "Now We Must Smash These Nazis," *Oxford Strumpet*, 14 February 1974, 2 in Proctor's Office Collection in the Oxford University Bodleian Library Special Collections, PR 1/23/26/5.

14. "Tariq Ali Ordered out of Student Sit-in Trial," *Oxford Mail*, 14 March 1974, 3 in Proctor's Office Collection in the Oxford University Bodleian Library Special Collections, 3 PR 1/23/31/2.

15. "900 March against the Proctors" *Oxford Strumpet*, 21 February 1974, 3; "Don't Just Sit There, Demonstrate!" *Oxford Strumpet*, 28 February 1974,

1; "Sit-in Trial Halted As Demonstrators Besiege Court," *Oxford Mail*,16 March 1974, 3; "Tariq Ali Ordered out of Student Sit-in Trial," *Oxford Mail*,14 March 1974, in Proctor's Office Collection in the Oxford University Bodleian Library Special Collections, 3 PR 1/23/31/2. "Oration by the Senior Proctor for 1973–4," *Oxford University Gazette*,1 August 1974, 1180 in Proctor's Office Collection PR 1/23/32/2.

16. "Oration by the Senior Proctor for 1973–4," *Oxford University Gazette*,1 August 1974, 1180 in Proctor's Office Collection PR 1/23/32/2.

17. Sir David Lindsay Keir, *Balliol College Record* 1960, 5 quoted in Keith Thomas, "College Life, 1945–1970," *The History of the University of Oxford: Volume III: The Twentieth Century*, ed. Brian Harrison (Oxford: Clarendon, 1994), 189.

18. Thomas, "College Life," 203–204.

19. Ibid., 205

20. Ibid., 190.

21. Ibid., 190.

22. "Cherwell Demands This Great Reform Bill," *The Cherwell*, 2 November 1963, 7.

23. Paul Taylor and Nick Illesly, *From May to October* April 1974, 3 in Proctor's Office Collection PR 1/23/32/2.

24. *Oxford Strumpet* 31 October 1973, 2–3 in Oxford University Bodleian Library University Archives, PR 1/23/30/2.

25. Boren, *Student Resistance*, 169–185; Dorothea Hauser, "Terrorism," in Klimke and Scharloth, *1968 in Europe*, 269–280.

26. Kirkpatrick Sale, *SDS* (New York: Random House, 1973), 652.

27. Fraser, *1968*, 327.

28. Green, *All Dressed Up*, 277–278.

29. Ibid., 277.

30. John Barker, "Anarchy in the UK, by Tom Vague [Review]", n.d., http://www.katesharpleylibrary.net/mw6n20 (accessed 16 December 2011).

31. Ibid.

32. Ibid.

33. Martin Bright, "Investigation: The Angry Brigade," *The Guardian/The Observer*, February 3, 2002, http://www.guardian.co.uk/theobserver/2002/feb/03/features.magazine27 (accessed 9 May 2012).

34. Green, *All Dressed Up*, 278.

35. Bright, "Investigation."

36. Quoted in Green, *All Dressed Up*, 281.

37. Quoted in Ibid.

38. Tom Vague, *Anarchy in the UK: Angry Brigade* (London: AK Press, 1997), 114.

39. J. C. Gunn, quoted in Ibid., 116.

40. Bright, "Investigation."

41. Gordon Carr, *The Angry Brigade: The Cause and the Case* (London: Victor Gollancz, 1975).

42. Hall et al., *Policing the Crisis*.

43. Colin Leys, *Politics in Britain* (London: Heineman Educational Books, 1983), 80.

44. Hall et al., *Policing the Crisis*, 284.

45. *Challenge* 25 (December 1970), 1.

46. *Challenge* 12 (February 1973), front.

47. Jim Phillips, "The 1972 Miners' Strike: Popular Agency and Industrial Politics in Britain," *Contemporary British History* 20: 2 (2006): 194–195.

48. Alex Callinicos and Simon Turner, "The Student Movement Today," *International Socialism* 75 (February 1977): 9–15.
49. Paul Taylor and Nick Illesly, *From May to October* April 1974, 3–7 in Proctor's Office Collection PR 1/23/32/2.
50. *Glasgow Guardian*, 29 October 1971, 1.
51. "Support," *Wyvern*, 5 November 1971, 4.
52. *Harden It Out* [undated Oxford IMG pamphlet], 9 in Proctor's Office University Archives of the Oxford University Bodleian Library Special Collections, PR 1/23/30/8.
53. "We Went," *Wyvern*, 17 February 1972, 4.
54. Editorial, *Wyvern*, 25 May 1972, 2.
55. Steve Chard, "Silence and Cry," *Wyvern*, 10 December 1971, 4.
56. Avishai Zvi Ehrlich, "The Leninist Organizations in Britain and the Student Movement 1966–1972" (Ph.D. Thesis, University of London, 1981), 148.
57. Ibid., 162.
58. Thomas, "The British Student Movement 1965–1972," 302.
59. "No Surrender," *Glasgow Guardian*, 15 December 1971, 1.
60. Ehrlich, "The Leninist Organizations," 148.
61. "No Surrender," *Glasgow Guardian*, 1.
62. Iain Noble, "Farewell, Farewell," *Wyvern*, 10 December 1971, 3.
63. "L. C. D. S. U.," *Wyvern*, 27 January 1972, 10.
64. John Carswell, *Government and the Universities in Britain, Program and Performance 1960–1980* (Cambridge: Cambridge University Press, 1985), 24–26; and "The Student Grant System," in "The National Union of Students Yearbook 1969," British Library of Political and Economic Science, London, 44.
65. C. Clarke, "President's Address," in "The National Union of Students of the Universities and Colleges of the United Kingdom April Conference held at Scarborough on the 5th, 6th, 7th, and 8th December, 1975: Minutes and Summary of Proceedings," Modern Records Centre 12.
66. Letter to the Editor, *Wyvern*, 4 May 1973, 2.
67. "400,000 Students Back Strike," *Glasgow Herald*, 15 March 1973, 1.
68. See for example, "Minutes of the Union Council," Hull University Archives, 19 March 1973, 4062 and "LSE Union Council Meeting Minutes" 11 March 1973.
69. "Essex," *Oxford Strumpet*, 21 February 1974, 4, Bodleian Special Collections, PR 1/23/31/2.
70. "General Defense and Justification of the Events Connected with the NUS Grants Campaign 15th November—12th December," *Wyvern*, December 1973, 7.
71. Ibid., 7.
72. Ibid., 8.
73. Lord Annan, *Report of the Annan Enquiry: Report on the disturbances in the University of Essex*, July 1974, National Library of Scotland, 3; and Executive Committee, University of Essex Students Union, "The Great Double-Act: A Reply to Lord Annan," September 1974, Essex University Special Collections, 3–7.
74. "It's a Rent Strike," *K3*, 29 November 1974, 1; Celia Pugh, of IMG, "A Left View of the Strike," *K3*, 29 November 1974, 2; and P.P. Fairbrother, "And a Right View," *K3*, 29 November 1974, 2 in Essex University Special Collections.
75. A good history of a London rent strike in this period is Jan O'Malley, *The politics of community action: a decade of struggle in Notting Hill* (Nottingham: Bertrand Russell Peace Foundation for Spokesman Books, 1977).

76. *Occupation News* 22 April, 8–14 May 1975 K. Jones Archive of Oxford University's John Johnson Collection, Box 3.
77. "3000 Students in Grant Protest," *Glasgow Guardian*, 26 October 1973, 1.
78. "Grants Action Call," *Glasgow Guardian*, 13 February 1975, 1.
79. Committee of Vice Chancellors and Principals of the Universities of the United Kingdom. *Student Participation in University Government* (1974), National Library of Scotland, Edinburgh, 6.
80. Ibid., 6–7.
81. John Fisk, "Control of the University: VP speaks out," *Beaver*, 20 May 1971, 3.
82. "The National Union of Students of the United Kingdom Executive Report: Presented to November Conference 1973," October 1973, NUS Archives, Modern Records Centre, 56–59.
83. Ibid.
84. Howard Malchow, *Special Relations: The Americanization of Britain?* (Stanford University Press, 2011), 206–208.
85. Lent, *British Social Movements Since 1945*, 69.
86. "Sexist Sennet," *Agitator*, November 1970, 2.
87. Ibid.
88. Louise Jacob, Letter to the Editor, *Beaver*, 14 March 1974, 2.
89. "LSE Union Council Meeting Minutes" 12 November 1974.
90. Christine Sheppard, "Women Unite," *Torchlight*, 13 May 1971, 7.
91. "Women's Lib—End of Femininity?" *Torchlight*, 4 March 1971, 5.
92. "Minutes of the Hull Union Council" 25 October 1971, 3678.
93. Judy Lown, Eve Hostettler, Jenny Rathbone, Jill Shankleman, "Women's Lib Here," *Wyvern*, 13 October 1971, 10.
94. Eve Hostettler, "Women's Lib," *Wyvern*, 19 October 1972, 12.
95. Judging from the frequent mention of gender, sex, and women's rights in Essex student publications from this period, Hostettler's assessment appears to be well-founded.
96. "Essex University Union Executive Minutes," University of Essex Archives, 16 January 1975.
97. "Delegation Leader's Report on NUS Easter Conference, Birmingham 1972," June 1972, University of Hull Archives, 3–4.
98. "NUS Women's Conference Report from Women's Liberation Group," *Beaver*, 29 October 1974, 7.
99. Lent, *British Social Movements Since 1945*, 72.
100. Malchow, *Special Relations*, 231.
101. "Gay Liberation," *Beaver*, 29 October 1970, 4; and "Gay Liberation Front Does It," *Beaver*, 10 December 1970, 7.
102. The Festival of Light was a demonstration organized by the National Viewers' and Listeners Association to reassert conservative Christian moral values. The GLF and contingents of the counterculture made a mockery of the event.
103. Reminiscences of David Fernbach (3 May 1984), on pages 39–43 in the CUCOHC.
104. "Gay is Good!" *Wyvern*, 26 November 1971, 8; and Simon Pringle, "A Report on the Gay Liberation Front's May conference at Essex University," *Wyvern* 85 [n.d. May 1973?]. At this point, the *Wyvern* had run out of money and was simple published as "News".
105. "NUS Backs Queers," *Glasgow Guardian*, 19 April 1973, 1.
106. "SRC Verbatim Minutes," Glasgow University Archives, 6 March 1975.
107. Mr. Stewart, "Report on Gay Rights Campaign," in "The National Union of Students of the Universities and Colleges of the United Kingdom April

Conference held at Liverpool on the 1st, 2nd, 3rd, 4th, and 5th of April 1974: Minutes and Summary of Proceedings," NUS Archives, Modern Records Centre, 38.

108. "National Union of Students of the United Kingdom Executive Report: Presented to November Conference 1973," October 1973, NUS Archives, Modern Records Centre, 23.
109. Fieldhouse, *Anti-apartheid*, 333.
110. "Minutes of the Union Council," Hull University Archives, 23 October 1972, 3920.
111. People First Society, "The Hull Sit-In 1972," Spokesman Pamphlet No. 30 (London: Bertrand Russell Peace Foundation, 1972), University of Michigan Special Collections, Graduate Library, University of Michigan, Ann Arbor.
112. "Minutes of the Union Council,"Hull University Archives, 8 December 1975, 4792.
113. Julian Brutus, "See You Saturday," *Beaver*, 14 March 1974, 2.
114. Peter Hain, "Away defeat for the Springboks," *New Statesman* 125: 4307 (25 October 1996), 28.
115. "The National Union of Students of the United Kingdom Executive Report: Presented to November Conference 1973," NUS Collection, Modern Records Centre, October 1973, 62.
116. Ibid., 61.

NOTES TO EPILOGUE AND CONCLUSIONS

1. *The Cherwell*,10 March 1976, 3.
2. *The Cherwell*, 21 May 1975, 5.
3. Digby Jacks, *Student Politics and Higher Education* (London: Lawrence and Wishart, 1975), 10
4. Seymour Martin Lipset and Philip G. Altbach, eds., *Students in Revolt* (Boston: Houghton Mifflin, 1969), xvi; Philip G Altbach, *The Student Revolution: A Global Analysis* (Bombay: Lalvani Pub. House, 1970), 8.
5. See Adam Lent, *British Social Movements Since 1945: Sex, Colour, Peace, and Power* (New York: Palgrave, 2001).

Bibliography

MANUSCRIPT COLLECTIONS

British Library, London.

McMurdo, Max. "Student Unrest and Its Educational Consequences for Higher Education, 1968–78: a Bibliography", 1978.

Radical Student Alliance. "A Radical Student Alliance (prospectus)". Radical Student Alliance, London, 1968.

The Committee of Vice Chancellors and Principals of the Universities of the United Kingdom and the National Union of Students of England, Wales, and Northern Ireland. *Joint Statement from the Committee of Vice-Chancellors and Principals and the National Union of Students*, October 7, 1968.

British Library of Political and Economic Science Archives, London.

Agitator. Journal of the L.S.E. Socialist Society. 1965–73. (Vol. 1–10)

Annual Report of the London School of Economics Students' Union, 1959–1971.

Beaver. Newspaper of the Students Union of the L.S.E. ., 1953–1974.

Clare Market Review. Journal of the L.S.E. Student Union. 1962–69.

LSE International Socialists. *LSE—A Marxist Perspective.* Pamphlet (undated, ca. 1973).

L.S.E.'s New Director: A Report on Walter Adams. L.S.E. Socialist Society Pamphlet, 1966.

L.S.E. Student Union Council Meeting Minutes. 1952–1975.

L.S.E. Students' Handbook. 1959–71.

Sennet. University of London Student Newspaper, 1973.

Students' Red Flag. Bulletin of the student fraction of the Revolutionary Workers' Party (Trotskyist) British Section of the IVth International. 1968–1969. (Issues 1–6)

Brynmore Jones Library, Hull University, Hull.

Hull University Union Council Minutes. 1959–1975.

Joynt. Hull Area Students Newspaper. 1972–74.

Torchlight. Student Union Newspaper of Hull University. 1960–72.

Edinburgh University Student Representative Council Offices, Edinburgh.

Minutes of the Executive Committee of the Student Representative Council of Edinburgh University, 1963–1971.
Copland, Stewart J.A. "Century of Activity: The History of Edinburgh University Students' Representative Council". Edinburgh University, 1982.

Glasgow University Archives, Glasgow.

Glasgow University Students' Representative Council Minutes and Verbatim Minutes. 1960–1975.
Glasgow University Magazine. 1955–1971. Glasgow University Library, Glasgow.
Glasgow University Guardian. Glasgow University student newspaper, 1960–75.
Glasgow University Students Handbook. 1956–75.

Modern Records Centre, University of Warwick, Coventry.

National Union of Students Archive [MSS 280, Boxes 21, 39, 51, 80, 86, 96, 99, 100, 101, and 109].

National Library of Scotland, Edinburgh.

Anti-Student. Antistudent Pamphlet Collective, London. 1972.
Committee of Vice-Chancellors and Principals of the Universities of the United Kingdom. *Student Participation in University Government*, 1974
Dutschke, Rudi. "The Students and the Revolution". Bertrand Russell Foundation, 1971.
Report of the Annan Enquiry: Report on the Disturbances in the University of Essex. July 1974.

Oxford University Bodleian Library Special Collections

University Archives: Proctor's Office.
John Johnson Collection (New Bodleian Library): Bulkeley Collection, K. Jones Archive, and Pateman Collection
The Cherwell. Oxford University student newspaper, 1955–1975.
Peace, Protest and the Nuclear Threat: Archives of the Campaign for Nuclear Disarmament, 1958–1972. Harvester Microfilm, Edinburgh University Library, Edinburgh.

University of Essex Special Collections, Albert Sloman Library, University of Essex, Wivenhoe

In Brief. University of Essex Students Council broadsheet, 1968–72.
M .J. Sommerlad Collection.
T. P. Hughes Collection.
University of Essex Tribunal of Enquiry, 1968.
University of Essex Union Council Meeting Minutes.
University of Essex Report of the Tribunal of Enquiry on the Events of May 7th 1968 and the events leading up to them, 1968.

Wyvern. University of Essex Union student newspaper, 1964–73. (Number 1–86)

University of Minnesota Archives, Walter Library, University of Minnesota, Minneapolis.

Ross Collection

University of Strathclyde Archives, University of Strathclyde, Glasgow.

University of Strathclyde Students' Association Minutes and Papers, 1968-1970.

H.M.S.O. DOCUMENTS

Committee on the Age of majority and John Latey, *Report of the Committee on the Age of Majority,* 1967.

Grants to Students, Report of the Committee Appointed by the Minister of Education and the Secretary of State for Scotland in June 1958, under the Chairmanship of Sir Colin Anderson, May 1960.

Higher Education, Report of the Committee Appointed by the Prime Minister under the Chairmanship of Lord Robbins, 1961–1963, presented October 1963, Cmnd. 2154, Parliamentary Papers xi–xiv, 1962–63.

Report from the Select Committee on Education and Science Session 1968–69: Student Relations. Vol. I-VII. London: House of Commons, 25 July 1969.

INTERVIEWS

Ali, Tariq. Interview by Ronald Fraser. Sound Recording, 3 April and 18 December 1984. Transcript C896/02. British Library Sound Archive.

Davin, Anna. Interview by Ronald Fraser. Transcript C896/06, 20 April 1984. Columbia University Center for Oral History Collection.

Fernbach, David. Interview by Ronald Fraser. Transcript C896/12, May 1984. Columbia University Center for Oral History Collection.

McAliskey, Bernadette. Interview by Ronald Fraser.Transcript C896/42, 27 July 1984.. Columbia University Center for Oral History Collection.

Rowbotham, Sheila. Interview by Ronald Fraser. Sound Recording, May 1984. Transcript C896/17. British Library Sound Archive.

Thompson, Willie. Interview by Caroline Hoefferle, 21 April 1997, Glasgow.

Triesman, David. Interview by Ronald Fraser. Transcript C896/05, 17 April 1984. Columbia University Center for Oral History Collection.

Wainwright, Hilary. Interview by Ronald Fraser. Transcript C896/30, 17 June 1984. Columbia University Center for Oral History Collection.

PUBLISHED SOURCES

Abrams, Philip, and Little, Alan. "The Young Voter in British Politics." *British Journal of Sociology* 16 (1965): 95–110.

Abse, Joan. *My L.S.E.* London: Robson Books, 1977.

Adams, Michael Vanny. "From Texas to Sussex: An Odssey of Campus Protest." *Encounter* 44 (1975): 83–89.

Adams, Walter. "LSE and the New Militancy." *British Universities Annual* (1969): 103–111.

Addison, Paul, and Harriet Jones, eds. *A Companion to Contemporary Britain, 1939—2000.* Oxford: Blackwell, 2005.

Albert, Judith Clavir and Stewart Edward Albert. *The Sixties Papers: Documents of a Rebellious Decade.* New York: Praeger, 1984.

Ali, Tariq. *1968 and After: Inside the Revolution.* 1st ed. London: Blond & Briggs, 1978.

———. *Street Fighting Years: An Autobiography of the Sixties.* London: Collins, 1987.

Ali, Tariq, ed. *New Revolutionaries: Left Opposition.* London: Peter Owen, 1969.

Altbach, Philip G. *The Student Revolution: A Global Analysis.* Bombay: Lalvani Pub. House, 1970.

Anderson, Terry H. *The Movement and the Sixties: Protest in America from Greensboro to Wounded Knee.* New York: Oxford University Press, 1995.

Andrews, Geoff, Richard Cockett, Alan Hooper, and Michael Williams. *New Left, New Right and Beyond: Taking the Sixties Seriously.* New York: Palgrave Macmillan, 1999.

Appleyard, Bryan. "I Remember '68, it was a Riot." *Times*, January 8, 1988, sec. 8.

Archer, Robin, Diemut Bubeck, and Hanjo Glock. *Out of Apathy: Voices of the New Left Thirty Years on.* Verso Books, 1989.

Ashby, Eric, and Mary Anderson. *The Rise of the Student Estate in Britain.* London: Macmillan, 1970.

Astin, Alexander W., Helen S. Astin, Alan E. Bayer, and Ann S. Bisconti. *The Power of Protest: A National Study of Student and Faculty Disruptions with Implications for the Future.* San Francisco: Jossey-Bass Publishers, 1975.

August, Andrew. "Gender and 1960s Youth Culture: The Rolling Stones and the New Woman." *Contemporary British History* 23: 1 (March 2009): 79–100.

Avorn, Jerry L. *Up Against the Ivy Wall: A History of the Columbia Crisis.* New York: Atheneum Press, 1968.

Barker, Paul. "Portrait of a Protest." *New Society* (31 October 1968): 631–634.

Barnett, Anthony. "People's Democracy: a Discussion on Strategy." *New Left Review* 55 (June 1969): 3–19.

Bell, D. A., J. Dunning-Davies, A.G. Martin, and F. W. Stephenson. "A Survey of Student Representation on University Senates." *Universities Quarterly* 27: 1 (Winter 1972): 40–45.

Beloff, Max. "The Myth of Student Power." *British Universities Annual* (1968): 86–89.

Best, John W. "Modern English Education." *Education* 84: 2 (October 1963): 70–73.

Black, Lawrence. *The Political Culture of the Left in Affluent Britain, 1951–64.* Basingstoke: Palgrave Macmillan, 2003.

Black, Lawrence. *Redefining British Politics: Culture, Consumerism and Participation, 1954–70.* Basingstoke: Palgrave MacMillan, 2010.

Blackstone, Tessa. "Students' Wish for Involvement." *New Society* (4 July 1968): 20–21.

Blackstone, Tessa, Kathleen Gales, Roger Hadley, and Wyn Lewis. *Students in Conflict, L.S.E. in 1967.* London: Weidenfeld and Nicolson, 1970.

Booker, Christopher. *The Neophiliacs: Revolution in English Life in the Fifties and Sixties.* London: Pimlico, 1969.

Boren, Mark Edelman. *Student Resistance: A History of the Unruly Subject*. New York: Routledge, 2001.

Bosi, Lorenzo. "The Dynamics of Social Movement Development: Northern Ireland's Civil Rights Movement in the 1960s." *Mobilization: An International Journal* 11: 1 (February 2006): 81–100.

Boulton, David. *Voices From the Crowd: Against the H-Bomb*. London: Peter Owen, 1964.

Boyle, Edward. "Student revolt, a lecture given in Canterbury Cathedral". Lecture, Canterbury, 5 November 1969.

Brienes, Wini. *Community and Organization in the New Left, 1962–1968: The Great Refusal*. New Brunswick: Rutgers University Press, 1989.

Brown, A., and M. Moss. *The University of Glasgow: 1451–1996*. Edinburgh: Edinburgh University Press, 1997.

Brown, Richard. *Knowledge, Education and Cultural Change: Papers in the Sociology of Education*. London: Tavistock, 1973.

Burkett, Jodi. "Re-defining British morality: 'Britishness' and the Campaign for Nuclear Disarmament 1958–68." *Twentieth Century British History* 21:2 (2010): 184–205.

Burns, Tom."The Revolt of the Privileged." *SSRC Newsletter* 4 (November 1968): 5–11.

Califano, Joseph. *The Student Revolution: A Global Confrontation*. New York: Norton, 1969.

Callaghan, John. *British Trotskyism: Theory and Practice*. Oxford: Blackwell, 1984.

Callinicos, Alex, and Simon Turner. "The Student Movement Today." *International Socialism* 75 (February 1977): 9--15.

Calvocoressi, Peter. *The British Experience, 1945–75*. New York: Pantheon, 1978.

Carr, Gordon, John Barker, and Stuart Christie. *The Angry Brigade—The Cause and the Case: A History of Britain's First Urban Guerilla Group*. London: Victor Gollancz, 1975.

Carswell, John. *Government and the Universities in Britain: Programme and Performance 1960–1980*. Cambridge: Cambridge University Press, 1985.

Caute, David. *Sixty-Eight: The Year of the Barricades*. London: Hamish Hamilton, 1988.

Chun, Lin. *The British New Left*. Edinburgh: Edinburgh University Press, 1993.

Cockburn, Alexander, and Robin Blackburn, eds. *Student Power: Problems, Diagnosis, Actions*. Harmondsworth: Penguin, 1969.

Cohen, Stanley. *Folk Devils and Moral Panics: The Creation of the Mods and Rockers*. East Sussex: Psychology Press, 1980.

Collins, Marcus. *The Permissive Society and Its Enemies: Sixties British Culture*. London: Rivers Oram Press, 2007.

Connery, C., and H. J. Spillers. "Introduction: The Still Vacillating Equilibrium of the World." *boundary 2* 36: 1 (March 2009): 1–5.

Connery, Christopher. "The End of the Sixties." In *boundary 2*, 36: 1 (March 2009): 183–210.

Cooper, David, ed. *The Dialectics of Liberation*. Harmondsworth: Penguin, 1968.

Cox, C. B., and Boyson, Rhodes eds. *Black Paper 1975: The Fight for Education*. London: J. M. Dent, 1975.

Crook, David. "The Cambridge Garden House Hotel Riot of 1970 and its Place in the History of British Student Protests." *Journal of Educational Administration and History* 38: 1 (April 2006): 19–28.

Crouch, Colin. *The Student Revolt*. London: Bodley Head, 1970.

Dahrendorf, Lord Ralf. *L.S.E.: A History of the London School of Economics and Political Science, 1895–1995.* New York: Oxford University Press, 1995.

Davis, James Kirkpatrick. *Assault on the Left: The FBI and the Sixties Antiwar Movement.* Westport, CT: Praeger, 1997.

Davis, Madeleine. "The Marxism of the British New Left." *Journal of Political Ideologies* 11: 3 (2006): 335–358.

DeGroot, Gerard J. *Student Protest: The Sixties and After.* New York: Longman, 1998.

———. *The Sixties Unplugged: A Kaleidoscopic History of a Disorderly Decade.* Cambridge: Harvard University Press, 2009.

———. "Street-Fighting Men." *History Today* 58: 5 (May 2008): 26–33.

Donnelly, Mark. *Sixties Britain: Culture, Society and Politics.* New York: Pearson Longman, 2005.

Duff, Peggy. *Left, Left, Left: A Personal Account of Six Protest Campaigns, 1945–65.* London: Allison and Busby, 1971.

Edmonds, Anthony. "The Viet Nam War and the British Student Left: A Study in Political Symbolism." *Vietnam Generation Journal* 5: 1–4 (1994): 81–84.

Ehrenreich, Barbara and John. *Long March, Short Spring: The Student Uprising at Home and Abroad.* New York: Monthly Review Press, 1969.

Ehrlich, Avishai Zvi. "The Leninist Organizations of Britain and the Student Movement 1966–1972". Ph.D. diss., University of London, 1981.

Evans, Sara M. "Sons, Daughters, and Patriarchy: Gender and the 1968 Generation." *American Historical Review* 114: 2 (April 2009): 331–347.

Evans, Sara. *Personal Politics: The Roots of Women's Liberation in the Civil Rights Movement & the New Left.* First Edition. Vintage, 1980.

Eynon, Bret. "Community, Democracy, and the Reconstruction of Political Life: The Civil Rights Influence on New Left Political Culture in Ann Arbor, Michigan, 1958–1966." Ph.D. diss., New York University, 1993.

Fawthrop, Tom. "Hull." *New Left Review* 50 (August 1968): 59–64.

Feuer, Lewis Samuel. *The Conflict of Generations.* New York: Basic Books, 1969.

Fieldhouse, Roger. *Anti-Apartheid: a History of the Movement in Britain: A Study in Pressure Group Politics.* London: Merlin, 2005.

Fink, Carole, Philipp Gassert, Detlef Junker, and Daniel S. Mattern. *1968: The World Transformed.* Cambridge: Cambridge University Press, 1998.

Fisher, Trevor. "The Sixties: A Cultural Revolution in Britain." *Contemporary Record* 3 (November 1989): 22–23.

Fowler, David. *Youth Culture in Modern Britain, c.1920–c.1970: From Ivory Tower to Global Movement—A New History.* New York: Palgrave Macmillan, 2008.

Fraser, Ronald. *1968: A Student Generation in Revolt.* New York: Pantheon, 1988.

Geary, Daniel. "'Becoming International Again': C. Wright Mills and the Emergence of a Global New Left, 1956–1962." *Journal of American History* 95: 3 (December 2008): 710–736.

———. *Radical Ambition: C. Wright Mills, the Left, and American Social Thought.* Berkeley: University of California Press, 2009.

Gitlin, Todd. *The Sixties: Years of Hope, Days of Rage.* Rev. ed. New York: Bantam Books, 1993.

———. *The Whole World is Watching: Mass Media in the Making and Unmaking of the New Left.* Berkeley: University of California Press, 1980.

Green, Jonathon. *All Dressed Up: The Sixties and the Counterculture.* London: Pimlico, 1999.

———. *Days in the Life: Voices from the English Underground, 1961–1971.* London: Heinemann, 1990.

Greer, Germaine. *The Female Eunuch*. New York: Farrar, Straus and Giroux, 2002.

Hadley, Roger, and Tessa Blackstone. "Who Occupied LSE?" *New Society* (December 5, 1968): 845–846.

Hall, Simon. "Protest Movements in the 1970s: The Long 1960s." *Journal of Contemporary History* 43: 4 (October 2008): 655–672.

Hall, Stuart. "The 'First' New Left: Life and Times." In *Out of Apathy: Voices of the New Left 30 Years On*, edited by Oxford University Socialist Discussion Group, 11–38. London: Verso, 1989.

Hall, Stuart, Chas Critcher, Tony Jefferson, John Clarke, and Brian Roberts. *Policing the Crisis*. London: : Palgrave, 1978.

Hamilton, Scott. *The Crisis of Theory: E. P. Thompson the New Left and Postwar British Politics*. Manchester: Manchester University Press, 2011.

Harrison, Brian. *The History of the University of Oxford: Volume VIII: The Twentieth Century*. Oxford: Clarendon, 1994.

Hayden, Tom. *Reunion: A Memoir*. New York: Random House, 1988.

Hennessy, Peter. *Having It So Good*. London: Allen Lane, 2006.

Hitchens, Christopher. *Hitch-22: A Memoir*. New York: Twelve, 2010.

Hoefferle, Caroline. "Students and Political Activism," in *the Vietnam War Era: Perspectives in American Social History,* ed. Mitchell K. Hall, 185–201. ABC-CLIO, April 2009.

———. "A Web of Interconnections: Student Peace Movements in Britain and the United States, 1960–1975" in *Peace Movements in Western Europe, Japan and the USA during the Cold War,* ed. Benjamin Ziemann, 129–146. Frieden und Krieg. Beiträge zur Historischen Friedensforschung, vol. 8. Essen: Klartext, 2007.

———. A Comparative History of Student Activism in Britain and the United States, 1960–1975." Ph.D. diss., Central Michigan University, 2000.

Holden, Richard James. "Democracy in British Student Politics: The National Union of Students". Ph.D. diss., University of Exeter, 1980.

Horn, Gerd-Rainer. *The Spirit of '68: Rebellion in Western Europe and North America, 1956–1976*. New York: Oxford University Press, 2007.

Horn, Gerd-Rainer, and Padraic Kenney. *Transnational Moments of change: Europe 1945, 1968, 1989*. Manham: Rowman & Littlefield, 2004.

Jacks, Digby. *Student Politics and Higher Education*. London: Lawrence and Wishart, 1975.

Jackson, Louise A. "'The Coffee Club Menace': Policing Youth, Leisure and Sexuality in Postwar Manchester." *Cultural and Social History* 5: 3 (July 2008): 289–309.

Jameson, Fredric. "Periodizing the 60s." In *The 60s without Apology*, ed. Sayers, et al., 178–209. Minneapolis: University of Minnesota Press, 1984.

Jarvis, Mark. *Conservative Governments, Morality and Social Change in Affluent Britain, 1957–64*. Manchester: Manchester University Press, 2005.

Jobs, Richard Ivan. "Youth Movements: Travel, Protest, and Europe in 1968." *American Historical Review* 114: 2 (April 2009): 376–404.

Jones, Bryn, and Mike O'Donnell. *Sixties Radicalism and Social Movement Activism: Retreat or Resurgence?* New York: Anthem Press, 2010.

Katsiaficas, George. *The Imagination of the New Left: A Global Analysis of 1968*. Boston: South End Press, 1987.

Kidd, Harry. *The Trouble at L.S.E. 1966–67*. London: Oxford University Press, 1969.

Kingsbury, Richard John. *The Realities of University Life*. London: University Tutorial Press, 1974.

Klimke, Martin, et al. *Between Prague Spring and French May: Opposition and Revolt in Europe, 1960–1980*. New York: Berghahn Books, 2011.

Klimke, Martin A., and Joachim Scharloth. *1968 in Europe: A History of Protest and Activism, 1956–1977*. New York: Palgrave Macmillan, 2008.

Klimke, Martin. *The Other Alliance: Student Protest in West Germany and the United States in the Global Sixties*. Princeton, NJ: Princeton University Press, 2009.

Lasky, Melvin J. "The Ideas of '68: A Retrospective on the 20th Anniversary Celebrations of 'The Student Revolt'." *Encounter* 71 (November 1988): 3–18.

Laybourn, Keith. *Marxism in Britain: Dissent, Decline and Re-emergence 1945–c.2000*. London: Taylor & Francis, 2006.

Lent, Adam. *British Social Movements Since 1945: Sex, Colour, Peace, and Power*. New York: Palgrave, 2001.

Levitt, Cyril. *Children of Privilege: Student Revolt in the Sixties: A Study of Student Movements in Canada, the United States, and West Germany*. Toronto: University of Toronto Press, 1984.

Leys, Colin. *Politics in Britain*. London: Heinemann, 1983.

Lindop, Fred. "Racism and the Working Class: Strikes in Support of Enoch Powell in 1968." *Labour History Review* 66: 1 (Spring 2001): 79–100.

Lipset, Seymour Martin. "Polls and Protests." In *Rebellion in the University*, 38–79. Chicago: University of Chicago Press, 1971.

Lipset, Seymour Martin, and Philip G. Altbach, eds. *Students in Revolt*. Boston: Houghton Mifflin, 1969.

Lowe, Rodney. *The Welfare State in Britain since 1945*. New York: St. Martin's, 1993.

MacArthur, Brian. "More Liberal Regime for Universities Advocated: Students' Right to Private Life." *Times*, October 14, 1969, 8.

———. "The Course of Student Protest." *Higher Education Review (UK)* (Autumn 1968): 68–74.

Malchow, Howard. *Special Relations: The Americanization of Britain?* Stanford, CA: Stanford University Press, 2011.

Maney, Gregory M. "Transnational Mobilization and Civil Rights in Northern Ireland." *Social Problems* 47: 2 (May 1, 2000): 153–179.

Martin, David A., ed. *Anarchy and Culture; The Problem of the Contemporary University*. London: Routledge & Kegan Paul Books, 1969.

Marwick, Arthur. *British Society Since 1945*. Harmondsworth: Penguin, 1982.

———. "How We Taught the World to Swing." *The Times* (UK), May 30, 2004.

———. "The 1960s: Was There a 'Cultural Revolution?'" *Contemporary Record* 2 (October 28, 1968): 18–20.

———. *The Sixties: Cultural Revolution in Britain, France, Italy, and the United States, c.1958–c.1974*. New York: Oxford University Press, 1998.

———. "Youth in Britain, 1920–1960: Detachment and Commitment." *Journal of Contemporary History* 5 (1970): 37–51.

Mausbach, Wilfried. "Historicising'1968'." *Contemporary European History* II: I (2002): 177–187.

Mills, C. Wright. *C. Wright Mills*. Edited by Pamela Mills and Kathryn Mills. Berkeley: University of California Press, 2000.

———. "Letter to the New Left." *New Left Review* 5 (September–October 1960): 18–23.

Mitchell, Juliet. *Woman's Estate*. New York: Pantheon Books, 1971.

Moodie, Graeme C. *Power and Authority in British Universities*. London: Allen & Unwin, 1974.

Morgan, Kenneth O. *The People's Peace: British History 1945–1989*. Oxford: Oxford University Press, 1990.

Mott, J., and N. Goldie. "Social Characteristics of Militant and Anti-Militant Students." *Universities Quarterly* 26: 1 (Winter 1971): 28–40.

Nagel, Julian (ed.). *Student Power*. London: Merlin Press Ltd., 1969.

Nehring, Holger. "National Internationalists: British and West German Protests against Nuclear Weapons, the Politics of Transnational Communications and the Social History of the Cold War, 1957–1964." *Contemporary European History* 14: 4 (2005): 559–582.

Nelson, Elizabeth. *The British Counter-Culture, 1966–73: A Study of the Underground Press*. New York: St. Martin's, 1989.

Ness, Immanuel. *Encyclopedia of American Social Movements*. Vol. 1. Armonk, NY: M. E. Sharpe, 2004.

Newens, Stan. "Memories of a seminal year." *International Socialism*, 12 October 2006. <http://www.isj.org.uk/index.php4?id=252&issue=112> Accessed 30 January 2012.

O'Malley, Jan. *The Politics of Community Action: A Decade of Struggle in Notting Hill*. Nottingham: Bertrand Russell Peace Foundation for Spokesman Books, 1977.

Osgerby, Bill. *Youth in Britain Since 1945*. Oxford: Blackwell Publishers, 1998.

Palmer, Bryan D. "Homage to Edward Thompson, Part II." *Labour / Le Travail* 33 (April 1, 1994): 13–68.

Parkin, Frank. "Adolescent Status and Student Politics." *Journal of Contemporary History* 5 (1970): 144–155.

———. *Middle Class Radicalism: The Social Bases of the British Campaign for Nuclear Disarmament*. Manchester: Manchester University Press, 1968.

Pateman, Trevor. *Counter Course: A Handbook for Course Criticism*. Harmondsworth: Penguin, 1972.

Payne, Geoff, and John Bird. "What Are Their Students Like?" *New Society* (October 23, 1969): 641–643.

Phillips, Jim. "The 1972 Miners' Strike: Popular Agency and Industrial Politics in Britain." *Contemporary British History* 20: 2 (2006): 187–207.

Polk, Kenneth. "Student Protest in the UK and the US." *Higher Education Review (UK)* (Autumn 1968): 63–67.

Prince, Simon. "The Global Revolt of 1968 and Northern Ireland." *The Historical Journal* 49: 3 (2006): 851–875.

Pullan, Brian, and Michele Abendstern. *A History of the University of Manchester, 1951–73*. Manchester: Manchester University Press, 2000.

Rigby, Andrew. *Communes in Britain*. London: Routledge & Kegan Paul Books, 1974.

Rojek, Chris. *Stuart Hall*. Cambridge: Polity, 2003.

W. J. Rorabaugh, *Berkeley At War*. New York: Oxford University Press, 1989.

Rowbotham, Sheila. *Promise of a Dream: Remembering the Sixties*. London: Allen Lane, 2000.

———. *Woman's Consciousness, Man's World*. Harmondsworth: Penguin, 1973.

Sale, Kirkpatrick. *SDS*. New York: Random House, 1973.

Sandbrook, Dominic. *Never Had It So Good: A History of Britain from Suez to the Beatles*. Little, Brown Book Group, 2006.

———. *State of Emergency: The Way We Were: Britain, 1970–1974*. London: Allen Lane, 2010.

———. *White Heat: A History of Britain in the Swinging Sixties*. London: Little, Brown, 2006.

Sayers, Sohnya, Anders Stephanson, Stanley Aronowitz, Frederic Jameson, eds. *The 60s without Apology*. Minneapolis: University of Minnesota Press, 1984.

Shipley, Peter. *Revolutionaries in Modern Britain*. London: Bodley Head, 1976.

Simon, Brian. *Education and the Social Order, 1940–1990*. London: Palgrave Macmillan, 1991.

Small, Melvin and Willian D. Hoover, eds. *Give Peace a Chance: Exploring the Vietnam Antiwar Movement*. Syracuse: Syracuse University Press, 1992.

Snowman, Daniel. *Britain and America: An Interpretation of Their Culture, 1945–1975.* New York: HarperCollins, 1977.

Statera, Gianni. *Death of a Utopia: The Development and Decline of Student-Movements in Europe.* New York: Oxford University Press, 1975.

Sterling, Salters, ed. *Reflections on Student Protest.* London: Student Christian Movement Press, 1969.

Straw, Jack, Albert Sloman, and Paul Doty. *Universities: Boundaries of Change.* London: Panther, 1970.

Students and Staff of Hornsey College of Art. *The Hornsey Affair.* Harmondsworth: Penguin, 1969.

Suri, Jeremi. *Power and Protest: Global Revolution and the Rise of Detente.* Cambridge: Harvard University Press, 2005.

———. "The Rise and Fall of an International Counterculture, 1960–1975." *American Historical Review* 114: 1 (February 2009): 45–68.

Taylor, Richard. *Against the Bomb: The British Peace Movement 1958–1965.* Oxford: Clarendon, 1988.

———. *Campaigns for Peace: British Peace Movements in the Twentieth Century.* Manchester: Manchester University Press, 1989.

Thomas, Nick. "Challenging Myths of the 1960s: The Case of Student Protest in Britain." *Twentieth Century British History* 13: 3 (2002): 277–297.

———. "Protests Against the Vietnam War in 1960s Britain: The Relationship between Protesters and the Press." *Contemporary British History* 22: 3 (2008): 335–354.

———. "Will the Real 1950s Please Stand Up? Views of a Contradictory Decade." *Cultural and Social History* 5: 2 (April 2009): 227–236.

———. "The British Student Movement 1965–1972". Ph.D. diss., University of Warwick, 1996.

Thompson, E. P. *Out of Apathy.* London: New Left Books, 1960.

———, ed. *Warwick University Ltd.: Industry, Management and the Universities.* Harmondsworth: Penguin, 1970.

Thompson, Paul, and Joanna Bornat. "Myths and Memories of an English Rising: 1968 at Essex." *Oral History* 22: 2 (Autumn 1994): 44–54.

Thompson, Willie. "Notes on Communist Work Among Students". Communist Party Great Britain, October 1965. Personal collection of Willie Thompson.

———. *The Left In History: Revolution and Reform in Twentieth-Century Politics.* London: Pluto Press, 1997.

Tickner, Lisa. *Hornsey 1968: The Art School Revolution.* London: Frances Lincoln, 2008.

Tischler, Barbara L. ed. *Sights on the Sixties.* New Brunswick, NJ: Rutgers University Press, 1992.

Turner, Alwyn W. *Crisis? What Crisis?: Britain in the 1970s.* Aurum Press, 2007.

Vague, Tom. *Anarchy in the UK: Angry Brigade.* London: AK Press, 1997.

Varon, Jeremy, Michael Foley, and John McMillian. "Time Is an Ocean: The Past and Future of the Sixties." *The Sixties: A Journal of History, Politics and Culture* 1: 1 (June 2008): 1–7.

Wandor, Michelene. *The Body Politic: Writings from the Women's Liberation Movement in Britain, 1969–1972.* London: Stage 1, 1972.

Webster, David. *Labour Party and the New Left.* London: Fabian Society, 1981.

Widgery, David. *The Left in Britain 1956–68: Volume 1.* Harmondsworth: Penguin, 1976.

Williams, Colin H. "Non-Violence and the Development of the Welsh Language Society, 1962–1974." *Welsh History Review* 8: 1–4 (1977): 426–455.

Williams, Raymond, ed. *May Day Manifesto 1968.* Harmondsworth: Penguin Books, 1968.

Wittner, Lawrence. *Confronting the Bomb: A Short History of the World Nuclear Disarmament Movement*. Stanford, CA: Stanford University Press, 2009.

———. "The Transnational Movement Against Nuclear Weapons, 1945–1986: A Preliminary Summary." In *Peace movements and Political Cultures*, edited by Charles Chatfield and Peter Van Den Dungen, 265–294. Tennessee: University of Tennessee Press, 1988.

Young, Nigel. *An Infantile Disorder: The Crisis and Decline of the New Left*. London: Routledge & Kegan Paul, 1977.

Ziemann, Benjamin. "Peace Movements in Western Europe, Japan and USA since 1945: An Introduction." *Mitteilungsblatt des Instituts fur soziale Bewegungen* Heft 32 (2004): 5–19.

Ziemann, Benjamin, ed. *Peace Movements in Western Europe, Japan and the USA during the Cold War*. Essen: Klartext Verlag, 2007.

Zweig, Ferdynand. *The Student in the Age of Anxiety; A Survey of Oxford and Manchester Students*. New York: The Free Press of Glencoe, 1963.

Index